I first met Pastor Daniel Del Vecchio in the late 1960s. At that time, the Lord used Pastor Daniel and his wife, Sister Rhoda, to begin the work of planting the Lord's message of the Great Commission into my heart. Those early years set the pattern and call of missions in our lives, and we have continued to train others to catch the call of missions and *go* into all the world with the gospel message.

—Dr. Dennis Lindsay, President and Chairman of the Board of Christ for the Nations, Inc., Dallas, Texas, which has trained over fifty thousand students to carry the Good News of Christ throughout the world

Pastor Dan Del Vecchio and his apostolic ministry has had the most profound influence on my spiritual walk. Wandering through Spain forty years ago, Pastor Dan became a "spiritual father" to me, like he did for untold hundreds of others of my generation. He discipled me in the tried-and-true values of faith and sacrifice, not just with words but by modeling these to me on a daily basis. His faith in action has in turn inspired me to do this for others, and it's why I have become the person of faith I am today.

—Dr. Daniel Lucero, Global Director Africa and Francophone Nations for the International Church of the Foursquare Gospel and President/Founder of the Foursquare Church in France

In 1972 I was hitchhiking through Europe. In Rotterdam I was invited to join a group of fellow hippies on a trip to Morocco. After spending a few weeks in Marrakesh, I decided to spend Christmas in Spain. Though I was a believer and a preacher's kid, I had a lot of questions. I was really trying to find myself. I came to ECC for the Christmas Eve service, and that night. God turned my whole life around. Sitting in the back pew, I received a clarion call to devote the rest of my life to full-time ministry. I am so deeply grateful to Pastor Dan for the significant part he played in influencing the trajectory of my life and ministry.

—Dr. Wayne Hilsden and his wife Ann partnered with another couple to pioneer the largest Christian fellowship in Jerusalem, King of Kings Community, and are co-founders of FIRM (Fellowship of Israel Related Ministries)

FLAME OF GOD

THE FIRE OF THE HOLY SPIRIT IN SPAIN

DARLA MILNE

FLAME OF GOD: THE FIRE OF THE HOLY SPIRIT IN SPAIN

The content of this publication is based on actual events. Names may have been changed to protect individual privacy.

ISBN: 978-1-4866-2271-9
eBook ISBN: 978-1-4866-2272-6

Word Alive Press
119 De Baets Street Winnipeg, MB R2J 3R9
www.wordalivepress.ca

WORD ALIVE PRESS

Cataloguing in Publication information can be obtained from Library and Archives Canada.

To my mother, Anne, who packed a Bible in my backpack.

ACKNOWLEDGMENTS

I am thankful for all those who have contributed to this book by sharing their lives through interviews, recordings, emails, and Zoom sessions. In 1985, I conducted interviews in person with Pastor Dan and his wife, Rhoda, and with many international and Spanish community members. Some material was gleaned from Barbara Fletcher's memoirs (later printed by her daughter, Dawn Bilbe-Smith, as *Unusual—believe it or not*) and from Rev. Del Vecchio's Spanish autobiography, *El Manto de José*. In 2021, I updated my notes to include events that have occurred more recently.

I wish to thank Word Alive Press for publishing this book and for their editorial input.

NOTE FROM THE AUTHOR

Forty-six years ago (*forty-six!*), my sister and I were backpacking around Europe when God led us to the evangelical Christian community in Torremolinos, Spain. We were actually on our way to Morocco, but for three days in a row, every time we boarded a bus in Málaga, we ended up in Torremolinos! Wandering through this tourist town, made famous by James Michener's *The Drifters*,[1] we noted the sign of a fish painted on a white wall.

"Christians must have been here," we remarked wistfully to each other. (A few months earlier in Greece, we had started reading our Bible from cover to cover and recommitted our lives to Christ.) We encountered a fellow Canadian, Mark, witnessing on the street, and I'll never forget seeing *Jesus* reflected in his eyes. Pastor Dan Del Vecchio came by and invited us to Barbara's villa, where we met other members of the Evangelical Community Church.

For several weeks we lived in this British aristocrat's villa, which she had generously opened to young people hungry to find out more about God. We were profoundly impressed with the

[1] James A. Michener, *The Drifters* (New York, NY: Random House, 1971).

practical expression of love we saw evidenced in the lives of these believers—it revolutionized my concept of Christianity! Here was a vibrant community imitating the radical New Testament church of Acts. At Easter, my sister and I were baptized at the Torremolinos church, witnessed by our mother, who had joined us for a few weeks of backpacking, traveling by train through Europe, and staying in youth hostels.

Several years later, our twin brothers also visited this community and helped to build a satellite church in Mijas, a town in the mountains to the west of Torremolinos. To say that the lives of us four siblings were profoundly changed in Spain by the power of the Holy Spirit would be an understatement! Later, my brother-in-law and sister-in-law were also introduced to this community.

In 1985, I visited Torremolinos again. Although I had returned for a time of spiritual refreshing, I soon became convinced that the extraordinary work God was doing here needed to be told. During the eight months that I lived in the community's renovated Hotel Panorama, I marveled at the transformation of new believers—most noticeably an Irish heroin addict who had been raised among the Costa Del Sol's wealthier expatriate residents. While living in the community, she had been set free from her drug abuse. After being a Christian for a mere six months, she had cared for another addict going through withdrawal—true discipleship in action.

These pages collected dust while I was serving as a witness in a restricted-access country. During the COVID-19 crisis, when, like most of the world, I was largely confined to my condo, I sifted through what I had written three decades ago. *Do these testimonies still resonate today? Are they relevant?* I decided that yes, the Holy Spirit still speaks through the lives of these Christians! His work in *ongoing*!

This inspiring story of Pastor Dan Vecchio's ministry, the chronicles of the evangelical Christian community, and the blossoming of the satellite Spanish churches also acted as a *plumbline* against which to measure my own life. *Are my priorities the priorities of Jesus Christ?* It's my desire that those who read *Flame of God* will also seek to bring their own lives into alignment with God's purpose. As followers of Jesus Christ, the Author of Life, we should be encouraged that we all have a role to play in God's divine plan. Each of us is an important link in God's chain of events to reach others.

Pastor Dan Del Vecchio is not a "marble" preacher perched on a "pulpit pedestal." Rather, he transparently allows others to see who he really is and to learn from his experiences. Although acquainted with suffering, discouragement, and persecution for the sake of Christ, he persisted in his calling. Through radical obedience to God and the empowerment of the Holy Spirit, Pastor Dan and this community of believers impacted the nation of Spain, South America, and seventy countries around the world. The young generation of Christians can learn from this modern-day example of the book of Acts. I pray that all of our lives be filled with a fresh anointing of God's Holy Spirit.

Interestingly, this year I've reconnected through Zoom calls with some of the far-flung community members spread over four continents. It's been fascinating to find out about their current lives, their memories, and the enduring impact of Pastor Dan's teachings on their spiritual foundation. This book records only a small portion of the remarkable stories of people whose lives were profoundly shaped by this ministry. My apologies to those who are not included!

I pray that readers of *Flame of God* will be inspired to study the Word of God, be led by the Holy Spirit, and step out in courageous faith to fulfill what Jesus Christ calls us to do—disciple the nations! May we also be challenged to open our hearts and homes to the lost and despised people of society. And during this time of change, when many churches are facing restrictions, may we *purposely seek out and find community!*

Darla Milne,
Toronto, Canada, 2021

FOREWORD
REV. JUHA KETOLA

I am delighted that the true testimony of Jesus is now available in this book for every thirsty soul. So many countless lives of both local and international people have been touched by the ministry of missionary and apostle Daniel Del Vecchio throughout the decades that he has been serving in Spain. So many have been saved, and so many have received and found their calling to the ministry while listening to him.

It's time to have this testimony in writing, especially now when the preaching and teaching of the raw and rugged cross of Jesus is being avoided. Without the faithfulness to the resurrected Lord and the Bible, with no compromise or political correctness, the power of the Holy Spirit would have never been available and the fire from heaven never fallen upon so many in the Torremolinos Community Church.

I also believe that the sufferings and pain Daniel Del Vecchio personally went through were constantly transformed by the Holy Spirit into life-changing words that burn, and into thoughts that breathe, creating new life and holiness in all who were exposed to his preaching and teaching of the true gospel. Daniel Del Vecchio truly has died together with Jesus so that Jesus's resurrection life could be received in the ones mentioned in this book and in many others, even passing the blessing on to the next generations.

I myself am one of those whose life was changed completely and permanently after coming to Torremolinos and getting under the influence of this ministry. I came to see my friend living in the community—and I met Jesus! I was baptized in water and in the Spirit in Torremolinos, and the teaching of Del Vecchio gave me a solid foundation in the Word. The holy and clear direction I received for my life has never departed from me, not even when I have stumbled or been unfaithful to Jesus. Since those days I have preached Jesus in more than fifty nations and in every continent of our world.

Today I am so very grateful to Jesus. He saved and cleansed me. Let the fire from heaven fall afresh on every reader of this book! And let every minister of the Word be encouraged.

A native of Finland, Rev. Juha Ketola was saved in Torremolinos in 1979 and has been in full-time ministry since 1985. He's a graduate of the International Bible Institute of London Kensington Temple and an ordained minister with the Pentecostal Assemblies of Canada and Finland. From 2012–2017, Rev. Ketola served as the International Director of the International Christian Embassy in Jerusalem, overseeing ICEJ's worldwide network.

He and his wife, Kati, now reside in Jyväskylä, Finland. They have three children and five grandchildren.

When the day of Pentecost had come, they were all together in one place. Suddenly a sound like a mighty rushing wind came from heaven, and it filled the whole house where they were sitting. There appeared to them tongues as of fire, being distributed and resting on each of them, and they were all filled with the Holy Spirit and began to speak in other tongues, as the Spirit enabled them to speak. (Acts 2:1–4, MEV)

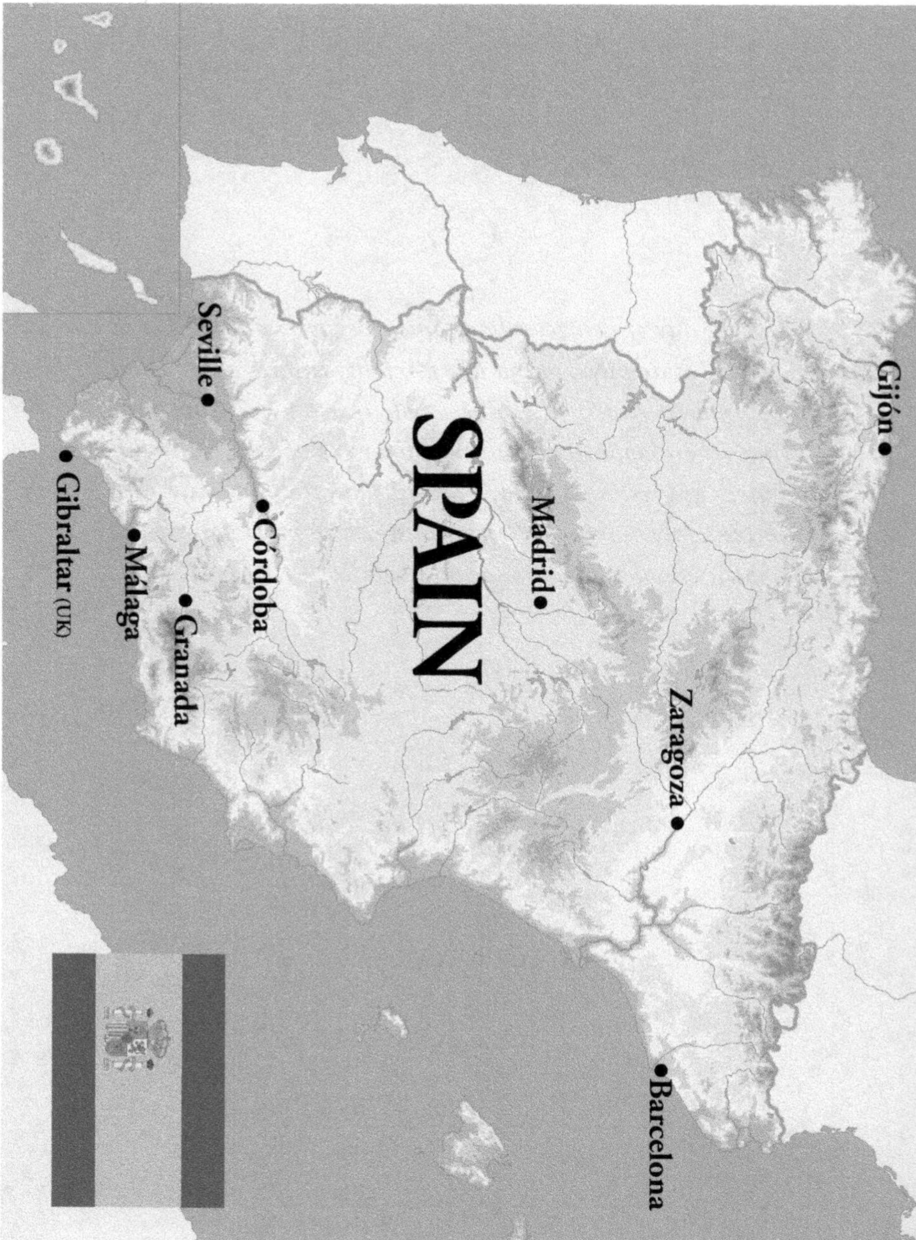
SPAIN
Gijón
Madrid
Zaragoza
Barcelona
Seville
Córdoba
Granada
Málaga
Gibraltar (UK)

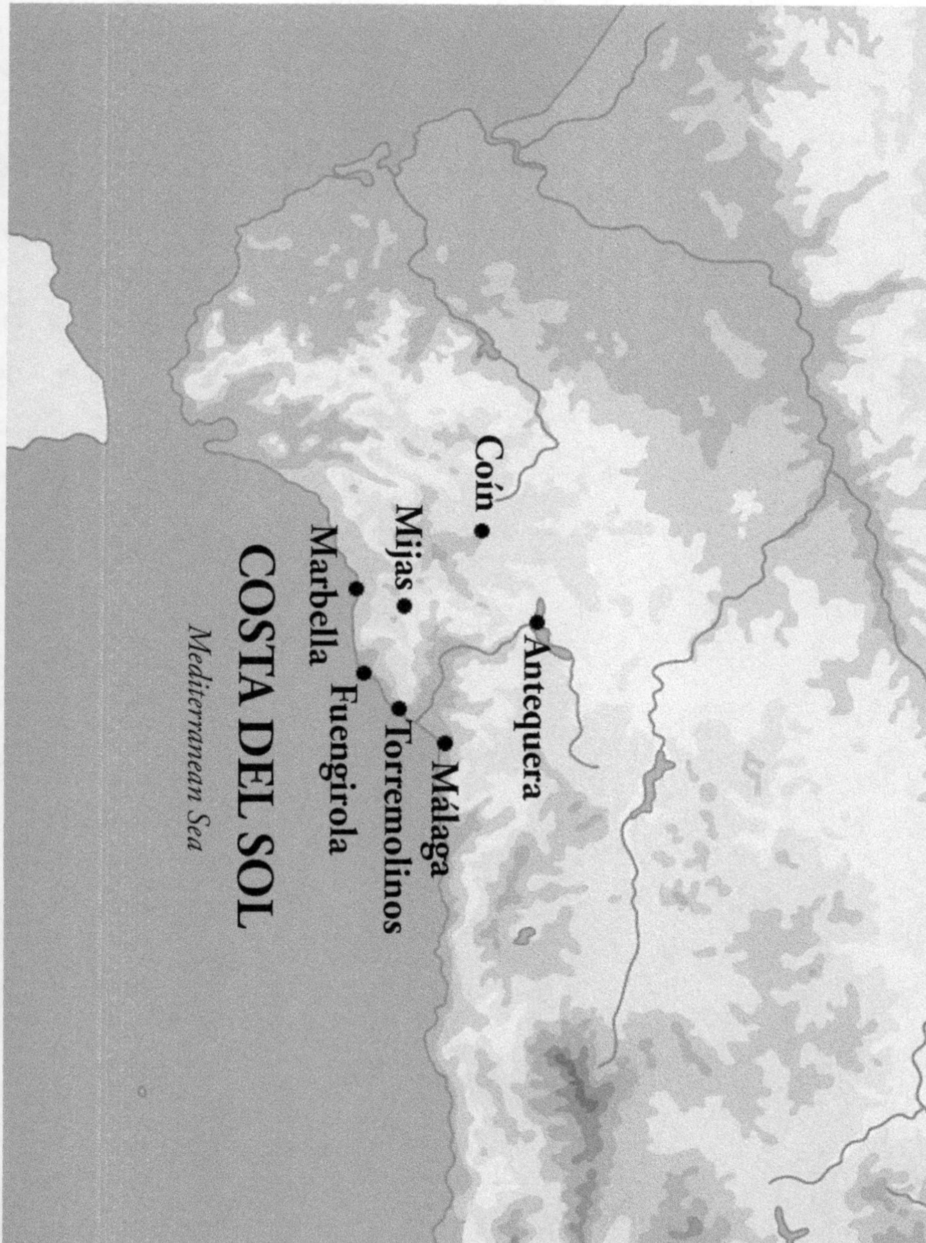
Antequera
Coín
Mijas
Málaga
Torremolinos
Fuengirola
Marbella
COSTA DEL SOL
Mediterranean Sea

CONTENTS

PROLOGUE
THE TRUE FAST

When Daniel Del Vecchio was fifteen years old, a minister friend named Brother Samuel visited his family's farm frequently. This Messianic Jew took it upon himself to teach the youth the way Jews study the Bible when they want their own children to learn it by heart. One day he asked Daniel to read the fifty-eighth chapter of Isaiah out loud:

Is not this the kind of fasting I have chosen:
to loose the chains of injustice,
and to untie the cords of the yoke,
to set the oppressed free
and break every yoke?

"You're going much too fast," Brother Samuel interrupted him. "Read it slowly."

Is it not to share your food with the hungry
and to provide the poor wanderer with shelter—
when you see the naked, to clothe them,
and not to turn away from your own flesh and blood?

> *Then your light will break forth like the dawn,*
> *and your healing will quickly appear;*
> *then your righteousness will go before you,*
> *and the glory of the Lord will be your rear guard.*[2]

The minister made Daniel read the passage over and over again. The young teenager obeyed, poring over the verses until they were pounded into his memory. He would never forget those words: "*To share your food with the hungry ... to provide the poor wanderer with shelter ... When you see the naked to clothe him ...*"

Isaiah 58 would be the guiding light of Daniel Del Vecchio's life. He was more impacted by the principles set forth here than by any other portion of scripture. God's words about a *true fast* were imprinted deeply upon his soul. He understood that they didn't just refer to fasting from food but to living a simpler lifestyle and sharing one's abundance with those in need: to give bread to the hungry, to give shelter to the homeless poor, to clothe the marginalized, and not to leave one's fellow man behind. God's *chosen fast* is a life dedicated to doing God's work and destroying the works of Satan.[3]

---

[2] Isaiah 58:6–8, NIV.

[3] Daniel Del Vecchio, *El Manto de José* (Guadalajara, Spain: REMAR, 2019) 169.

PART ONE
MANIFESTO FOR MIRACLES

CHAPTER ONE
CUBA

Daniel Del Vecchio was born in July 1932 on a farm in Mullica Hill, New Jersey into an Italian immigrant family. It was the time of the "Great Depression," and he was the sixth child. His father was already in his fifties, and his mother was in her forties. His family was very poor: their living conditions on the farm were humble, with no bathroom or running water. They lived off the land, eating or selling what they produced: vegetables, corn, chickens, eggs, sausages, meat, milk, bread, and soap. From an early age, Daniel learned the virtues of hard work and perseverance—character qualities that marked his life.

It was there on that garden farm that God called Dan to preach. As a young man of twenty-four, fresh out of the Navy, Dan was lying awake in his bedroom one night when he had an unmistakable, life-changing encounter with the living God. An awesome glory filled his room. Terrified, he wanted to crawl under the bed. Instead, trembling with fear, he addressed the Presence at the foot of his bed:

"Speak, Lord, thy servant heareth," Dan quoted the young prophet Samuel.[4] As he uttered these words, the anointing power

[4] 1 Samuel 3:10.

of the Holy Spirit swept through him, and a strong inner voice said: *Listen to My words. Be attentive to the words of My lips. For I will raise you up, and you will bring My words to the ends of the world.*

These words struck Dan's heart with such force that he never, then or later, doubted this call. With the Holy Spirit's fire burning in his soul, he immediately started to preach the gospel, reaching out to migrant workers. At night, he visited their camps at the largest farms nearby, strumming his electric guitar, singing, and preaching. On his first outing, seven laborers gave themselves to the Lord, throwing away their cigarettes.

Of all the workers he met, his heart was most drawn to the Hispanics. Even as a teenage boy working side-by-side with them in his father's fields, he'd been attracted to these warm, lively people. Over the years, he developed a special love for Hispanics—a love God was working in his heart. Very early, Dan sensed that he was being called to serve these people.

For the next three years, Daniel Del Vecchio followed this pattern of life: by day, laying bricks and learning the building trade, and by night, singing and sharing the gospel. As the months passed, he felt a growing conviction that God was calling him into full-time service.

"Dan, a missionary from Cuba, spoke at church tonight," his older brother casually informed him one evening. "He said there are seven churches there with only one pastor."

His brother's words had a profound impact on Dan. For the next week, they echoed over and over in his heart: he couldn't forget them. A growing desire to go to Cuba gripped his innermost being.

"I believe God is calling me to Cuba," Dan boldly told the Italian Council of the Christian Churches of America, the denomination that had ordained him. "And I need your help to get there."

One of the elders eyed him. "What will you do if we don't support you?"

"Then I'll swim!" Dan replied, the desire to go to Cuba burning so fiercely within him that he was prepared to go to any measure to obey it.

The civil war had already begun in Cuba. Dan sensed that there'd be only a short time to preach the gospel before communism took over. Without guarantee of support but certain that God was sending him, he was confident that God would supply all his needs.

In February of 1957, twenty-five-year-old Daniel arrived with his sister Erma in Unión de Reyes, province of Matanzas, Cuba. She was to be his much-needed prayer support.

"It's too noisy around here for me to pray," the restless young man informed his sister shortly after they had checked into their hotel. "I'm going for a drive in the country."

The young missionary drove his car along a dirt road through acres of sugar cane swaying in the fields. At a particularly deserted stretch, he pulled over to the shoulder, thankful for a peaceful place to pray. Stretching himself across the front seat, he was soon totally absorbed in prayer. Suddenly, without opening his eyes, he knew that he was being watched.

Dan jerked upright to see guns pointed at his head. He was surrounded by Cuban soldiers, and they didn't appear friendly. With more boldness than he felt, Dan complained to them in heated Spanish: "I came all the way out here to find peace, and you won't leave me alone!"

The soldiers had mistaken the missionary for one of Fidel Castro's rebel guerillas. When they realized the angry American was not who they were searching for, they disappeared as quickly as they'd arrived. This was the young missionary's rude introduction to Cuba—a country in the deathly throes of revolution. It was here that Daniel Del Vecchio's ministry was to mature, forged in the fires of persecution.

For thirty days, Dan preached in the streets of Alacranes in a chaotic time of bomb attacks and blackouts. His sister stayed behind in the apartment they had rented, interceding for him. Although Erma was only in Cuba for six months, her fervent prayers laid the foundation for the seven churches the Lord enabled Dan to start in just three years.

Fidel Castro and his rebels were hiding out in the mountains, terrorizing the people. Every night when the guerillas planned to cut the electricity, the Holy Spirit impressed upon Dan not to go outside. Conversely, whenever he felt at liberty to go, the power lines were never cut. The street lights remained on, and no terrorist act ever happened. In this way, God protected him from dangerous situations.

In Alacranes, Dan rented a former theater to begin holding meetings in, and later he built a small church. One evening when about ninety people had gathered, Dan began praying for them to receive the Holy Spirit, and they started falling prostrate on the floor. As he walked among them, the building was suddenly plunged into darkness. Rebel forces had arrived in town and had cut the electrical wires. The young missionary didn't know what to do. He was surrounded by prone bodies, and he couldn't make it back to the pulpit to light a candle without tripping over them. Then faith in the Lord's power welled up within him:

"I command these lights to go on in the name of Jesus!"

Instantly light flooded the church. Most of the people were so intent on worshiping the Lord that they didn't even notice the miracle. One by one they rose to their feet and began to remove the religious medallions from around their necks: it was a sovereign work of the Holy Spirit.

Dan's home in Cuba was nothing more than a rickety shack. Whenever it rained, water dripped through the roof, increasing the young man's discomfort and misery. Every morning before he could wash, he had to remove frogs from the bathtub. One day as he was shaving, Dan examined his reflection in the cracked mirror above the basin. His face had turned a sickly yellow. For the past eleven days, he hadn't been able to keep his food down. As he attempted to leave the shack, which doubled as his home and church, Dan fainted on the path near the door. As consciousness slipped away, the young man pleaded, "God, don't let me die alone."

Later that morning, two passing Cuban women, members of his congregation, discovered the unconscious, emaciated missionary. They dragged him back into the shack and managed to revive him. "We're going to get a doctor," they told him.

Dan stopped them. "No, I don't need a doctor. Just lay your hands on my stomach and pray for me," he instructed, for he was a firm believer in divine healing.

For the next few days, Dan felt better, but then he suffered a relapse and was forced to see a doctor. The doctor took one look at the missionary's yellow skin and eyes and immediately diagnosed infectious hepatitis. He inserted a needle into Dan's arm and set up an intravenous line.

Later as he stumbled across the main plaza, Dan saw a man collapse face-down to the ground. For some reason, a nearby policeman approached the sick missionary. "Can you help him?" he asked Dan, probably assuming all the Americans left in his country were doctors. "He's having a seizure."

Despite his own poor health, the missionary knelt down in the dust beside the man. Laying his hand on the Cuban's forehead, Dan bound the devil in the name of Jesus. The man opened his eyes and slowly rose to his feet.

"How long do these attacks usually last?" the missionary asked him.

"Four hours," the man replied. "I need a doctor."

"I know a good doctor," Dan smiled weakly. "Come with me."

Dan took the man back to his shack and prayed for him—the beginning of his deliverance ministry. As Cuba was a country steeped in superstition and voodoo, many of the people were bound both in mind and body by evil spirits. The young missionary exercised the authority Jesus had given to His followers: "*And these signs will follow those who believe: In My name they will cast out demons; they will speak with new tongues … they will lay hands on the sick, and they will recover*" (Mark 16:17–18).

On another occasion, Dan offered to drive a woman from his church to a family funeral wake in the hill country. When they arrived at the house where the wake was in progress, Dan saw a large man being held down. One man was holding his head while the others grasped his arms and legs. The man was thrashing around violently. It took the combined strength of five men to restrain him. Dan immediately walked over to these men. Although a crowd of 120 had gathered in the house to mourn the passing of an old woman, nobody was paying attention to the thrashing man, the deceased woman's son.

"May I pray for him?" Dan asked the struggling men.

They shrugged their shoulders. Taking their indifference for consent, Dan placed his finger on the man's forehead. "Satan, loose him in the name of Jesus!"

Instantly the man's head dropped limply to his chest as the violent power left him. The men, still expecting him to struggle, maintained their tight grip on his body.

"Let him go," Dan said. "He's all right now."

The missionary was uncomfortably aware that a hush had descended on the crowd as people stared at him in wonder. Embarrassed, Dan slipped out the door. He was still too young and inexperienced to use opportunities like this to preach the gospel.

The delivered man and his father both rushed out the door to catch up with the missionary, thanking him profusely. "This is your home," the father said, expressing his gratitude. "Do what you want here."

Dan began to preach the gospel in that house, and so a church was planted in the hill country of Unión de Reyes. Many of the Christians who gathered in that home were later sent to prison or executed for being anti-Castro and anti-revolutionary.

Dan began preaching in Sabanilla, a town of four thousand people in the province of Matanzas. Alone with his guitar, an amplifier, and a microphone, he began singing on the street. A crowd soon formed. There had never been a gospel witness in this town. It was wholly given over to idolatry and witchcraft, and many people were suffering from sickness.

After preaching the Word, Dan asked for a show of hands of those who were in pain. The young evangelist knew that as a believer he had the authority, in the name of Jesus Christ, to cast out these evil spirits of infirmity. "*Behold, I give you the authority to trample on serpents and scorpions, and over all the power of the enemy, and nothing shall by any means hurt you*" (Luke 10:19). With the power of the Holy Spirit and faith in the name of Jesus, Dan exercised his authority as a child of God: "I command the spirits of infirmity to come out in the name of Jesus!"

Many in the crowd gave testimony of healing. After a few days of open-air meetings, he moved into a rented building. In one of the first services, a woman attended who was known as a "healer." Although she was a good and sincere woman, she'd been using evil powers to heal and prescribe cures. Dan noticed that she was having a hard time keeping her eyes open. The demons in her didn't want her to hear the gospel. He and his co-worker went over to her and cast out those evil spirits. The following service, the woman returned with many of her clients and friends. Because of her obvious deliverance, they were eager to hear the Good News. When Dan gave the altar call, they rushed forward to receive Jesus Christ as their Savior and Deliverer.

The church in Sabanilla continues to this day. In 2008, Dan returned to preach there again. This woman's grandson is now superintendent of about three hundred churches in Cuba. To God be the glory!

One day, as Dan was leaving the church he'd planted in Sabanilla, the Holy Spirit impressed upon him: *Drive down this road.* Obeying, Dan drove his Volkswagen van for eight or nine miles down the dirt road. Each time he was tempted to turn around, the inner voice compelled him to go further. Finally, he reached the brow of a hill overlooking the beautiful valley of Montserrat, with its fields of sugar cane dotted with cane-roofed cabins.

Stop here, the inner voice urged. *Start a church.*

Surprised, Dan looked around him. There was nothing but a small country store on one side of the road, and the ruins of an old castle on the other. Having learned not to question this inner voice, however, Dan began holding open air meetings in that unlikely location. People of all ages turned up to listen, including *guajiros,* local cowboys who would pass by on their horses. One night some rowdy young cowboys gathered on the sidelines, intent on disturbing the meeting and creating trouble. They'd brought a very spirited horse along with them.

"Ride *Americano*," they challenged the missionary.

Dan looked at the snorting stallion, which had no saddle or bridle—just a rope halter around its nose and a blanket over its back. "I can ride," he told the leader. "I was riding before you were born, young man."

"Then ride!" the brash boy sneered.

"I'll ride him," Raúl, Dan's assistant pastor, bravely volunteered. He mounted the horse, rode him up and down the road, and then slid off.

"Now you, *Americano,*" the young man smirked.

As Dan jumped on the stallion's back, the leader of the group maliciously shot his hand under the blanket. The large sand burr he'd placed there instantly goaded the horse, and it began to buck wildly. Dan held on to the rope tightly as the stallion kicked and pawed the air in frenzied circles. Finally, the spirited horse bucked the missionary off. Dan slid down his back and landed on his feet, dazed but unhurt. The horse, however, fell over backwards and lay on the ground, his sides heaving.

"There you have it." Dan faced the cowboy triumphantly. "I'm on my feet, and the horse is on the ground!"

The cowboys roared with laughter. The missionary had passed their test, and after that, they gave him no further opposition.

The castle ruins on the other side of the road intrigued Dan. He had discovered that an eccentric woman, the daughter of a Spanish count and a black slave, had inherited thousands of acres of sugar cane fields surrounding the ruins. She was one of the wealthiest landowners in Cuba. One day Dan decided to visit this woman. Near the castle, in front of a simple cane-roof hut, he found an unassuming, elderly Black woman, her head wrapped in a turban, hoeing the rich earth.

"I'd like to build a church on your property," Dan proposed.

The woman wasn't very receptive until she found out that the missionary was from the United States. When she had visited his country, she'd been treated very well. She proudly informed Dan that she even had an American flag. By the end of his visit, the woman had agreed to give him one of the castle "rooms" in which to build a church.

As he left the property, Dan surveyed the ruins of the "castle," which was only a three-foot-high foundation of what was originally intended to be a replica of Havana's famous landmark, *El Morro* Castle. The wealthy woman had abandoned the building project years before. Dan chose the "living room" as the best location for his church.

A few days later, a truck dumped the solid limestone blocks Daniel had ordered in a ravine near the ruins. The blocks were two feet wide, a yard long, and weighed four or five hundred pounds. Each one would have to be fitted and cut with a hand saw.

"How will we ever move these?" José, Dan's first convert in Cuba, asked in despair. He had offered to help the missionary build this new church in Montserrat.

"Let's try the old pivot method," Dan suggested. Painstakingly, the two worked together in the 120-degree heat, sweat pouring down their backs. One would place a rock and stick under a limestone block, raising it a little, and then the other would quickly shove another rock under it, lifting it even more. When the block stood on its side, they would push it over. They repeated this process until all the rocks were rolled over to the castle foundation.

The blocks that had tumbled down into the ravine posed another problem. No matter how much effort they exerted, Dan and José couldn't move them. Dan had even tried tying a rope from his VW van to one of the rocks, but it wouldn't budge an inch.

"God, I can't go any further," Dan groaned. The persistent missionary, who usually didn't give up without a fight, was ready to do just that.

"Having any trouble?" A farmer passed by driving a team of oxen.

"Yeah," Dan replied, his voice heavy with discouragement. "We can't move these rocks."

The farmer glanced at the pile of limestone blocks in the ravine. "When I finish work, I'll come back and have my oxen move them."

Dan laughed incredulously. "Your oxen are going to pull these rocks?"

"Don't worry, you'll see!"

Dan and José waited in the shade for the farmer to return. After six, he came back and, true to his word, hooked his oxen to the rocks. The missionary and his assistant stared in astonishment as the oxen dragged the solid limestone blocks up the ravine as if they were cardboard boxes.

Dan and José cut and fitted the stones, erecting the church block by block, and topping it off with a sugar-cane roof. Because of the American trade embargo with Cuba, building material in the country was in short supply, so Daniel and José had to scrounge wood from abandoned houses. They constructed wooden pews, and to add the finishing touch, the missionary nailed a couple of two-by-fours together for a cross, which he placed above the entrance.

A local priest tried to convince the owner to evict the missionary from her property. "This is 'America,'" the woman retorted, proudly referring to her land. "And I'm not going to throw anybody out!" While the priest and the owner were engaged in conversation, Dan witnessed to her nephew, who was visiting from Havana. He accepted the Lord right there. Later Dan facilitated the nephew's entry into the United States and helped him enroll at Wheaton College to study for the ministry.

In the church in Montserrat, Dan began to step out further in faith in the area of divine healing. He preached with conviction that Jesus would heal the sick and invited everyone to come forward for prayer. As the people formed a line, Dan and his assistant, Raúl, prayed for each one. To their growing dismay, nothing much appeared to be happening. Then with dread, Daniel noticed that the next person in line was an old deaf woman who, according to the locals, was "so deaf she couldn't hear a cannon go off."

"Oh God, what am I going to do?" the missionary groaned. He turned to Raúl. "What should we do now?"

"Send her to the back of the line," Raúl whispered without hesitation.

The deaf woman's turn came again all too quickly, and Dan faced her in frustration. He wanted above everything to give glory to God, but he was afraid that if this woman wasn't healed, not only would he look foolish in the eyes of the people but, more importantly, the gospel would appear foolish.

Dan raised his arms to the ceiling. "God," he implored in absolute desperation, "You know I can't heal this woman." He prayed in English, a language he sometimes reverted to when he was in a tight situation. As he confessed his own inadequacy to meet this woman's need, the power of the Holy Spirit descended on him like a thousand volts of electricity. Knowing with certainty that he was endued with power from on high, Dan placed his fingers in the old woman's ears.

"Open in the name of Jesus!" he commanded.

Instantly the Cuban woman's ears popped open and she cried with joy.

Daniel Del Vecchio had learned a lesson that was to be repeated over and over in his life: when God was his only source, *God always came through*. God would never fail him.

There is *power in the name of Jesus!*

CHAPTER TWO
RHODA

The heat, his ill-health, the squalid living conditions, and the constant struggles in spiritual warfare often combined to depress Dan. Sometimes the young missionary felt as if he was carrying a burden beyond what he could bear. Often when he suffered these black moods of despair, he read and re-read his mother's letters. They were a constant source of encouragement to him.

Dan had been thinking a lot about a certain young woman who had been writing to him. Although only three letters had been exchanged between them, Dan already sensed there was something special about this young lady, whose name was Rhoda. Kneeling by his bed one hot, humid evening in the summer of 1959, a mosquito net wrapped around him, Dan placed Rhoda's letter on the sheets before him. Something about her letter had struck him deeply—somewhere within him was a strange but exciting stirring.

"Lord," he prayed, "who is this woman?"

After waiting on God in silence for a few moments, a distinct word of knowledge came to the young missionary. The words surprised Dan yet filled him with a deep peace: *This is your wife. You will marry in the fall.*

Back in New Jersey, an energetic young woman named Rhoda and her friend Twyla were traveling around the country conducting children's outreaches. They'd been visiting various churches and camps for almost a year. Every day, three times a day, they prayed together: first for their ministry, then for their financial needs, and lastly for their social needs.

"Lord, if You want Twyla and I to be married," Rhoda would pray, "You'll have to provide a husband for each of us."

Privately, Rhoda asked the Lord for some very detailed qualities in her future husband. She specified that he should be like the Apostle Paul: raising up churches, healing the sick, and casting out devils. As if that wasn't enough, she boldly added: "And please, Lord, have him be a Spanish-speaking missionary." By now she had ministered to Hispanic children and had developed a God-given love for them. "And have him be Italian, musically-inclined, an artist like my dad … kind and faithful …"

Rhoda and Twyla were invited to minister at Rev. Jim Del Vecchio's church in New Jersey. As the two young evangelists entered his home, Rhoda immediately noticed a painting on the wall. "Isn't this lovely," Rhoda remarked appreciatively to the pastor's wife. "I see it's signed Del Vecchio. Is this your husband's work?"

"No." Mary Del Vecchio smiled at the young woman's interest. "It's my brother-in-law's."

"Does he paint for a living?" Rhoda asked, intrigued.

"No, he's a missionary," the woman replied. "In Cuba." Mrs. Del Vecchio then put on a record, and a male and female voice blended in a harmonious duet.

"Who's that singing?" Rhoda inquired.

"That's my brother-in-law," Mrs. Del Vecchio answered proudly. "He has a good voice, hasn't he?"

Rhoda agreed, and then she couldn't help asking with undisguised curiosity, "And who is that accompanying him? His wife?"

"No," Jim Del Vecchio interjected, amused. "He's not married."

Rhoda and Twyla exchanged conspiratorial glances. Twyla sensed her friend's heightened interest in this mysterious singer, artist, and missionary.

Because his modest home had no extra space for guests, Jim Del Vecchio arranged for Rhoda and Twyla to stay on his parents' farm. The elder Mrs. Del Vecchio had her son's oil paintings displayed all over the large farmhouse—it was like an art gallery. While Rhoda boarded with the Del Vecchios, she felt surrounded by the absent missionary's presence: she slept in his bed, waking every morning to gaze at his framed photograph on the dresser. Something about the handsome, wavy-haired young man captivated her attention. She was drawn to his warm blue eyes and intrigued by his artistic talent and creativity.

One day, the elder Mrs. Del Vecchio approached Rhoda and Twyla. "Would one of you girls write a letter for me? To my son Danny in Cuba?"

The Italian mother eyed her two boarders speculatively. She explained that she wasn't very literate in English and found it difficult to compose sentences.

"Go ahead," Rhoda nudged Twyla.

Twyla shook her head mischievously. "No, I've already found my guy," she said, referring to the young gentleman she'd met in the previous church they had visited. "This one is yours, Rhoda."

Rhoda wrote the letter exactly as Dan's mother dictated, and then she gave it to her to sign. Mrs. Del Vecchio handed the letter back to the young woman. "Please, on the other side write who you are and what you're doing here."

Rhoda obeyed. She wrote Dan that her father was a co-pastor of a church in a nearby town, that he also was a painter, and that she admired his paintings. She mentioned that she and another woman were working as children's evangelists in Dan's brother's church. "We're praying for you. If there's anything we can do to help, please let us know."

Before she sealed the letter, Rhoda felt prompted to enclose her last three dollars as an offering to the dedicated Cuban missionary. The two girls weren't given much money from the churches they worked with, but they were learning to trust God to meet their financial needs. For Rhoda, this was an important initiation into the life of faith—and the lessons she learned would prove to be highly beneficial in the coming years.

Although Rhoda didn't expect to receive a response to her letter, deep down in her spirit she knew she would. In less than two weeks, she received the missionary's reply, thanking her for the offering. In his letter, Dan alluded to the suffering and sacrifice involved in the kind of front-line evangelism he was doing, but Rhoda didn't pay much attention to that aspect. Instead, she found the mention of mosquito nets and palm trees thrilling—and, of course, the miraculous healings and deliverances touched a responsive chord. *Was this her Apostle Paul?*

"I'll be coming home in June," Dan ended his letter. "If your father thinks I could be a blessing to his church, I'd be happy to visit."

In June, Dan phoned Rhoda and made arrangements to meet at her house at six that evening. With excitement, Rhoda baked a chocolate marble cake. "Truly a masterpiece," she giggled, removing her apron. She was just about to change her dress when the doorbell rang.

"It's only five o'clock," Rhoda gasped in alarm. "He's an hour early!" Horrified at their disheveled state, both Rhoda and her sister Ella scurried to their bedroom, leaving their poor mother to answer the door.

On the porch, Dan straightened his tie and smoothed down his wavy hair and wondered why nobody was responding to the bell. Finally, Rhoda's mother opened the door, and Dan caught a glimpse of two giggling girls disappearing into a bedroom. Rhoda's mother escorted the distinguished guest into the living room.

"Would you like a cup of coffee?" she asked nervously, anxious to please this potential son-in-law. "Or maybe you'd prefer tea?"

Eventually a tall, slender woman entered the room and walked over to greet the missionary. *Oh no,* Dan groaned inwardly. *She's too tall for me.*

"I'm Rhoda's sister Ella," she introduced herself. "Rhoda will be out in a moment, so just make yourself comfortable."

Daniel tried to relax, but as the minutes passed, he grew tense with anticipation. Finally, Rhoda emerged from the bedroom—a young woman whose shoulder-length, wavy dark hair and merry, olive eyes helped relieve the primness of her Bible-schoolish dress. She sat demurely on the sofa and the two exchanged covert glances. Certainly there was no instantaneous attraction between them.

At least she's not too tall, Dan consoled himself, secretly appraising the young lady.

Rhoda was equally disappointed with her suitor. He was still emaciated and pale from his bout with hepatitis. *He's so gaunt,* she thought. *He looks so ill and tired.* Yet despite her negative first impression, Rhoda became intrigued by the man beside her. After dinner and the delicious chocolate cake, Dan showed Rhoda photographs of Cuba. As the missionary opened up and began to speak about his life there, Rhoda found him more and more interesting. She admired him. *There's a lot to this man*, she conceded. *I mustn't be thrown off by first appearances.*

After the third date, when nothing seemed to be happening between the courting couple, Dan thought, *I must have made a mistake, but Lord, I'm open to Your will. If she's to be my wife, please confirm this to me.*

On what Dan surmised would be their last date, they attended a wedding together. During the ceremony, Rhoda sang, and as Dan listened to her vibrant voice, he was moved with an intense emotion. Surprised, he realized he was deeply drawn to this petite woman. He was, in fact, falling in love with her.

After that, their dates usually revolved around church meetings: Dan preached and Rhoda sometimes complemented his ministry by singing. Then on one memorable occasion, Dan invited Rhoda to travel with him to New York, where he was scheduled to speak. As Rhoda's sister was going to Ohio, Dan offered to take them all out for a Chinese dinner and then drop Ella off at the bus station.

Rhoda was delighted. She thought it extremely generous for a missionary to treat not only her but her sister as well. She was secretly pleased to see that the restaurant he chose was one of the best. "This will be too much for you to afford," Rhoda protested.

Dan laughed and then looked straight into her eyes, "Oh, I believe that the Lord takes my girlfriend into consideration."

Girlfriend. Rhoda savored the word but said nothing. "Ella and I will just share a plate," she offered, but the gallant young man wouldn't hear of it.

On the drive home, Rhoda found herself thinking of this man and her relationship with him. She knew that she didn't love him, and she had always believed that it was the will of God that she should be deeply in love with the man she would marry. *Oh Lord, what should I do?* she prayed silently as they drove down the freeway. *I appreciate all of his qualities, but I don't love him.* At that moment, the Spirit of God came upon Rhoda in a mighty way and broke the resistance in her heart. She suddenly felt a great outpouring of love for the man at the steering wheel, and she burst into tears.

Dan glanced quickly at the weeping young woman. "What's the matter?" he asked awkwardly. "Why are you crying?"

Rhoda shook her head, not knowing what to say. How could she tell Dan about the sudden love she felt for him? Since he hadn't made an announcement of his feelings towards her, she thought it would be presumptuous to declare her feelings first. "Oh, it's nothing," Rhoda answered shyly. "I just feel the presence of God."

The following week, Dan offered to drive Rhoda and Twyla to the camp in upstate New York where they were scheduled to be counselors. The missionary stayed overnight in one of the guest cabins, shivering so much in the brisk weather that he wore his hat to bed. Before he left, Dan gave Rhoda a dozen roses. By now, a deep affection had grown between the couple, and although Dan had not yet verbally expressed his love to Rhoda, his eyes said everything. She knew.

"I want to speak to you about something important, Rhoda," Dan said earnestly. "We can talk about things over at the Christian retreat center in Rome, New York."

Dan and Rhoda spent a lovely, romantic time walking in the mountains along trails cut through dense pine trees. In a peaceful spot by a stream, Dan stopped and took Rhoda's arm. "I have three questions to ask you," he declared, looking deep into Rhoda's eyes and watching her every response. "The first one is—will you marry me?"

Rhoda opened her mouth, but Dan interrupted quickly. "Don't answer yet until I finish." He paused and took a deep breath, "The second is—will you marry me in the fall? And the third is—will you go back with me to Cuba immediately after we're married?"

Rhoda flung her arms around Dan. "Yes, yes, and yes—to all three!"

Dan drew her into his arms and kissed her firmly, sealing their declaration of love for each other.

In October of 1960, Dan and Rhoda became husband and wife, fulfilling the word of knowledge the Lord had given to the young missionary. After a brief honeymoon in Florida, the newlyweds returned to Cuba. At the Miami airport, the Del Vecchios watched as Cuban refugees disembarked from their plane. Many were weeping. They'd been separated from their families and had lost their possessions and homes. Ironically, while these unfortunate people were fleeing Cuba, Dan and Rhoda were waiting to enter their country, in chaos because of the revolution. The US government had severed diplomatic relations with Cuba and lifted state protection over American citizens. Despite the danger, the missionaries were willing to risk their lives.

When the plane landed in Havana, Dan and Rhoda were greeted by dark, bearded revolutionaries dressed in khakis and wielding bayonets and machine guns. Fidel Castro was now firmly in control of the country; officials from the previous government had either been hanged or imprisoned. To Rhoda, who had never ventured beyond New York, New Jersey, and Pennsylvania, these brooding soldiers looked especially fierce and threatening.

I know, I know the Lord has called us together, Rhoda nervously reminded herself, feeling the electrifying tension as they passed through the terminal. *This is not our moment of death.*

Shortly after their arrival in Cuba, Rhoda had a vivid dream. She woke up in a cold sweat, shaking with fright. "Dan, wake up," she nudged her sleeping husband.

"What is it, honey?" he murmured drowsily.

"I just had the most awful nightmare! Firemen were banging on our door and yelling 'Fire! Fire! Escape!' What do you think it means? Is it a warning?"

Dan switched on the lamp beside the bed and sat up. After considering the dream, he tended to agree with Rhoda's interpretation. "Maybe it's God's way of telling us to get out of the country. It's too dangerous for us to stay here."

Fidel Castro's government was very anti-American. Angry demonstrators were burning effigies of newly-elected President John F. Kennedy in the streets. Dan realized that their presence created a serious hazard for the national church leaders and their congregations. After only ten brief days in Cuba, the Del Vecchios returned to the States. They waved goodbye to all their weeping friends, committing them into the hands of the Lord. These warm-hearted Cubans sensed they would never see the two American missionaries again.

For three intense years, Daniel Del Vecchio had labored in the ripe field of Cuba. In all, he had pioneered seven mission outreaches in that country, including the four churches of Alacranes, Unión de Reyes, Sabanilla, and Montserrat. The fruit of his work would withstand, by God's grace, the ensuing years of persecution under Fidel Castro's pro-Communist regime—although many believers would lose their freedom, and some, even their lives.

After more than six decades, the church Dan had planted in Sabanilla still continues to this day, with twenty key leaders having emerged from that assembly. The congregation in Alacranes built a larger church, which is also still active with hundreds of converts and house meetings in the area. Sadly, Castro's Communists confiscated the church in Montserrat, using the building as a labor hall. The wealthy landowner had to flee for her life, losing all her property. Many Cubans had been saved there and went on to follow the Lord. Only eternity will reveal the whole story.

Dan too had paid a price: his health had suffered. Hepatitis had affected his liver, and for a long time he could only consume small portions of food throughout the day. But despite the ravages to his health, for the missionary, Cuba had been a training ground in the development of his ministry—a crash course in healing and deliverance, faith and perseverance.

CHAPTER THREE
MEXICO

After Dan and Rhoda returned from Cuba, they stayed with friends in Florida while they built their "honeymoon cottage." Being the stubborn, independent person that he was, Dan thought he could build their home by himself. While working on the roof joists, he fell nine feet, landing directly on his head between two tree stumps. If he had landed fifteen inches on either side, he would have cracked his skull. Dan struggled to get up but screamed with pain, collapsed, and lost consciousness.

When he came to his senses, Daniel found himself in an ambulance with its sirens blaring. He overheard his wife anxiously asking the medic: "We just got married. Is my husband going to become a paralytic?"

At the hospital, the X-ray revealed that Daniel had suffered a compressed fracture of his spine. He was placed in traction for a few days with weights on his legs—extremely uncomfortable for him, as he couldn't move. When he was released from the hospital, he had to wear a spring steel and leather brace every day to support his spine indefinitely.

Returning to their half-constructed "honeymoon cottage," Dan was amazed to discover that his wonderful Christian neighbors had completed the roof while he'd been in the hospital. Only a brick façade on the front half of the house still needed to be finished. Rhoda helped by carting bricks in a wheelbarrow over to her husband. Unable to bend over because of the steel back brace, Dan had to kneel down on his knees to lay the bricks.

During the past year, a burden for Mexico had been working in Dan's heart. The desire to go had increased until he couldn't ignore it. He had contacted a missionary who operated a children's orphanage in Monterrey, and he made a commitment to be there in June. In spite of his back injury, he wanted to keep his word.

Exhibiting the dogged determination that characterized the man, and wearing the uncomfortable brace that dug into his groin, Dan finished building their home. He was proud of the result: a cozy cottage with two bedrooms and two bathrooms, and a lovely bay window overlooking a garden. Rhoda was pleased that they would have a place to call "home" when they returned on furlough from Mexico, especially now that she was expecting their first child.

The young missionary couple packed up their little van and left for Mexico. After a three-day journey, the Del Vecchios arrived in Monterrey in June of 1961. Feeling foolish, Dan realized that he didn't have a street address for the missionary, only a post box number. Hoping that the post office would give him the address, he drove there, arriving near closing time.

"We can't give out personal information," the man at the counter said, turning down his request.

Dan wasn't sure what to do now. Here they were in a strange country, with little money. They didn't know where this family lived, and they didn't know anybody else in Mexico. As he faced this dilemma, a voice from behind him in the line piped up: "I know where they are. I'll take you."

This helpful stranger guided the Del Vecchios to a place a far distance out of Monterrey. They found the orphanage very late at night, and then the stranger vanished. They never saw this "person" again. Dan was convinced he was an angel.

"I've never heard of you," the missionary told Dan bluntly when he knocked on the door. "I'm leaving for Washington early in the morning, and I don't have time to talk now."

With no place to go, Dan and Rhoda slept on the mattress in the back of their van. At two in the morning, the missionary relented. "You can come inside now."

In the morning, the missionary drove the Del Vecchios back into the city of Monterrey. "I'm taking you to my wife," he said. "She'll tell you what's going on."

"Oh, everyone says they're coming to visit us and they never come," the wife explained. "So I just wait until they come and then worry about it. But I'll try to organize something."

"Forget it," Dan replied. He remembered the name of another missionary that someone had given to him in New Jersey. "Do you know who he is?"

"Yes," she answered and gave him that missionary's phone number.

Pastor Harold welcomed the Del Vecchios warmly and invited them to stay at his house. Although he could barely speak Spanish, he had hired young men to preach at the little churches he had started. Dan preached to these small groups of stoic Mexicans, who seemed to be falling asleep half of the time.

While driving through Monterrey with Harold that first week, Dan spotted a large boxing arena with a seating capacity of six thousand.

I want you to rent that place, the Lord told him very clearly.

Going from preaching to thirty sleepy Mexicans to six thousand people was a huge leap of faith for Dan. In obedience to

God's voice, the missionary approached the city's Ministers' Alliance and met with all the pastors representing many denominations. They told Dan that they would support a united campaign if he obtained permission from the mayor's office in writing. The law didn't allow any kind of religious services to be held in a public building like the coliseum. Open air meetings were illegal.

The heat in Monterrey was intense, like an inferno. The metal and leather brace Dan wore to support his spine was extremely uncomfortable in the suffocating heat. At night, he lay on the floor because the sheets felt like fire to his skin. Overhead, the water-fed fan whirred, dispersing cool air.

One night, in agony because of his excruciating back pain and a raging fever, Dan suddenly saw a vision. With his eyes wide open, he was transported in the Spirit to the coliseum. Alert and wide awake, he witnessed a sequence of events take place with such vividness that it was like watching a three-dimensional movie. As if he was an outside observer, Dan saw the coliseum filled with thousands of people. He saw Rhoda, dressed in white, singing to the crowd. Then he saw the choir singing, and finally he could see himself standing behind the pulpit and preaching with great clarity. He could hear every word of the powerful, anointed sermon he preached based on a verse taken from Isaiah 53: "*Who has believed our report? And to whom has the arm of the Lord been revealed?*"[5] At the end of the message, he watched himself give an altar call, and over one hundred people streamed down the aisles in response.

"Honey, look, they're coming!" Dan joyfully cried out loud, waking up his wife. "They're coming to Christ."

Rhoda had no idea what was happening. She thought that the fever was making her husband delirious and that he was hal-

[5] Isaiah 53:1.

lucinating. Quickly she pressed a bag of ice cubes on his burning forehead, hoping it would cool his temperature and quiet his thoughts. Dan tried to shake her off and explain the vision he had seen, but she insisted that he calm down.

"It's not the fever!" he protested. "It's a revelation from God!"

The vision Dan had received strengthened his faith and resolve to rent the coliseum for an evangelistic campaign, to preach the gospel and pray for the sick. At the same time, doubts tormented him: *Pray for the sick? When you yourself have a broken back?*

For three months Dan had prayed for the healing of his back, and God had not healed him. In his inner struggle of faith, he heard the voice of the Lord whisper to his heart the words from Exodus 15:26: "*I am the Lord who healeth thee, Jehovah Rapha.*"[6] The Lord clearly showed Dan that he couldn't pray for healing while he was wearing his metal brace. It wouldn't be faith-inspiring for people to see the ugly form protruding so visibly from under his shirt. He realized that something dramatic needed to be done.

"Lord, if You are my healer, if You are my physician," Dan boldly prayed, "then You are responsible for my back. By faith, I'm going to remove my brace, and I'm going to walk."

Slowly Dan unbuckled the steel and leather brace, tears streaming down onto his hands. It was an intense emotional strain to take off his brace and trust God for his healing. In the short time he'd been wearing it, he had developed a psychological dependence on its support. He thought that without the brace, his back might buckle like a hinge.

The Ministers' Alliance had agreed to cooperate with him if he received written permission from the mayor to use the coliseum.

---

[6] "*For I am the Lord who heals you.*" Other translations have "*Your Healer.*"

The City Hall was located high up above many steps. Every step the missionary climbed was pure agony.

When Dan arrived at the mayor's office, he found it crowded with people. As there were no empty seats, he was forced to stand. Every now and then, the mayor's male secretary came into the waiting room and called people one by one into the inner office. Dan felt faint. His pain was so great that he could hardly stand. Moving to the door where the secretary went in and out, he leaned heavily against it, bracing himself against its frame.

He's going to have to knock me over, the missionary gritted his teeth, *because I'm not going to let him out of there until he sees me!* When the secretary next appeared, Dan blocked his path and introduced himself. The secretary promised to present his request before the mayor.

"The mayor can't give you written permission," the secretary finally informed him, "but he gives his word. He will not send the police or stop you in any way."

The word of the mayor was good enough for Dan. He had granted his unofficial permission to get around the law, which forbade use of public buildings for religious purposes. When Dan presented the mayor's response to the Ministers' Alliance, however, most backed out from their support of the campaign. Without official documents, they were afraid of being thrown out of the country.

Only one man was brave enough to stand publicly behind the young evangelist—a superintendent of the Nazarene Church. Dan visited this man in the hospital, where he was recovering from an operation. His legs had just been amputated after a terrible car accident. Even though he was in excruciating pain, this man of faith mustered the strength to encourage the missionary: "Brother, you hold the campaign. I'll send my choir to back you up. Those pastors are cowards. They're hiding behind the doors before the stones come!"

The only other source of encouragement to Dan was a group of ten dedicated women who had decided to meet in a church cellar to fast and pray for the crusade for ten days. God had told them: *Fast and pray. You will see miracles you have never seen before.*

To advertise the campaign, Dan printed fifty thousand pamphlets. Using a magazine cover with Castro addressing a crowd, the pastor had ingeniously cut out the Cuban dictator's picture and replaced it with his own photograph, holding an open Bible in his hands. The caption boldly proclaimed: "The deaf hear, the blind see, the lame walk, and the poor have the gospel preached to them."[7] Dan gave street children selling gum a few pesos to distribute the pamphlets. Instead of tossing them away, these honorable little angels spread them all over Monterrey.

The first night of the meeting, Dan watched in amazement from behind a small ticket booth window at the lines of Mexicans filing into the coliseum. They seemed to be coming in anticipation, bringing sick people of all kinds with them. He observed cripples, blind people, and even lepers among the crowd. *Oh God*, he gulped.

The first evening of the evangelistic service took place exactly as Dan had seen in the vision. Rhoda sang dressed in white, and the choir from the Nazarene Church sang. On the platform, except for the choir, he found himself virtually alone. The other local pastors were dispersed among the crowd so that in the event of a police raid, they couldn't be accused of any involvement. As Dan preached, the amplification system broke down. He had to turn slowly in circles and shout so that everybody in the audience could

[7] Based on Luke 7:22: "*Jesus answered and said to them, 'Go and tell John the things you have seen and heard: that the blind see, the lame walk, the lepers are cleansed, the deaf hear, the dead are raised, the poor have the gospel preached to them.*'"

at least catch fragments of his sermon. Over one thousand people were seated on the ground floor of the coliseum. He preached to the north, the south, the east, and the west, shouting out the gospel message. Despite these difficulties, the Lord blessed the service. When Dan gave the altar call, 120 Mexican souls responded, streaming to the front to receive Christ—just as he had seen in his vision.

The first meeting left Dan totally exhausted. Because of the problems he'd faced trying to get the campaign off the ground, the lack of cooperation, and the breakdown of the public address system, he felt completely worn out, emotionally and physically.

The evangelist lay on the floor of Pastor Harold's home with his face in the crook of his arm and wept. Despite the previous evening's measure of victory, Dan felt crushed and broken in spirit. Under tremendous spiritual pressure, he cried out to God. As he lay on the floor, broken before the Lord, suddenly Dan knew that Jesus was standing behind him. Although he didn't look up, he was acutely aware that *He was there*. It wasn't just the Presence of the Holy Spirit. It was *the Presence of Jesus Himself.* He spoke to Dan's heart in a voice so strong and clear, it was almost audible:

"*My son, why did you doubt?*" Jesus gently rebuked the weeping, prostrate man in words similar to those He had expressed to Peter, His disciple. Dan wasn't even aware that he'd been doubting. Then Jesus exhorted him: "*If you will trust Me and not doubt, then I will cause you to ride upon the high places of the earth and give you the heritage of Jacob your father.*"

At the time, Dan had no idea what those words meant, but later he would discover that this incredible promise came from Isaiah 58:14. God had always spoken to Dan through scripture, and he claimed this promise for his life. Years later he would understand just what the heritage of Jacob involved: the spiritual and material blessings of God, meaning the blessings of heaven and the blessings of earth; prosperity and provision; and the anointing of the Holy Spirit, the "dew of heaven." And he would be able to declare that God had indeed mightily and abundantly fulfilled His promise to him.

The second night on the platform, Dan was a new man because *Jesus had spoken to him!* He was so filled with faith that everybody noticed the amazing change in the evangelist. Empowered by that word from God and on fire with the Holy Spirit, Dan rose and boldly declared: "If God doesn't do miracles tonight and heal the sick, then I am a liar. Jesus is dead, the Bible is not true, and I'm an imposter!"

But the Lord confirmed His word! Hundreds of souls came to Christ. The pastors wouldn't allow Dan to pray for the sick by the laying on of hands. They had warned him that many of the people had infectious diseases like tuberculosis and leprosy, and if he touched them, he could spread the disease. The department of health would then be forced to shut the meetings down.

Following this advice, Dan prayed for the sick, not individually but en masse. Although he didn't realize it at the time, this method helped to create an atmosphere of faith among the people, building up their expectation that at any moment God would heal them. As the evangelist moved among them and prayed, God did begin to heal the sick.

On the last day of the meetings, Dan decided, *I'm going to pray for them individually no matter what happens—even if the police come!*

That night, 240 people stood in the healing line for prayer. As he touched the people, the gift of healing began to operate, and Dan could feel strength flowing out of his hands. Miracles were happening. He had never witnessed anything like it before in his ministry. The blind could see, cripples walked, and lepers were healed! Over 90 percent of those who came forward were instantly healed by the power of God.

Dan was especially touched by one child, a polio victim whose hand was twisted and deformed. As he held the boy's withered hand, it suddenly straightened out before everyone's eyes. Dan marveled at the power of the Lord so present to heal. He attributed this to three main factors: Jesus's word to him and his faith in that word; the ten women who were fasting and praying and holding off demonic forces; and the trusting, believing Mexican people themselves. Dan gathered 220 signed testimonies of miraculous healings.

As an added blessing, Dan noticed that his own back was no longer giving him any pain. The first night of the meeting, his back had been healed! The day he had gone to the mayor's office, suffering great agony, had been a crucial test. By removing his brace, he had stepped out in faith, and from that time forward, he never put it on again. Although the fracture is still present in his spine, Dan was able to lead a normal life during many more decades of ministry.

Once a month, a group of missionaries and pastors met together to pray for the people of Monterrey. After witnessing the miracles of the crusade, they now had faith to pray for the sick. A woman whose abdomen was grotesquely swollen came to one meeting and requested prayer for healing. Although she was scheduled to have an operation to remove a section of her bowel, she believed that God would divinely touch her body. One of the pastors prayed what he thought was the prayer of faith for this woman's healing. As soon as he finished praying, he insisted that the meeting end. They had prayed in faith, he stated, and now it was up to the Lord to heal her.

"Now wait just a minute," Dan interjected before everyone dispersed. "The Holy Spirit hasn't come yet; please sit down."

"But we said the prayer of faith," the pastor insisted. "The rest is the work of the Lord."

"Please take a seat," Dan repeated, taking authority over the situation. "The Holy Spirit has not yet fallen upon us. We're going to continue to wait on the Lord."

As the group waited on the Lord, worshiping and praising Him, they became truly united in spirit. Before long, everyone sensed the undeniable Presence of the Holy Spirit. Now with true harmony and accord amongst themselves, they prayed once again for the woman's healing.

Instantly before their eyes the woman's swollen abdomen deflated, rendering her operation unnecessary. This set a certain precedent for the mystery of divine healing: the prayer of agreement, the true unity of the Spirit. As Matthew 18:19–20 states:

> *... if two of you agree on earth concerning anything that they ask, it will be done for them by My Father in heaven. For where two or three are gathered together in My Name, I am there in the midst of them.*

As a result of the campaign, Pastor Daniel Del Vecchio's reputation as a man who had faith to pray for the sick spread throughout Monterrey, and people flocked to the churches where he preached. As he had no desire to draw a personal following, he decided that the best plan would be to leave Monterrey and move on to other cities.

In Cuernavaca, Dan held an evangelistic and healing campaign, preaching in a local theater. The Del Vecchios had rented a two-story house, and it was here that they experienced a personal miracle. Before hand-washing Daniel Jr.'s diapers, Rhoda took off her wedding rings, wrapped them in tissue, and put them in her purse. Ten-month-old Daniel, with his typical curiosity, emptied all the contents of her purse on the floor. When she realized what the child had done, she picked up the scattered items and accidentally flushed the tissue paper down the toilet.

"Honey, where are your rings?" Dan asked Rhoda at dinner that night.

"Oh, they're upstairs."

"Are you sure?" he asked his wife, who replied in the affirmative.

After dinner, Rhoda rummaged through her closets and drawers, turning everything upside down. Suddenly it dawned on her that she had flushed her rings down the toilet! She spent the night in turmoil, sometimes crying and sometimes praying.

In the morning, Rhoda read the scripture: "*My soul magnifies the Lord, and my spirit has rejoiced in God my Savior … For He who is mighty has done great things for me, and holy is His name*" (Luke 1:46–47, 49). God spoke to her: *Today I will do something great for you.* And then He repeated the promise.

Although the toilet had been flushed several times and the rings would now be lost, Rhoda wanted her husband to find them. Dan didn't know that his wife had heard the voice of God and that His words had given her faith for the impossible. She urged Dan to ask the gardener if there was a septic tank where they could search for the missing rings. Although the request seemed ridiculous, he conceded, not wanting to dampen her spirits. The gardener explained that there was no cesspool; all the wastewater flowed into the city's sewage system. Rhoda did not give up.

"Is there some place with a lid where we can observe the wastewater drain into the city sewage?" Rhoda persisted. The gardener answered yes.

Rhoda asked her husband to throw buckets of water into the two toilets above and below and then block the drain pipe with a board to stop the water from flowing. Dan knew that she was asking for the impossible. Even if the rings were still at the bottom, when he lifted the board, they would pass by undetected in the dirty water. After a few hours of this labor, Dan said impatiently, "Forget the rings. I'll buy you others!"

"Please, just one more bucket," Rhoda pleaded, clinging to her hope.

"One more bucket, but no more!" Dan conceded.

As Dan poured the last bucket of water, he saw something shining in the clear waters, resting on the toilet's ledge. The two rings were together, one on top of the other.

"Hallelujah!" he shouted, amazed at this miracle. Like the prophet Elisha[8] who had commanded an axe head to float in the river where it had sunk, Rhoda's faith in God's promise had caused the two rings to be recovered! Over the years this miracle, which defied natural laws, served to remind Dan and Rhoda of God's love and care for every detail of their lives, even things that may seem "insignificant."

Dan was invited by a pastor to preach in Saltillo, in the province of Coahuila. The pastor intended to rent a hall that belonged to the labor union, with a seating capacity of five hundred. He asked for money in advance to organize the outreach, and Dan gave it to him. The Del Vecchios then traveled to minister on the Pacific Coast. When they returned to Saltillo for the date set for the meetings, they found the hall empty.

"Where are the chairs?" Dan asked the guard in surprise.

[8] 2 Kings 6:1–7.

"What chairs?" he responded suspiciously. "Who are you?"

"I've rented this place for meetings."

When the guard told him he knew nothing about the arrangement, Dan called all the pastors of the churches in Saltillo together and presented the situation to them, telling them how this pastor had taken his money and disappeared. The pastors were frightened of renting the hall, as any kind of meeting outside of a registered church was illegal in Mexico. The leader among the pastors, a retired general, carried the strongest voice. He quoted Romans 13: "*Let everyone be subject to the governing authorities, for there is no authority except that which God has established.*" [9]

"Don't stop there. Keep reading," Dan instructed the general, who thought the issue was settled.

"*For rulers hold no terror for those who do right, but for those who do wrong. Do you want to be free from fear of the one in authority? Then do what is right and you will be commended.*" [10]

"This is what I'm doing," Dan exhorted the pastors. "I'm not afraid of the authorities. I'm doing what is good. I'm preaching the gospel and healing the sick, so I have no reason to be afraid of the powers that be."

The pastors, however, bowed to the general's influence. They were frightened to be involved in the evangelistic campaign because of police reprisals. "Well then, my wife and I will conduct the meetings by ourselves," Dan told them.

When the Del Vecchios arrived at the hall, they found that everything was set up and all the chairs arranged. The pastors were gathered together on the platform. "What are you doing here?" Dan asked them in happy surprise.

"You shamed us," they replied. "We couldn't leave you on your own."

---

[9] Romans 13:1a (NIV).

[10] Romans 13:3 (NIV).

God sent people to the hall until it was almost full. During the first meeting, a young man came running down the aisle, screaming in terror. He ran towards the altar and collapsed on the floor, shaking like he was having an epileptic attack. The pastors on the platform were shocked.

"Don't be afraid," Dan urged the pastors. "C'mon, let's get this out!"

Dan jumped off the five-foot high platform and cast the tormenting spirit out of the young man. Within minutes, the man stood to his feet, raising his hands and praising the Lord. The glory of God was all over him. The incident broke open the meetings. At the same time, the group of women who had interceded for the evangelistic campaign in Monterrey were fasting and fervently praying. The Lord had opened the way for spiritual breakthrough.

Every meeting, a woman was dragged in a chair all the way to the front row and placed before the platform. Paralyzed from her waist down, she hadn't been able to walk for five years. Dan noticed this woman, but he knew that his faith wasn't strong enough to pray for her. He waited on God for the anointing to come. He waited for the faith of the whole congregation to rise to the point where they could pray for miracles.

By the fifth night, Dan knew that the power of God was present to heal. Ever since the young man had been delivered, the people were increasingly looking towards the power of God, and God was healing and performing miracles to the degree of their faith. Dan now perceived that there was collective faith for this woman to be healed. He jumped off the high platform and took the woman in the chair by her hands: "In the name of Jesus Christ, walk!"

For the first time in five years, the woman began to walk. She was weeping; her daughter was weeping. That night, the woman knelt down by her bed and thanked God for her miraculous healing.

The Del Vecchios made the province of Puebla their home base for six months, within sight of the Popocatépetl volcano. Dan wanted to evangelize two towns: Chipilo and Cholula. The agricultural village of Chipilo was unusual in that most of its inhabitants bore the tall, blond, blue-eyed features of their European forefathers, Italians from Venice, in striking contrast to the darker complexion of the typical Mexican. The Del Vecchio family was very popular in the town; the locals adored their young son—blond, blue-eyed Daniel Junior.

Dan and his Italian assistant, Antonio,[11] attempted to show a film in Chipilo's plaza, but the opposition from the locals was so intense, they decided a safer approach would be to open a Christian bookstore instead. Dan placed a Californian-Mexican named Guadalupe in charge of this enterprise—a woman who ministered in the local jail.

The day after it opened, a nun, who had previously been very friendly, entered the store and wagged her finger under Dan's nose. "Don't you dare bring your Protestant propaganda into my town," she threatened.

"Please take a look around," Dan invited, hoping to appease her. "Tell me which books you don't like." He had lots of Catholic books on display.

The nun refused his offer and angrily left the store. A few hours later, a crowd of screaming women had gathered outside the front door. "*Comunista! Comunista* go home!" they shouted wildly, waving gasoline cans and appearing ready to burn the bookstore down at any moment.

[11] Antonio had been so moved by the message the Del Vecchios had shared at their church in Mullica Hill, New Jersey, that he had given up his job and, along with his wife and two children, joined their mission work in Mexico. Fasting and prayer were part of his life. Eventually he returned to Sicily, where he and his family started forty churches.

"Guard the store with your life," Dan had told Guadalupe when he'd left earlier, never dreaming she would take him at his word. Bravely, she stood in the doorway and fought the riotous mob off. Fortunately, a passing bus driver and ticket collector came to her rescue. They got her inside the bookstore, locked the door, and protected her until she managed to escape through the back exit. After midnight, Dan and some helpers returned to the shop and collected all the books.

After being driven out of that town, Dan moved on to another village called Cholula, which originally had 365 Aztec temples, one for every day of the year. The Spanish *conquistador* Hernán Cortés had destroyed them and built cathedrals on the ruins, seventeen of which were still functioning. A pyramid where human sacrifices had once been offered still stood.[12]

Cholula was a strong bastion of Roman Catholicism, and Protestants were fiercely persecuted. Guadalupe had told Dan about a small group of Christians of the latter denomination that had been meeting in a home for prayer. Fanatics had surrounded the house. "Come out or we're going to burn you alive inside," they shouted, waving sticks.

The non-Catholic believers knew that the angry mob was waiting outside to beat them to death. They didn't know what to do. If they stayed inside, they'd be burned alive; if they ventured out, they'd be beaten to death. Guadalupe, who'd been among those trapped in the home, recounted to Dan how they had fallen on their faces and cried out to God. Suddenly an eclipse took place! In the cover of darkness, the group managed to jump over a wall and escape. Their persecutors, confused, started beating each other.

Dan wasn't sure how to begin an outreach in Cholula. It was very dangerous because the persecutors had driven the non-Catholic Christians out into the mountains. Throughout Mexico

[12] For more history, see Wikipedia.org/wiki/Cholula.

it was a perilous time. Many people were being killed for the gospel's sake. In one church that Dan had preached in, nine Christians had been martyred. Then Dan met a missionary who was traveling around with a truck and projector showing an old silent film, *The Passion of Christ*. They decided to show this film together in Cholula.

"I want to go with you," Rhoda pleaded with her husband as he packed their Chevrolet station wagon for the trip into town. She held their son, Daniel Junior, in her arms.

"No, honey, it's too dangerous," Dan replied, not wanting to risk the lives of his wife and child. "They've attacked everyone who's come with the gospel. Stay home."

"Where you go, I go," Rhoda stated with determination.

"If you insist," Dan gave in to his wife. "But stay in the car. If they attack, I'll jump in and we'll get out of town fast!"

Dan drove to the main plaza of Cholula. "Why don't we project the film on the wall of the cathedral?" He suggested to the missionary assisting him.

"It's too dangerous!" the missionary warned. "Let's use that garage wall over there."

While Rhoda waited in the car some distance away, they set up the equipment so that the film could be projected on the whitewashed wall of the nearby garage. The film, which was about Christ's crucifixion, drew hundreds of spectators into the plaza until nearly one thousand had gathered. The people openly wept as they watched *The Passion of Christ*, deeply moved and stirred with a desire to know more.

"How many of you want to read the story of Jesus? I've got the Gospel of St. John to give you for free," Dan announced over the loudspeaker at the film's conclusion. Hundreds mobbed the truck, pushing and shoving to reach for the literature. In their eagerness, they knocked over the film projector. The mental image of all those Mexican hands desperately grabbing for the Gospel left a profound impression on the evangelist. He had never witnessed such hunger for God.

After the successful film showing, Dan rented a hotel hall with an entrance on the main street and once again set up a Christian bookstore. He left the very capable and faithful Guadalupe in charge of the venture. In the months following, although violent mobs tried to burn the bookstore down with gasoline, Guadalupe refused to be shaken. When a mob threatened to bomb the hotel, however, the owner forced her to close down.

The brave Guadalupe stayed in Cholula and kept witnessing about Jesus. The first church she helped to plant with some brothers from Puebla was burned down four times during its construction, but Guadalupe refused to give up. Her unswerving faith, literally tried by fire, bore results. Eventually she helped establish two churches and a Bible school in the town—a testimony of the Mexican believers' longsuffering, sacrifice, and perseverance.

The Del Vecchios ministered for three years in the nation of Mexico. During that time, they witnessed incredible miracles—in little church meetings of thirty people to thousands in the coliseum where God had confirmed His Word with such signs and wonders as amazing healings and conversions. The Lord used Dan to spearhead a work in Mexico that broke through the strong opposition to any non-Catholic denominations.

While in Mexico, Dan's primary focus had been on evangelism. He had judged his success by the number of conversions. After the meetings, however, he had no idea whether lives had truly been transformed. Increasingly dissatisfied, he longed to disciple people one by one, to encourage their spiritual growth and to build up their faith. God was slowly working in his heart, changing his desires and ministry. Instead of evangelistic fervor, he experienced a growing desire to be a spiritual *father.*

Years later, God would speak deeply into his heart: *I will make you a father of many nations.* This *fatherhood desire* also bore witness to the apostolic gifting emerging in Daniel Del Vecchio's life. God would soon open doors to a new nation.

CHAPTER FOUR
SPAIN

Dan spread the map of the world on the living room floor of the brick farmhouse in New Jersey. After serving six years on the mission field, the thirty-two-year-old had returned with his wife and toddler son to his childhood home to seek God's further direction. His eyes scanned all the nations that lay before him.

Lord, he prayed silently, *where should we go?*

His eyes came to the nation of Spain and rested there. It was natural that he should be drawn to this country, progressing from Cuba to Mexico and now to Spain. The desire to go to this land had been growing in his heart even as he had labored in the Mexican heat. He knew the Lord was calling him to this nation.

Where, Lord? he repeated as he studied the map of Spain. His eyes ran up and down the southern coast and stopped on the port of Málaga.

You will be in Barcelona one month and then you will go to Málaga, the Holy Spirit clearly impressed upon him. Málaga was just a name on the map to Dan. He knew nothing about the city or what he would find there. [13]

[13] An ancient trading seaport on the Mediterranean with a rich three-thousand-year-old history, Málaga was colonized by the Phoenicians, Greeks, Carthaginians, Romans, and the Moors. It was one of the last Muslim cities to fall during the siege of the Catholic monarchs Isabella and Ferdinand in 1487. (For more information see: www.wikipedia.org/wiki/history_of_Málaga).

In February of 1964, Dan, Rhoda, and their two-year old son, Daniel Jr., flew to the nation of Spain, sent not by an official missionary organization but by the strong call of God on their hearts. They had virtually no financial support, but they had faith in the God who had commissioned them.

As the plane circled over the shimmering turquoise waters of the Mediterranean, Dan had no idea that Spain was going to be his cross. Spain would prove to be to him what Egypt had been to Joseph, and he would be able to echo Joseph's words: "*For God has caused me to be fruitful in the land of my affliction*" (Genesis 41:52b).

After spending one month in Barcelona with another missionary couple, Dan, Rhoda, and young Daniel Jr. drove into Málaga on Easter Friday, arriving right in the middle of a Holy Week procession. Forced to halt because of the pressing crowd, the Del Vecchio family sat in their newly purchased Simca car observing the somber pageantry. Shocked by the superstitious nature of the processional, they watched incredulously as groups of men passed by, hoisting on their shoulders massive statues of the Virgin covered in candles. The men marched slowly to the dreary, depressing beat of drums. The parade resembled a funeral dirge more than a religious celebration. Following the Virgins, men dressed in long robes and pointed peaked hats brought up the rear, dragging heavy chains behind them.

"It's like something straight out of the Middle Ages," Dan remarked to Rhoda.

Dan and Rhoda had come face to face with the rituals and traditions of the centuries' old religious power in Spain that would not, as they were soon to discover, be easily broken.

When the Del Vecchios first arrived in Spain, the nation was under the dictatorship of General Franco. Except for Roman Catholicism, no other public expression of religion was permitted. Protestant churches were not tolerated. The baptism of the Holy Spirit was pretty much unknown. Throughout the whole country, Dan learned that there were only two dozen people filled with the Holy Spirit—a group of eleven in Barcelona and a few others scattered here and there. In major cities like Madrid, Seville, and Málaga there was no charismatic ministry.

Dan and Rhoda found a little apartment on the outskirts of Málaga and set up their home. The Director of the Assemblies of God in Europe and the Italian Assemblies of God in the USA had given Dan letters of recommendation, even though he wasn't a member of their denomination. Soon Dan was in contact with a Protestant group and invited to preach. Afterwards, the leading elder's sister, who had been a nun for eleven years, approached him.

"You're different from these other people," Adelaida commented curiously. "You have something. What is it?"

Dan studied her thoughtfully. "Come on over for lunch. You can share your testimony, and I'll give you mine."

Adelaida joined the Del Vecchios for lunch in their apartment. Over the meal, the former nun told the couple how, during her first six years in the convent, she hadn't been allowed to have a Bible. After she had taken her final vow, her brother had given her a Bible and she had begun to read it. For the next five years as she'd studied it, she'd become increasingly aware of the tremendous differences between what she believed and what the Bible declared. Later, while on duty as a nurse, she'd also listened in secret to Radio Monte Carlo's gospel broadcast.

At Adelaida's request, Dan told this former nun about his missionary work in Cuba and Mexico. When he shared with her how the Lord had miraculously healed people, she listened in rapt astonishment. Dan could see that she had a keen spiritual hunger, but he was reluctant to bring up the subject of the Holy Spirit.

"Take this book and read it," Dan finally said, handing her the booklet he had written and published in Mexico about the baptism of the Holy Spirit, *El Espíritu Santo y Su Obra.*[14]

Adelaida eagerly accepted it. That night she read the booklet until three in the morning, weeping as she devoured its pages. She came back the next day to see Dan, and the two of them knelt on the floor of his apartment and prayed. Adelaida received the promised Comforter and joyfully spoke in a new tongue, the first in Málaga to do so. With excitement, she shared the news with her brother, and soon after, he too received the baptism of the Holy Spirit during his lunch *siesta.*

Sadly, when other church members found out about their experience, a controversy erupted. The leaders of their denomination not only threatened to expel Dan from the country but firmly closed the door to any further ministry through him. Dan was hurt by their hostile reaction. He'd done nothing but echo what the Apostle Paul had asked the Ephesians: "*Did you receive the Holy Spirit when you believed?*" (Acts 19:2a).

One vivid memory of those early years involved a very famous colonel who had directed military operations in North Africa for many years. He was dying, and Dan was asked to come and pray for him. In those days, it was very unlikely that such an important man of high position in Spanish society would invite a pastor to pray for him. The nurse who was attending him, however, had received the gospel and thought that Dan might be able to help him. Unaware of the religious intolerance and prejudice that existed at the time, Dan visited this dying colonel. As Dan walked up the winding steps to his house, the priest, who had just administered the last rites, passed him on his way down.

[14] Daniel Del Vecchio, *The Holy Spirit and His Work* (2019). Available through Amazon.

When Dan entered his room, the colonel received him warmly and kissed his hand. Dan did not give any significance to this gesture; he merely thought he had been told that he was a man of God and this was the customary way of showing respect to a priest. On the wall, Dan noticed the photographs of the colonel with *Generalissimo* Francisco Franco, the dictator who would rule Spain with an iron fist for thirty-six years.

Dan found this high-ranking military officer, who spoke many languages, to have a clear mind. As he shared with him, the colonel received the gospel like a dying man hanging on to a life raft. What Dan didn't know was that earlier in the week, the colonel had seen a vision of a man standing at the foot of his bed.

"Who is that man?" he had asked his daughter.

"There's nobody there," she'd told him, perplexed. "Nobody is there."

When Dan had walked into his room, the colonel had immediately recognized him as the man he'd seen in his vision, which was why he'd received him with such respect and an open mind. After Dan found out about this supernatural experience, he was reminded of Cornelius in the Book of Acts.[15] Cornelius, of course, was also a military officer, and God had sent the Apostle Peter to share the gospel with him in response to his prayers.

The colonel's daughter, who had led the pastor into her father's room, was a lady of high social standing herself, married to a celebrated acrobatic pilot. More than a decade later, she would accept Christ into her life, and Dan would pray for her to be filled with the Holy Spirit.

During this period, Dan struggled with finding ways to evangelize the Spanish people who were far from God. He couldn't preach

[15] Acts 10.

the gospel publicly, but the Lord gave him an idea. With toddler son Daniel Jr. in tow, Dan and Rhoda visited the RCA studios in Madrid, the best recording facilities in the country. Miraculously, they were able to produce two 45 rpm records. On one side, they recorded Rhoda singing gospel songs with her beautiful voice, and on the other side, Dan preached. On the first record, he preached an evangelistic message, and on the second, he preached on divine healing.

With a small battery-operated record player, Dan ventured into the back alleys of Málaga's housing projects. Cranking up the volume, he played the record with his wife singing and then turned it over for his preaching. People gathered around curiously. Although he couldn't preach the gospel openly, this intrepid missionary was able to "preach" through these records, which were borrowed and passed out all over Málaga. Dan has kept a couple of those old scratched records as a reminder of his pioneering days in Spain.

The nation's laws forbade literature distribution. Undeterred and after numerous delays, Dan was able to get a Bible study booklet called *The New Birth* legally recognized through the Ministry of Justice for printing. Although officially this booklet was meant solely for the internal use of his church, Dan decided that a one-page message from the booklet would make an excellent tract. The missionary knew that the only way he could publish it was to print it covertly.

At a printing shop, Dan found an old small hand press that was perfect for his purpose. He installed it in one of the bedrooms, turning their tiny apartment into an underground printing house. Painstakingly, through trial and error, the missionary taught himself how to operate the press, which was more complicated than he thought. Each lead letter of every word had to be tied together with a little cord, and every line wrapped with string and placed in the printing press. Dan then rolled on the ink and pressed it down, eventually learning to set the pressure just right. In this way, Dan printed his first tract: *How to Be Born Again.*

One day, a Spaniard in his early forties came to the Del Vecchios' apartment selling insurance. Dan invited the man into their home. Before long, Manolo was pouring out his troubled life to the sympathetic pastor. Although polite and obviously a man of culture, the Spaniard admitted to being an alcoholic. A few years earlier when his wife had died while giving birth to their third child, Manolo had been so shattered that he had tried to drown his sorrow with a case of whisky. After that, he drank more frequently until he could no longer hold down a steady job. He had drifted from town to town, sleeping on park benches or under bridges. He had been so desperate for alcohol that he'd even sold his blood to buy it. Dan and Rhoda were so moved by compassion for this self-confessed alcoholic that they offered him a place to sleep for the night. Manolo ended up living with them for several months.

Dan showed Manolo how to operate the printing press. During the day while Manolo printed the gospel tracts, Dan distributed them all over Málaga. The tract captured Manolo's interest and soon he started reading the New Testament. Shortly after, he made a genuine commitment to Jesus Christ. Dan and Rhoda were overjoyed to see that the alcoholic immediately stopped drinking—something that had been impossible for him to do before.

"Manolo, would you mind staying at a hotel *pensión* tonight?" Dan asked one day a few months later when a visitor from America arrived. "I'll give you the money to pay for it."

Later, Dan realized that giving money to Manolo had been a costly mistake. He had thought that the Spaniard had overcome the desire to drink, but that night, instead of paying for a hotel room, Manolo entered a bar and got drunk. A few days later, he showed up at the Del Vecchios' apartment.

"I'm sorry. I'm not worthy to be in your home." Manolo hung his head in bitter regret. "I'm drunk and I'm leaving."

Dan tried to convince this Spaniard to stay. Manolo, however, wouldn't change his mind, and he left.

"Go get him, honey!" Rhoda urged her husband. "Don't let him get away!"

Dan pursued Manolo down the street and found him in the corner bar. "Come on back with me, Manolo," Dan pleaded. "God forgives you. We forgive you. Don't throw your life away again."

"No, leave me alone," the Spaniard shrugged hopelessly, sipping his drink.

Dan tried to pull Manolo out of the bar, but the man resisted all his efforts. Sadly and with a grieving heart, Dan walked away.

Manolo had been the first person in Spain that the Del Vecchios had taken into their own home. Through this experience, they realized what an impact simply living out their Christian faith on a daily basis could have on an unbeliever. Secondly, they realized the need to minister on a long-term basis to broken, substance-dependent people. After conversion, those people needed to be sheltered and watched over until they were really secure and disciplined in their Christian faith. Although he had failed with Manolo, Dan absorbed these vital lessons, which would prove invaluable to his future ministry, especially in caring for heroin addicts.

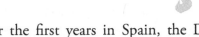

For the first years in Spain, the Del Vecchios lived a hand-to-mouth existence, often not knowing where their next meal was coming from. One day when their money had run out, Dan came home discouraged. He had just spent their last few pesetas on a bottle of milk.

"Who can I go to?" Dan agonized. Living in this foreign country, he had no one to turn to. Dan knew that he could phone his father in America and ask him to send money, but this didn't seem right to the young missionary. "God has called me to minister here," he reasoned. "It's God's *responsibility* to supply our needs."

The situation would have been dire enough if he only had himself to feed, but now the missionary had a growing family to care for: son Daniel Jr. and newborn daughter, Deborah, whom Rhoda was nursing. This crisis was a tremendous test of their faith.

"Honey, we have just one bottle of milk left," he informed his wife, dejected. "I don't know where to go from here." They were facing starvation.

Rhoda took in her husband's downcast demeanor. "Oh, don't worry about it," she declared. "I still have half a pound of rice!" Dan was so grateful for his wife's faith. She didn't complain or put extra pressure on him.

That evening a *guardia civil* officer, a member of Dan's struggling church, couldn't get to sleep. He tossed and turned. Finally, he told his wife, "I have to get up and give the pastor two hundred pesetas."

"But he's American," she countered. "He's rich!"

"I don't understand it, but I have this voice inside of me. I *have* to give him two hundred pesetas." The police officer got out of bed, dressed, and drove across town to the Del Vecchios' apartment.

"The Lord won't allow me peace until I give you this. Here," he said, depositing the two hundred pesetas into the surprised pastor's hand.

The Del Vecchios praised God for His timely provision. The money was enough to purchase groceries for the next week. Then Adelaida gave them ninety pesetas, and they lived on that for another week. Through these experiences, Dan and Rhoda learned to trust God, to really trust Him to meet all their needs. They endured many tests, then and later, terrible testing times, but God always came through.

In those early years in Spain, anything that looked like a Protestant church was strictly forbidden. To avoid being closed down, Dan bought two adjoining apartments in Málaga and removed the dividing wall. He constructed his own pews, altar, and pulpit and began to hold services in the enlarged room, which could now seat fifty. All the residents in the apartment building, however, soon joined together and threatened him. Unless he stopped holding meetings, they would throw him out.

In frustration, Dan went to the housing authorities, and without revealing his own position, he presented a potential situation. "What happens if I pray with others in my house?" he asked innocently.

"We can take your house away from you," they replied curtly.

"But it's my home!" Dan insisted.

"That makes no difference. These buildings aren't made for commercial purposes."

Dan was stunned that they considered prayer meetings to be commercial concerns. Soon after, a tenants' meeting was held in the Del Vecchios' home. After seeing the group was solidly against him, Dan asked politely: "I'd like six months to re-locate."

"No, you have to leave immediately," the leader, a schoolteacher, insisted.

Dan realized that if he refused to move, they would certainly report him to the Housing Department, and he would be in danger of forfeiting the $6,000 he'd borrowed from his father to pay for the apartment.

What can I do? Dan thought in despair and prayed silently.

The apartment's semi-legal advisor, who was sitting next to him, suddenly leaned over and whispered, "Why don't you offer to repair the roof and keep the drains clean? In exchange for this, maybe they'll let you stay."

Dan's face visibly brightened at the suggestion. He knew immediately what the man was referring to. Every day, residents of the seven-story apartment building would toss scraps of food to the "herd" of cats that lived on the patio below. This patio, located in front of the Del Vecchios' first floor apartment, was actually the roof of the commercial properties on the ground level of the apartment building. The garbage thrown from the balconies clogged the drainage system. When it rained, the drains flooded, and the leaking water was destroying the property below. At a previous tenants' meeting, a tremendous conflict over this situation had arisen. Nobody wanted to fork out any more money for repairs.

Dan made some quick calculations. As a builder, he realized he could repair the roof himself for less than $60. He stood up and faced the angry residents. "I'll collect the garbage, clean the drains, and repair the roof," he volunteered, "if you'll let me stay."

The residents took a vote, which resulted in a tie. "Quick, get down on your knees and pray," Dan instructed Rhoda and Adelaida. "We're going to vote again."

When the outcome of the second vote was announced, Daniel, Rhoda, and Adelaida waited with bated breath. One person had changed their mind in favor of Dan's proposal, and the Del Vecchios were allowed to stay. The three rejoiced, hugging each other.

By New Year's, attendance at the services had already outgrown their double apartment. Dan bought larger facilities in another section of Málaga on Los Rosales Street and named this new church *Casa Ágape*. Eventually a church with over one thousand members would grow out of this humble beginning.

After three years in Málaga, Dan bought an apartment in Córdoba to begin a ministry there. The Del Vecchios wanted to hold meetings in their private home, which was located near a site where Christians had suffered death and torture during the diabolical Inquisition.[16] The blood of martyrs had been shed in this city.

Dan found that pioneering a work is exciting, but it's also difficult and full of pressure. The police raided their house church and confiscated all their literature and Bibles, burning and destroying everything. During the raid, they also seized the Del Vecchios' records, but later, when they realized that these recordings were legalized, they were forced to return them.

When faced with trying situations, Dan often recalled a prophecy that an American pastor friend had prophesied over him in Málaga: "*For I will show him how many things he must suffer for My Name's sake*,"[17] quoting words God gave to Ananias regarding Saul of Tarsus upon his conversion. Remembering these words helped Dan to keep persevering in the midst of trials.

Dan believes that intolerance and persecution act as a wind that makes the *fire* of the gospel burn more intensely: "*These things I have spoken to you, that in Me you may have peace. In the world you will have tribulation, but be of good cheer, I have overcome the world*," (John 16:33).

[16] The "Spanish" Inquisition endured from 1478 until the reign of Isabel II in 1834. The brutality began with the persecution and expulsion of the Jews and then extended to those deemed "heretics," including Protestants. Confiscation of property, forced conversions, and torture were used to terrorize victims. At least 2,000 people were burned at the stake and 32,000 were executed. (For more information see: www.britannica.com/topic/Spanish-Inquisition).

[17] Acts 9:16.

CHAPTER FIVE
TORREMOLINOS

When he saw the crowds, he had compassion on them, because they were harassed and helpless, like sheep without a shepherd. Then he said to his disciples, 'The harvest is plentiful but the workers are few. Ask the Lord of the harvest, therefore, to send out workers into his harvest field.' (Matthew 9:36–38, NIV)

One day in 1966 after two frustrating years of trying to start a work in Málaga, Pastor Dan was walking down Calle Larios when he suddenly became aware of all the foreigners passing by. He had never seen them before. His whole mind and heart had been centered on the Spanish people, but suddenly the Holy Spirit highlighted these tourists and expatriate residents to him. Up until that moment, Dan had merely seen the crowds as bargain-hunters or pleasure-seekers, but now he saw them in a new light—as ripe fields ready for harvest. He saw them as Jesus would see them.

"As sheep without a shepherd," Dan mused, pondering the Bible verse from Matthew 9:36 that had struck his mind. "Who is meeting their spiritual needs?"

Dan was filled with compassion for these lost people who were wandering aimlessly through life without purpose or direction. He knew of only one Protestant church along the whole Costa del Sol, an Anglican one in Málaga. With the sudden boom in the tourist industry, people from all over the world, especially from Europe and North America, were pouring into the Costa del Sol, Spain's famous southern coast. The town of Torremolinos was just being discovered. It was to this tourist-mecca, a fifteen-minute drive from Málaga, that Dan felt himself increasingly drawn.

When Dan searched for suitable premises in Torremolinos to hold meetings, he encountered great difficulty. Nobody wanted to rent to a group of Protestants. Finally, the French director of one hotel agreed to allow the missionary to hold English services in the bridge room. Within a month, Dan was pleased that this hotel congregation had grown to fifty people. He was finding that after the pressure of the Málaga work—a lot of effort with few results—the ministry to tourists in Torremolinos was a welcome relief.

After the fourth meeting, the director of the hotel met the pastor at the door. "I'm sorry," the man said curtly, "but we have to do renovations in this room. You won't be able to use it anymore."

Dan, accustomed by now to these excuses, prodded the director. "Give me the real reason."

"Well, to tell you the truth," he admitted, "the owner is coming, and I nearly lost my job for allowing you in. I got up late on purpose this morning so you could have your meeting, but you can't come back." He was adamant.

The next Sunday, Dan met the congregation on the steps of the hotel. (Not knowing the services had been cancelled, they had returned.) He gathered his flock by the side door of the hotel, near the garden, and they prayed together, asking God for direction. Many were experiencing the sting of intolerance for the first time, and tears were flowing freely.

After weeks of searching, Dan found another hotel that would allow them to use their lounge for one thousand pesetas per hour.

He asked the Persian owner, "What guarantee do I have that you won't throw me out?"

"As long as you pay, as long as the police don't come, you can stay."

Announcements were printed up and a highway sign erected. Dan held one meeting there on the Sunday before Easter, but then, within the week, he was once again asked to leave. The Persian owner's two Spanish associates were afraid that the Ministry of Tourism would close them down if they allowed the Protestants in.

The next Sunday, Dan gathered his wandering congregation at the back of the hotel. With the blue sky as their canopy and the surf of the Mediterranean as their backdrop, Dan conducted an unusual outdoor service for his transient congregation that they would not quickly forget.

Six months of fruitless searching for new premises followed. At each new place Dan found to rent, he always received the same answer: as soon as the owner was told what the place would be used for, it was suddenly unavailable. Dan tried every hotel, hall, and public place in town, but all the doors were slammed shut.

Finally, Dan located a small hall that could seat fifty people near the "Happy Buddha" Chinese restaurant. As usual, the owner asked Dan, "What are you going to use it for?"

"An information center for tourists," Dan replied, not saying what kind of "information" he would be spreading—biblical information.

Dan rented these premises for the next three years, ministering to people who came from many parts of the world. Although he couldn't publicize the meetings, he placed leaflets in hotels, and tourists found their way to the little hall. A couple who ran a restaurant in town came to the Lord. (Years later, they invited Dan and Rhoda to their native Indonesia, where the Del Vecchios ministered to many churches throughout the country for forty-five days.)

One morning, Dan arrived at the hall to find a body curled up on the pavement in front of the door. As he was about to step over the old drunk, the pastor looked more closely at the grizzled face and was shocked to recognize the man. It was Manolo, the alcoholic whom he and Rhoda had befriended and taken into their home. Stooping down, he tried to shake him awake.

"Manolo! Manolo! It's me. Dan Del Vecchio," the pastor tried to rouse the Spaniard. "Do you remember me?"

Groggily, Manolo tried to focus his eyes on the face of the man bending over him. Dan was horrified to see how much the once dapper Spaniard had aged in the four years since he'd last seen him. His face was ashen, and it was obvious that he was very sick.

"Were you waiting for me, Manolo?" Dan asked. "Did you know this is a church?"

"No, no. I had no idea," Manolo muttered. He told the pastor that he had slept under the roof to keep out of the rain. "I don't believe in God. I don't believe in anything anymore."

"But Manolo," Dan protested gently, "can you imagine how many doors there are in this town? Yet God brought you right here. Come and live with us again!"

But despite Dan's desperate attempt to coax the Spaniard into coming back, Manolo refused all his offers of help. The pastor could do nothing more for the alcoholic. He knew that in all probability, within a few months the man would be dead. Indeed, that was the last time he ever saw him.

After a few years of living in rented apartments in Málaga and Benalmádena Costa, Dan asked God for a house of his own.

Build My house first and then yours, God answered him.

Dan had raised enough money from offerings to consider buying property on which to build a permanent facility, a proper church. Franco had designated Prince Juan Carlos to be his successor, who then granted religious liberty in Spain. Taking advantage of this new freedom, and in obedience to the voice of the Spirit, Dan made a down payment on a lovely piece of land across from the Mansion Club Apartments. He bought this strategic property in the heart of Torremolinos for 600,000 pesetas, which was about $12,000. Such a purchase of land for a Protestant church would have been impossible before.

With a congregation composed of transient tourists, Dan and Rhoda had no idea where the remaining money would come from to pay for the property and the church building. They trusted God, however, to supply each payment as it fell due. They were confident that God's direction would also mean God's provision.

During this time, Dan received the shocking news that his older brother, Jim, had suddenly died of a massive heart attack. Dan was devastated. Although they were separated by eleven years in age, Dan had been very close to his brother, who had been his main guiding influence and example. Jim, a lay pastor and builder, had taught him both how to preach and how to build homes.

Unable to return to the States for the funeral, Dan was finally able to go several months later. As he walked into his brother's garage and saw all his familiar tools hanging on the walls, the tools they had used so often together in building, a great grief seized him. Dan wept.

Eventually Dan made his way to the cemetery. It was a cold March afternoon and the bitter wind lashed his face as he searched for his brother's grave. Finally, he found a simple metal plaque with his brother's name inscribed on it. Dan sunk to his knees, overcome with unbearable grief at losing his closest friend and mentor.

"*Thy brother shall rise again.*" [18] Into the emptiness of his broken heart, the Holy Spirit gently wafted these words of hope—the words that Jesus had spoken to Martha after her brother Lazarus had died. Dan was greatly comforted.

The death of his beloved brother brought many questions. "Does God care what happens to my brother's family?" Dan agonized, grappling with doubts about God's love. "Does He really care what happens to me or my children?"

Dan began to fear that the abdominal pain he'd been recently experiencing was caused by cancer. In a tract entitled *Fruitfulness and Crippling Fear*, he would later write: "I feared a devastating cancer was eating my very life. I could not think positively or creatively. I allowed bitterness to obsess me. I began to fear God, but not in the proper sense. I feared for my own life and for the future of my wife and children. I had given my *all* for the Lord and now I was afflicted, with seemingly no cure. All joy drained from my Christian service, life became a chore, the darkness was indeed black."

Fortunately, Dan heard a well-known Bible teacher preaching on Proverbs 4:20–22 (NIV):

> *My son, pay attention to what I say;*
> *turn your ear to my words.*
> *Do not let them out of your sight,*
> *keep them within your heart;*
> *for they are life to those who find them*
> *and health to one's whole body.*

For the first time, Dan started studying the Bible—not just for devotions or sermon material, but for his health. He began to receive the words of the Bible as he would receive medicine, be-

[18] John 11:23b (KJ21).

lieving that as he read, God's Word was literally healing him. His depression and doubt faded away, replaced by a stronger faith and a fresh resolve to serve the God of love and mercy. He sailed back to Spain on an Italian ocean liner, returning with an organ and a design for the new church dancing in his mind.

Dan hired a builder to construct the foundation of the new church and another one to erect the steel beam girders, forming the skeleton of the building. Then he started on the brickwork. Although the property had been paid off within a year, without more funds, he had to do much of the manual labor himself.

Slowly, Dan unloaded the second truck-load of five thousand bricks. He'd carried so many bricks that the skin was worn right off his fingers. "Oh God, send someone to help me," he pleaded in desperation. "I can't go on anymore."

Discouraged, Dan got into his car. As he was backing up onto the main highway, he almost ran over a young man walking by. The man had his eyes on the ground and wasn't watching where he was going. Dan studied the Spaniard, an emaciated forlorn figure, his head hung in hopeless despair. He asked him, "Do you want to work?"

"*Sí,*" the Spanish youth nodded, his shoulders straightening.

Thanking God for this answer to prayer, Dan brought Andrés over to help unload the bricks from the truck. He gave the gaunt youth an apple and watched in amazement at the difficulty he had in eating it—the poor fellow's throat was so constricted he could hardly swallow.

As Dan taught the Spanish youth how to mix cement, he found out more about his past. Andrés had just been released from prison after serving a sentence for robbery. He'd hunted unsuccessfully for work, and finally, in complete despair, he'd decided to kill himself. He confided to Dan that he was on his way to commit suicide when, through the providential near accident, he had met the pastor.

Dan took Andrés into his own home and treated him like a son, even having patience with him when he stole money from Rhoda's purse or the children's piggy bank. The Del Vecchios led him to Christ and sent him to Bible school. Later, Andrés fell away from the Lord and eventually became the prosperous owner of one of the biggest steak houses in Torremolinos.

While Andrés mixed the cement, Dan laid the bricks. Brick by brick, the pastor built the church, laying by his own hands all 25,000 of them! He was still meditating on Proverbs 4:20, taking it as his daily medicine and receiving strength both for his spirit and body. As he built this house of worship, his energy seemed to be revitalized every day. With such a clear-cut goal before him, Dan poured all of himself into the work and noted with satisfaction the structure's progress. At last, there was something tangible to show for his efforts in Spain.

When it came to the roof, the architect opposed the pastor's plans. Dan envisioned a slanted American-style roof constructed of two-by-fours between steel girders, with plywood on top. This would then be covered with the tarpaper-and-gravel method Dan had found to be so effective in Florida. As most Spanish roofs were constructed of cement and tile, however, the architect ridiculed the missionary for his foolish idea.

"You could make extra money by renting umbrellas when the roof leaks," the architect mocked scornfully. In the end, however, the insistent pastor got his way. The roof indeed proved to be inexpensive, light, and effective. And God had the last laugh because the cathedral that this architect later built in Málaga was flooded after a heavy rain, with four inches of water surrounding the altar.

Dan worked on the roof with a young German helper. Although he was wary of heights because he had fallen off of scaffolds several times, and had injured his back while building his honeymoon home, Dan forced himself to climb up on the steel girders. To protect the roof, they had to paint the plywood sheets with linseed oil, which made them extremely slippery and dangerous. One day the German youth lost his grip and slid all the way down the roof, fortunately hitting the ground on his feet, unhurt.

Dan hired a mason to make a solid stone wall at the front of the church behind the pulpit, on which he placed a simple but very predominant cross. The stones came from a quarry, and each had to be hand-chipped right at the church. At the back of the church, Dan designed a floor-to-ceiling stained glass window. The carpenter he had hired, one of the best in Málaga, argued with Dan that this window wouldn't fit in esthetically with the rest of the church design.

Dan lifted the problem to God. Later, he showed the carpenter: "This is the way it can be done." The pastor never forgot this moment when he—who knew practically nothing about carpentry—could tell a professional carpenter how to solve the problem. And so Dan had his beautiful stained glass window, allowing light to stream in at the back of the church. The ceiling he covered with imported California redwood.

As Dan leaned upon Him, the Holy Spirit took over the design of the church, down to the minutest details. Dan faced many difficulties, but with the vision of the finished church building always before him, he found the strength to carry on. At this time, nine words were burned into his soul: "*Take God's side. Expect a miracle. Never give up.*"

In November of 1969, the Evangelical Community Church in Torremolinos was officially inaugurated, with the mayor in attendance and a police escort directing traffic. Although the church's seating capacity was a comfortable 150 to 200 people, for this grand occasion, 400 packed the building. From that time on, the church began to grow, with visiting tourists from Great Britain, Holland, Scandinavia, Germany, and North America—a truly international congregation. During the winter months there was usually standing-room only, with people spilling into the side rooms and out the front door onto the streets. Since there were few places where other congregations could meet, Dan allowed the Dutch and Germans to hold their services during the week. Later, a chapter of Alcoholics Anonymous met in the church.

To complete the construction of the church, Dan had asked an English sister, a member of the congregation, to lend him $5,000. In an unforeseen way, God intervened and supplied this need.

Gordon Lindsay, a renowned servant of God and founder of Christ for the Nations, a Bible school in Texas, visited Torremolinos. He had been given an apartment in town and didn't know what to do with it.

"What should I do with this place?" he asked Loren Cunningham, the head of Youth with a Mission.[19] YWAM was just beginning their ministry, and one of their first outreaches was in Spain. "It's a hassle to pay the mortgage and other expenses. It's just costing me money."

"Give it to Del Vecchio. He's a good businessman," Loren replied, putting Gordon in touch with Dan.

---

[19] Youth with a Mission (YWAM) is a "global movement of Christians from many cultures, age groups and Christian traditions, dedicated to serving Jesus Christ throughout the world" (ywam.org). Founded by Loren Cunningham in 1960, it is now a global ministry with over twenty thousand workers.

After visiting with Dan and his family, Gordon decided to give the apartment to the pastor. As they had prayed, Dan had been aware of the strong presence of God. Gordon was a real man of God. Dan sold the apartment, paid off the mortgage, and with the remaining money was able to pay off the debt to the church member.

As a follow-up to this story, Gordon's son, Dennis Lindsay, passed through Torremolinos not long after. At the time, the young man was backslidden in his faith. Dennis ended up sleeping on Dan's couch in the church office and recommitting his life to Jesus.

"It was at that time that the Lord used Pastor Daniel and his wife, Sister Rhoda, to begin a work of planting the Lord's message of the Great Commission into my heart," Dr. Dennis Lindsay recalls of the late 60s. "They provided me with an opportunity to live and work out of their assembly in Torremolinos. From there I joined Youth with a Mission's School of Evangelism, and for three years I worked during the summer in outreach ministry with Pastor Del Vecchio. During those years, my wife, Ginger, and I were blessed to use the pastor's office floor to hold our air mattress bedding. Each morning we would roll up our sleeping bags and leave before the pastor arrived. Those early years set the pattern and call of missions in our lives, and we've continued to train others to catch the call of missions in their hearts and to *go* into all the world with the gospel message."

Dr. Dennis Lindsay is now President and Chairman of the Board of Christ for the Nations Inc. in Dallas, Texas, carrying on the legacy of his late parents, Gordon and Freda. CFNI is a worldwide missions organization and Bible Institute that has trained over fifty thousand students who are spreading the Good News of Christ around the globe.

After the construction of the church was finished, Dan reminded the Lord of their need for a house of their own. The Del Vecchios found a large, two-story house in Churriana, which had a carved stone façade and a vegetable garden, all for a bargain price. They bought it and moved to the quiet countryside near Torremolinos.

CHAPTER SIX

TRIALS OF FAITH

Often while driving through the countryside, Dan watched the primitive method of threshing wheat still used in some parts of Spain. Horses or mules are driven round and round on the cut wheat until it's broken into mulch. When the strong winds come, the men, using ancient-looking winnowing forks, throw the mixture high into the air. The wind separates the chaff from the wheat. The chaff falls at a distance, while the heavier wheat falls into a golden pile. Finally, the chaff is gathered and burned.

Dan often thought about how John the Baptist used this analogy to describe the work of the Holy Spirit in the life of the believer. He said,

> *... One mightier than I is coming, whose sandal strap I am not worthy to loose. He will baptize you with the Holy Spirit and fire. His winnowing fan is in His hand, and He will thoroughly clean out His threshing floor, and gather the wheat into His barn; but the chaff He will burn with unquenchable fire.* (Luke 3:16–17)

Chaff is necessary for the growth and development of the wheat, but before the grain can be ground into flour for bread it must be purged and burned. It's the Lord who baptizes the believer with the Holy Spirit and with fire, who fans the smoldering flame into a burning blaze that's destined to devour all impurities.

Dan was about to endure two devastating trials, a "purging" of his faith. What emerged, after the "chaff" was burned away through suffering, became pure and unshakeable—a faith ground by pain and pressure into "flour," providing spiritual "bread" for thousands.

For seven years, Dan had been aware of a lump buried under his left jawbone. At first he hadn't paid much attention to the hard mass of tissue, but as it grew larger, so did his concern. He and Rhoda often prayed for it to be healed, but nothing happened. Finally, when the lump started to interfere with his ability to swallow, and when he began to get headaches, Dan considered an operation.

"Honey, what do you think I should do?" he asked his wife.

"No matter what you decide, whether you go for an operation or wait until God heals it," Rhoda comforted him, "it's still under God's healing power," Rhoda said, comforting him.

Deciding to consult surgeons in America, Dan flew to the United States while Rhoda, in her eighth month of pregnancy with their fourth child, remained at home in Spain.

"It's a brachial cyst," the specialist at a hospital in Philadelphia informed Dan after examining the lump. "It's nothing to worry about, just a matter of a minor operation."

As Dan was wheeled into the operating theater, he was full of faith and confidence.

"Suppose something goes wrong?" asked a nurse dryly, having overheard him praising the Lord.

"What can go wrong?" Dan smiled. "I'm in the hands of the Lord."

During the operation, part of Dan's jawbone was removed. The growth had wrapped its tentacles around his jugular vein and various nerves, choking the supply of blood to his brain. These tentacles had to be unraveled.

When he regained consciousness after the operation, Dan discovered that he couldn't move the muscles of his face. *It must still be the effect of the anesthetic*, Dan thought, trying to reassure himself. But after a couple of days, when the left half of his face remained paralyzed, Dan worried that something had gone wrong.

After three weeks, the doctors concluded that the motor nerve had been accidentally severed. A second operation, this time to reconnect the damaged nerve, took place on the twentieth day, as a nerve lasts twenty-one days before it's completely dead.

A new surgeon performed the delicate procedure, a brilliant Armenian professor at Johns Hopkins University Hospital in Baltimore. For four and a half tedious hours, the surgeon searched painstakingly for the loose half of the nerve that had slipped somewhere behind Dan's ear. If it hadn't been for this man's valiant determination and the concerned prayers of loved ones, the missing nerve may never have been located. After the operation, the surgeon emerged from the theater and leaned up against a wall, exhausted.

"I found it," he reassured Dan's anxious sister.

For six months, Dan wouldn't know whether the second operation had been a success. That's how long it would take for the nerve to regenerate itself and reactivate his facial muscles again. This waiting period was to be one of the toughest trials of his faith.

Why has God allowed this to happen? he wondered. *What did I do to deserve this?*

The more Dan questioned, the more his doubts grew and the deeper the darkness he found himself in.

Before the first operation, Dan had gone to a Kathryn Kuhlman[20] service with the expectation that God would divinely heal his tumor. As miracles happened all around him, he felt confident that at any moment God was going to touch his face, and the tumor would instantly disappear. He had great faith for healing—yet nothing happened.

After the operation, with the left half of his face paralyzed, Dan attended another Kathryn Kuhlman service in Pittsburgh, full of hope that God would surely perform a miracle this time. He believed in divine healing, he had preached it, and he had witnessed the results with his own eyes.

But once again, he left disappointed.

Why doesn't God heal me? he asked himself. *I have faith.*

During this time of dark depression, an African American deacon visited Daniel.

"I asked God, 'What shall I tell our brother Dan?'" the deacon told him. "The Lord gave me this word from Job 23:10 for you." He paused to open his Bible. "'*But He knows the way that I take; when He has tested me, I shall come forth as gold.*'"

After the deacon left, Dan pondered the words. They offered the first ray of hope in his dismal situation, the first glimpse of understanding of God's purposes. In them, he found some comfort. "When He has tested me, I shall come forth as gold." He clung to this promise.

A few days later, God spoke to Dan in an almost audible voice: *Go preach in Nutley, New Jersey.* The words surprised the minister. He recoiled in fear at their implication. Ever since the operation,

[20] An American evangelist who was known for her miraculous healing services.

he had locked himself inside his sister's home, not wanting to see anybody. He was ashamed of his distorted face, and the last thing he wanted to do was preach! In fact, he wanted to give up the ministry.

The quiet inner voice persisted: *Go to Nutley.*

"Why should I go there?" Dan resisted. "To walk into a church and say God has sent me is the last thing I will do!" The insistent inner voice wouldn't leave him in peace. At last, he yielded. Obediently, but not entirely willingly, he went to the church. The pastor didn't greet him with enthusiasm.

"Well, brother, God sent me," Daniel told the pastor plainly. "If you want me to preach, fine! If not, I'll leave. But God told me to come here, and I'm here."

The pastor grudgingly gave permission for Daniel to preach. He introduced the unexpected guest preacher to his congregation: "W-we're v-very h-h-happy to h-have B-b-brother D-Daniel h-here."

My God, he's worse than me, Daniel thought as he heard the man's stuttering.

The pastor had suffered a nervous breakdown in his last church and hadn't recuperated fully. Instead of asking his elders to pray for him, he had stubbornly refused to acknowledge his speaking problem. The Lord used this situation to show Daniel another need that was as great as his own. As he ministered, the power of the Holy Spirit fell upon the congregation, and they came forward to the altar, weeping. As the Holy Spirit melted the church and broke down all resistance, the pastor himself came down from his platform and asked the elders to pray for him.

After this, Daniel was directed to a church in Burlington, New Jersey. The pastor of the church had a son who had been working for the summer in construction. The previous week, this son had fallen from a fifty-foot steel bridge onto a solid concrete embankment, crushing his spine. He would have to spend the rest of his life in a wheelchair.

As Dan preached to the church, holding up his paralyzed face, he was able to identify with their questions about senseless tragedy. As he ministered to both these churches, which were experiencing trial and suffering, Dan himself was ministered to. God was working something deep into his life—helping him to feel for those who are hurting, making him into a softer man.

What are my kids going to think? Dan worried as he flew back to Spain after the operation. Physically he felt ugly; emotionally he felt scarred. *Will they be afraid of me? And Rhoda? Will she reject me?* Self-consciously, he touched the nasty stitched-up wound.

Embarrassed, he wore dark glasses and pulled his hat down low in a futile effort to cover his face. At the Málaga airport, a very pregnant Rhoda and their three children rushed to greet Daniel. They surrounded him and hugged him and took no notice of his drooping face.

"Oh Daddy," they cried, "you're beautiful!"

Relieved at their response, Daniel attempted a smile, but as only half of his mouth obeyed, it resembled more of a crooked grimace. The continuing loving support of his wife and children meant a lot to him.

The next months were traumatic for the pastor as he struggled to come to grips with his facial handicap and struggled to preach. If there had been any avenue of escape from preaching, Dan would gladly have taken it. Before he had prayed: "Lord, if You heal me, then I will preach." But as the Lord in His wisdom had chosen not to heal him, Dan found that he resented God for allowing his face to be disfigured.

"It's not fair that I have to preach under these circumstances," Dan complained to His Maker. He wanted desperately to run and hide from people—not face a Sunday morning congregation. In his absence, Rhoda and Theo, an elder, had taken turns preaching every week. Now if he could find someone to take his place permanently, Dan would gladly have backed out. The Lord, however, would not allow him to desert his position of responsibility. Dan knew that he had no choice but to be obedient to the voice of the Holy Spirit. He obeyed, but not with a willing heart.

The first Sunday morning as he preached, occasionally pressing a handkerchief to his cheek, Dan looked over the congregation, intensely aware of their reaction. He was amazed to see several people holding the side of their faces—an unconscious sympathetic identification with their pastor. They listened to his sermon with rapt attention, and all the more so because they could see he was having such difficulty speaking. Instead of losing his audience as he had feared, Dan was surprised to discover that they were more engaged than usual. His handicap was actually making his sermon more effective.

Dan also forced himself to shake hands with people at the front door. Although he had never possessed an effervescent personality, he now found that he was even reluctant to smile. With his drooping eye and cheek, he was acutely aware of how unattractive he appeared.

"Smile," visiting tourists would urge him as they prepared to snap a photo of him in front of the church.

"I can't," Dan would mutter, smiling the best he could: a lopsided grimace.

Dan had been recording programs for various family radio stations in America, including a powerful 50,000-watt station that covered California and parts of Mexico, and lesser stations in New Jersey, Pennsylvania, and Florida. He had an excellent fifteen-minute slot between Kathryn Kuhlman and Billy Graham. Dan recorded the programs on an old-fashioned four-track recorder loaned to him by a Baptist missionary who had used it for

Radio Monte Carlo broadcasts into North Africa. Alone in the "radio" room at the church, Dan preached into the microphone, holding up the side of his face. With his facial paralysis, it was hard for him to speak without popping sounds coming from his lips. Discouraged, he quit.

Every day, Dan gave his face electric shocks with a machine to keep his muscles from atrophying. The electric shocks that he administered to his forehead were particularly painful. At night, he had to wear a patch over his left eye, as it wouldn't close, to get some sleep. Even years later, he wouldn't be able to close his eye without scrunching up the whole left half of his face. Saliva often dripped from the side of his mouth and formed ulcers on his lip. Dan always carried a handkerchief to mop his cheek, especially when he was eating.

It was during this time that Pastor Dan absorbed what he learned about the "cross" of Christianity. It took him years before he adjusted to his facial appearance, years before he could see the benefits gained from this handicap. From his own experience, he discovered he was better able to identify with and understand the various forms of suffering he encountered in those who visited his office.

Soon after Dan had returned to Spain, a woman from the Málaga church visited him wanting prayer for healing. Dan was dismayed to see that she had an identical lump at the base of her ear. *How can I pray for her? How can I have faith for her healing when I wasn't healed?* With only a small amount of faith, Dan prayed for the woman. As he did, a surge of faith mounted in his spirit. "Lord, avenge me of my face!" Dan boldly asked, feeling like Samson.

Fifteen days later, the woman's cyst disappeared.

Although Dan had prayed for countless numbers of people in his Mexican outreaches who had been miraculously healed, in the last few years—and especially after his operation—his healing ministry had tapered off. It was as if God was allowing him to see another side of His grace: how He develops a person's character through suffering.

He was also more aware of God's sovereignty in his life, which didn't depend on whether he had faith for healing or not. Dan began to see that sometimes He might have a higher purpose than healing, a higher purpose for spiritual development and growth. He concluded that God was allowing him to suffer as discipline, as part of forming His own character within.

"If you don't get deliverance," Dan would later preach, "you'll get *development*."

In his sermons, Dan began to share the lessons he was learning in the "darkness" that he would never have learned in the "daytime." He could enter into the suffering of others, sympathizing with their pains and comforting them. Gradually he became aware of the great need for emotional healing in those he counseled, a field that in those days was largely ignored by the church. Increasingly his ministry began to shift in this direction.

CHAPTER SEVEN
FLAME OF GOD

On September 9, 1972, only a month after his facial operation, Dan paced back and forth restlessly in the corridor of a small private clinic in Torremolinos. Rhoda was in labor with their fourth child, and Dan was anxiously waiting for news of the long overdue birth. After what seemed like hours to the nervous father, the doctor appeared.

"If the baby doesn't come quickly, I'm going to have to perform a caesarean section," the doctor informed Dan curtly. He was clearly disturbed. "The baby is in the wrong position, and I can't do anything about it."

Dan digested this news in silence. "Please wait for another twenty minutes," he begged the doctor, feeling intuitively that it would be best for Rhoda and what she would have wanted. Dan continued his nervous pacing up and down the corridor. Fear nagged the back of his mind as he remembered that a Roman Catholic doctor may sometimes decide to save the infant if he's faced with a desperate choice.

"Oh God, save Rhoda and the baby!" Dan pleaded. "Deliver them both from harm."

Finally, the tension was broken by the appearance of a nurse. "Your wife has given birth to a baby boy," she announced perfunctorily.

Dan slumped against the wall, relieved. Strangely, the joy that had always accompanied the birth of one of his children was missing. Instead, he felt numb, a feeling he couldn't explain. The doctor appeared, tired and upset. He ignored Dan completely and instead approached Adelaida, who had come along for moral support. The former nun had known this doctor when she had worked in the hospital with him as a nurse.

"The baby has Down Syndrome. He's terribly deformed. His liver is distended and his spleen is enlarged. He can't possibly live for more than twenty-four hours," the doctor told Adelaida tersely, unaware of the traumatic impact his words were having on the father.

Dan sat down heavily, his throat suddenly dry and constricted. This cruel blow had been totally unexpected. Dan's frantic mind raced ahead, already making funeral plans.

"Be sure not to tell the mother." The doctor's stern advice interrupted his thoughts. "In her weakened condition, she could go into shock or hemorrhage."

With leaden feet, Dan climbed the stairs, his eyes avoiding the operating room where his son was being given auxiliary attention. As Dan entered Rhoda's room, he saw that she was lying quietly, still under the effects of anesthesia. Her face was white and drained, her lips parched. Dan kissed her gently.

Rhoda opened her eyes and a smile flashed across her tired face. "How's the baby?"

Already Dan had to face the dreaded question. He searched for words.

"Is it a boy?" Rhoda asked eagerly. "It *is* a boy, isn't it? How is our David Paul?" They had planned to give him this name months, even years, before. Such a lovely name seemed senseless to Dan at this point.

"He *is* well, isn't he?" Rhoda persisted.

When Dan didn't reply immediately, a look of concern crossed her face.

"Is he all right? How is my baby?" her voice was rising now. Dan tried to comfort her, but she wouldn't be quiet. "Does he have all his fingers? Is there something wrong with his leg?"

"No, dear," Dan said, trying to keep his composure. "Nothing is wrong with his leg."

"There *is* something wrong with my baby!" Rhoda cried.

Seeing her anguished face only compounded the agony in Dan's heart. He fought to keep his emotions under control. The doctor had warned him that his wife must not know. She needed time to regain her strength. In the tense silence, the truth slowly dawned upon Rhoda.

"He has Down Syndrome," she whispered, and she seemed to call on an inner reserve of strength. She later told Dan that she had seen a strange look of pity in the nurse's eyes.

Dan nodded and rushed to the bathroom, where all his pent-up pain came flooding out in torrents of grief. "Where is God? Why did this happen to us? *Why? Why? Why?*" Later Dan composed the words to a song:

Is there a God who understands?
Is there a God who holds my hands?
Is there a God who feels my pain?
Is there a God? I ask again.
Though darkness hides His lovely face,
And pain becloud His saving grace.
Yes, there's a God, I still believe
There is a God!

Someday I'll understand,
Someday in that bright, other land,
Where there's no pain, no death, no night,
Where God Himself shall be the light.
Then He will tell me of His plan
To form my life at His command
Yes, there's a God, I still believe
There is a God!

David remained in the hospital under intensive care. Three days later, the pediatrician, a boyish man in his early thirties, came to examine the baby. Unlike the obstetrician, he spoke very encouragingly to Dan and Rhoda. Finally, Dan, unable to keep the burning question inside any longer, blurted out, "But Doctor, will he live?"

"Live? Why yes, he'll live," the pediatrician responded in surprise. "He's recuperating rapidly. He'll live for at least thirty years!"[21]

Dan nearly fainted on the empty bed next to Rhoda's. Devastated, he had resigned himself to the terrible tragedy of his son's death.

Rhoda took the news very calmly. After the doctor had gone, she insisted on going to the nursery. "I want to see my baby," she declared. "I want to hold him!"

Dan couldn't bear the thought of holding their son. After the obstetrician's very vivid description, the distorted image Dan had formed of their child was tormenting his mind. Sensing his wife's inner bravery, he reluctantly agreed.

He had no idea then of the desperate battle that had been raging within Rhoda for the last three days. The Holy Spirit had insisted, *Go get your baby.* Rhoda hadn't yielded to this inner urging. She hadn't yet been able to accept her son's supposed "deformity,"

[21] At the time of this writing, David is almost fifty years old and lives in a group home near his parents.

a challenge she had instinctively recoiled from. She could see no joy beyond this "cross," only pain and shame and hopelessness.

Then the Lord had given her a solemn warning, words recorded in Matthew 18:10: "*Take heed that you do not despise one of these little ones, for I say to you that in heaven their angels always see the face of My Father who is in heaven.*"

Rhoda took their baby son in her arms and brought him back to the privacy of her room. As she held David, the Holy Spirit covered her with a glorious canopy, a protection from the terrible pain. His Presence was so strong in the room that she felt enfolded by His warm love. In her mind, she could see Jesus hanging on the cross with His bleeding hands, His arms opened wide, not held there by nails. She understood as never before that it was because of His love. With those embracing arms, He had willingly received us. He hadn't been ashamed to draw us, vile and deformed creatures, into His bosom. And now He spoke gently to Rhoda's heart: *Will you not receive your own child?*

Rhoda pressed tiny David to her breast, holding him tight. The Lord impressed upon her that His love would strengthen her and give her the ability to turn the situation into a blessing. Faith began to rise in her heart, and she began to hope that God would heal her son.

It is for the glory of God, she thought. *He will perform a miracle.*

Dan and Rhoda were to learn later that even though God may not perform a miracle by changing our outward circumstances, He can perform a miracle in our hearts. Though He may not choose to deliver us from our trials, He can use them to deliver us from ourselves. They discovered that when the Lord allows the heart of one of his children to be broken, He deposits within it something of Himself.

A few days later, the Lord spoke to Dan. Up until then, the pain had been so severe that he could not, would not hear ... but finally the message came through: "*Whoever receives one little child like this in My name receives Me*" (Matthew 18:5).

Over the next few months, Dan and Rhoda wondered how to tell their other three children that David would never be a "normal" child. Their fears were unnecessary. The children loved him and doted on him.

The experience of loving their uniquely-gifted son opened up a new world to Dan and Rhoda. It unstopped the fountain of God's love in their hearts so that it could flow unhindered to people who are "different" and "unloved." It also gave them a greater appreciation for all children—the incalculable worth of the precious gifts God bestows on parents.

Dan remembered the words God had spoken deeply into his heart: *I will make you a father of many nations.* Dan was discovering that in both the natural and spiritual realms, *being made* into a father was a process—often a heart-breaking one. The suffering Dan endured worked a deeper cleansing and purifying in his heart. Through the crucible of his pain, the flame of God's love burned away the "dross" in his heart, releasing His love in a brighter, purer form. During this intense time, Dan composed this song:

Flame of God

Burn deep within my heart, O flame of God,
For I am barren clay without Thy love;
Burn deep within my heart, O flame of God
And baptize me afresh, O heavenly dove.
Burn deep within my heart, O flame of God.
Lord, cleanse my way until I am pure gold;
Burn deep within my heart, O flame of God,
And may I be the fuel to light the world.
Send Thy cleansing flame, burn up the dross,

And may I now with love embrace my cross.
Burn deep within my heart,
Lord, let the glow of heaven shine from me.

PART TWO
CHRONICLES OF A COMMUNITY

CHAPTER EIGHT
FIRSTFRUITS

In the beginning, the congregation of the church in Torremolinos was mostly composed of elderly tourists and pensioners. But God had greater plans in store for this church. On this rather shaky foundation, He would build the evangelical community churches of Spain. One key figure in the growth of the Spanish work was to be a handsome young bartender with black hair and bushy sideburns …

In 1971, Benito wiped the counter clean while his fellow bartender spoke to him about the dramatic change that had recently occurred in his life. Benito knew that only a short time ago, his fellow bartender had been bitterly angry at a certain Rev. Del Vecchio for converting his girlfriend. Then this pastor, accompanied by his young son, had begun visiting his friend at his bar, and over Cokes talked to him *not* about "religion" but about a living Christ. In a complete about-face, his friend had begun regularly attending the pastor's church.

Benito wished his friend would stop talking about Jesus. For the past three years, Benito had been working in hotel bars along the Costa del Sol, enjoying his easy-going lifestyle. *What do I need God for?* Whenever he attended mass, he would experience a temporary desire to change his life, but he didn't have the strength to follow his convictions.

When Benito started his mandatory military service, his friend sent him a Bible and tracts. At the end of one tract, he was invited to give his life to Jesus Christ. Because of the guilt he carried from his immoral lifestyle, Benito wasn't sure if God would forgive him. He cried out to Jesus and then experienced tremendous joy, as he knew with inward certainty that the Lord had forgiven him! The first change he noticed in his life was that now he had power to resist sexual temptations. His fellow soldiers called him crazy and fanatical, but Benito knew he was a different man.

After finishing his military duty, Benito worked in construction, purposely not going back to hotel work where he could be placed in the path of temptation. He attended Pastor Dan's church, and before long, he felt the call of God on his life. Increasingly his mind was occupied with the salvation of souls. For Benito, the decisive turning point came one evening when he visited the pastor's home on the outskirts of Torremolinos. Rhoda greeted the weeping man at the door.

"The Lord has spoken to me," Benito burst out, "that I must give up my savings to His work."

"Then why are you crying?" Rhoda asked with concern.

"I'm supposed to be getting married, and this money was to be invested in an apartment for us," Benito explained tearfully. "But I don't understand. I feel this tug of God on my heart that I have to give up this money to His work. What am I going to do?" Benito sunk into a chair, torn with great inner conflict. He was trembling under the powerful conviction of God.

"What's the matter, Ben?" Dan entered the living room and sat beside the troubled Spaniard. Benito poured out his heart to the concerned pastor, whom he fondly regarded as a father. Dan shared what he thought about the woman in question, Benito's intended fiancée. For various reasons, Dan believed it would be a serious mistake for Benito to marry this woman.

"Are you willing to give up this relationship?" Dan questioned the anxious Spaniard. "Are you willing to give everything over to the Lord, Ben? It's up to you."

Benito nodded his head. Wiping the tears from his face, he handed Dan a fistful of money—forty thousand pesetas, half of his entire savings. "Here, take this," Benito insisted.

When Pastor Dan was convinced that the young man had fully counted the cost, he accepted the money gratefully. The coming evangelical outreach in Málaga was going to cost seventy thousand pesetas. Benito's tearful offering would go a long way towards meeting the expenses.

As Dan talked further with him, he discerned that this sincere Spaniard meant business with the Lord. The step of financial sacrifice Benito had just taken expressed his whole-hearted desire to serve Christ—and not the god of money. Dan reflected that his own ministry had begun in this way, and now here was a young man willing to give up everything for the sake of the gospel.

Is this the man I'm looking for? Dan thoughtfully studied Benito. *Is he the key man I need to reach the Spaniards?*

Benito confided to Dan that he believed God was calling him into full-time ministry.

"Why don't you move in with us?" Dan offered, sensing that God had a special plan for this young man's life.

Benito gave up his job and apartment and moved into Pastor Dan's garage, which had been hastily turned into a bedroom. The Spaniard lived with the Del Vecchios for the following two years, becoming like another son to their family.

Pastor Dan discipled Benito daily. He firmly believed in being transparent, living and working closely with Benito and others he would mentor in the future—not being a "marble" preacher kept at a safe distance from his congregation on some "pulpit pedestal." As Benito ate with Dan and Rhoda, and talked and prayed with them, he absorbed a great deal about the Christian way of life and the courageous journey of faith.

Often Dan would take Benito to preach with him on the crowded streets of Torremolinos, Málaga, and Marbella. Usually, the pastor would begin preaching and then step back and encourage his young disciple to take over—a very practical training for ministry. Benito appreciated the time, energy, and wisdom that the pastor poured into his life. As the Apostle Paul had taught Timothy, so Dan instructed and corrected Benito. He eventually sent him off to Bible school.

Dan's deposit and investment into Benito's life would reap dividends. The earnest young Spaniard would play a pivotal role in the future evangelization of his own countrymen. Benito's financial sacrifice, the surrender of his job and fiancée, the relinquishment of his own dreams, and his willingness to give his life to the service of Christ would result in much fruit. It's a time-tested spiritual principle: *out of sacrifice flows life.*

The Evangelical Community Church in Torremolinos attracted people from many countries. While most of those who attended the services were tourists, others were English-speaking residents living along the Costa del Sol. One of the first converts to come to this international church was a young man named Robby, who managed a furniture shop in town. When Dan baptized him, he was full of joy. Much later, Robby would be ordained by the Methodist Church and serve as a minister in Scotland.

For a number of years, Rhoda directed the choir, and Robby played the Hammond organ Dan had imported from England. One day Robby told Dan about two English nurses who had run out of money and were looking for a place to stay. "What can we do? Where can we put them?" he asked with concern.

Dan wasn't sure how to help them. There was no place in the church for the young women to stay. Later, when he heard that their lives had taken a downward turn, with one becoming pregnant, their situation weighed heavily upon him.

If only we had a house for them, Dan thought. *Maybe their lives could have been saved.*

The silver-haired English woman in her mid-fifties sat on a stool in the darkened bar, stirring her drink morosely. Outside in the hot afternoon sun, tourists crowded San Miguel, the main walking street of Torremolinos, intent on enjoying their vacations. Barbara was oblivious to her surroundings. Recently she had suffered her fourth heart attack, and the experience had forced her to face up to death.

This wasn't a subject the socialite had paid much attention to. Eccentric and bohemian in lifestyle, Barbara had spent most of her life pursuing pleasure and adventure. Born into a wealthy English family, she'd been brought up by an endless stream of governesses. After finishing her education in Paris, she'd been presented at Court in Buckingham Palace—her official debut into the social whirl of high society in Britain.

The young men she had met bored Barbara with their class-consciousness and conceit. She fell in love with an unassuming fellow who worked on a nearby farm. Although her father had opposed her choice of partner and threatened to disinherit her, Barbara had married the young man anyway. The marriage had lasted only a few brief months before, disillusioned, the young bride had returned home.

Soon after, she gave birth to a beautiful baby girl. Before the child was three months old, however, Barbara had become ill with tuberculosis and had to send her daughter to live with her husband's parents. From the age of twenty-five to thirty, Barbara was in and out of hospital. The doctors eventually had to remove most of her left lung and many of her ribs.

After traveling around for several years, Barbara had settled down and married again. Her second husband had turned out to be emotionally unbalanced, and after a particularly brutal attack, Barbara had fled to Torremolinos and bought a villa on a hill. Here she hoped to find the "something" she was inwardly seeking. Frequenting bars and nightclubs, she'd found the drinking crowd to be just like herself—unhappy people with broken marriages, desperately lonely yet pretending everything was fine.

Is this all there is to life? Loneliness? Depravity? Barbara sighed in despair, staring listlessly at the glass in her hands. *Another soul-destroying drink to drag me down to the grave?*

She was about to signal to the bartender for another when she spied a pamphlet on the counter. *Earthman, Spaceman*, she read the strange title, intrigued. Turning it over, she noticed that it had been written by a Rev. Daniel Del Vecchio of the Evangelical Church in Torremolinos. Curious, she started to read it. Suddenly her attention was caught: "Jesus Christ is ALIVE today. Jesus Christ is ALIVE IN US!"

Could this be true? the astonished woman wondered. Something inside her stirred with excitement. *Could this be the "something" I've been looking for? If this man speaks as well as he writes,* Barbara decided, *I want to hear him.*

The following Sunday morning she entered the packed church and slipped unnoticed into a back pew. As Pastor Del Vecchio preached the gospel with power, tears began to flow down Barbara's cheeks—tears of remorse and repentance. She felt an overwhelming longing to know more about this Jesus who gives abundant life here on earth. On Monday morning, she rushed into a second-hand bookshop and purchased the only New Testament they had. She took it home and read it right through. When she came to Romans 8:38–39, she thought it was the most beautiful passage she'd ever read:

> *For I am persuaded that neither death nor life, nor angels nor principalities nor powers, nor things present nor things to come, nor height nor depth, nor any other created thing, shall be able to separate us from the love of God which is in Christ Jesus our Lord.*

Suddenly Barbara understood Jesus's love for her—that He was standing by her with an outstretched hand, offering her His healing power, His life, and His infinite love. Falling to her knees, she asked Jesus to forgive her for all she had done to hurt Him and to be Her Lord and Savior—to come into her heart, to change her, and to make her a daughter of His family.

Four days later, Pastor Del Vecchio met with a small group who were interested in receiving the baptism of the Holy Spirit. Barbara eagerly followed the others into the kitchen of the church through a side door just behind the pulpit. She had given up alcohol as soon as she had realized that her body was God's temple, and now she was fully expecting Him to fill her.

Pastor Dan prayed for the small group gathered around him. The Holy Spirit fell with such power on Barbara that she began to shake. The pastor laid his hands on her and she cried out with joy, praising the Lord in a new language.

"Barbara, you will never smoke again," Pastor Dan told the radiant woman.

At home, after an hour of worshiping the Lord, Barbara spied a cigarette on the mantelpiece. Out of sheer habit, she lit the cigarette. "Ugh, this tastes frightful," she grimaced, throwing the cigarette away. "The pastor was right."

That night with a New Testament in her hand, Barbara slept peacefully. When she awoke the next morning, she was drenched with foul-smelling sweat—even her hair was wet and clinging to her forehead. Barbara pulled back her damp sheets and then noticed in amazement that they were stained yellow with the nicotine that had been pressed out of her pores. The Lord had cleansed her body! Although she'd been smoking at least two packs daily, her craving for tobacco vanished, and she never smoked again. She also never had trouble with her heart after that. "I am indeed a new creation," Barbara rejoiced.[22]

On February 20, 1972, Barbara was baptized in water. "I want to follow in the footsteps of Jesus," Barbara testified publicly. "To walk as He walked, to love as He loved." With characteristic abandonment, she offered herself up to Him, to the destiny He had planned for her life. She didn't know how soon she would be taken up on her offer.

"Now that I'm a Christian, what can I do for the Lord?" Barbara asked Pastor Dan.

Knowing that hashish-smoking hippies hung out at her large villa, Pastor Dan suggested, "Throw the hippies out and instead open your house to young people who are looking for God."

God had placed a burden on the pastor's heart to help backpackers who were passing through Torremolinos, traveling without direction or purpose. Some were curious university students who had read about the town in James Michener's novel *The Drifters.* [23]Others were on their way to Morocco in search of drugs. Before, Dan had only seen these young people as adventure-seekers,

[22] Adapted from Barbara Fletcher, *Unusual—believe it or not* (1981), printed by her daughter, Dawn Bilbe-Smith (2010), 6–7.
[23] James A. Michener (Pulitzer Prize winning author), *The Drifters* (New York, NY: Random House, 1971).

but now he viewed them as candidates for ministry. When Jesus had encountered fishermen mending their nets on the shores of Galilee, in His Spirit He had seen *apostles* who would go with the gospel into all the world.

"Many of these backpackers need a place to stay. You could give them food and shelter and then give them the Good News too."

Barbara stared at Pastor Dan, trying to decide if he was serious or not. "How could I possibly do that?" she blurted out. "For one thing, I don't know one end of the Bible from the other. I've only read through the New Testament once. I need much more time to mature in the Lord."

Pastor Dan laughed. "That would take all your life, my dear. Just your way of living would be a witness for the Lord. Leave the teaching to me."[24]

Within months, Barbara's villa was filled with fifteen people, the boys sleeping in the garage and the girls in the bedrooms. Most of these long-haired hippies were delighted to find a crash pad where they could eat and sleep for free. Pastor Dan and Barbara decided it was best if these boarders had a definite time limit. They were allowed to stay only a month and then they had to move on. During this time, they were confronted with a choice—whether to enter into a personal relationship with Jesus or not.

One of the first young men invited to move into Barbara's garage was a Canadian hitchhiking through Europe. In Rotterdam, Wayne had joined a group of fellow hippies on a trip to Morocco. After a few weeks in Marrakesh, he'd decided to spend Christmas in Spain. Although he was a believer and a preacher's kid, Wayne had a lot of questions and was on a spiritual quest. During the Christmas Eve service at the Evangelical Community Church in Torremolinos, God turned his whole life around. That night,

---

[24] *Unusual—believe it or not,* 11.

sitting in the back pew, Wayne received a clarion call to devote the rest of his life to full-time ministry. Years later, Dr. Wayne Hilsden and his wife, Ann, partnered with another couple to pioneer the largest Christian fellowship in Jerusalem—King of Kings Community.

CHAPTER NINE

SHEEP NOT GOATS

In September of 1973, a young French girl in her early twenties slipped into the darkened interior of the little church off San Miguel. Every day for the last few weeks, during siesta time, Anne-Marie had come to this quiet sanctuary to read her New Testament. As a strong Catholic, she wanted to devote her life totally to God. Over the years, she had a growing desire to enter a convent, the only place she felt she could live with God every moment of the day. Lately, as she had read her Bible, this desire had deepened. Today she decided she was finally ready to ask the priest which convent she should go to.

As Anne-Marie read the scriptures, she suddenly realized with a startling clarity that Jesus had not called his disciples to *withdraw* from the world but rather *to go* into the world and bring the Good News to people. Before this she'd always thought that giving her "life" to the Lord meant entering a convent, but now she realized that it meant giving her "will" to Him. For the next three days, Anne-Marie struggled with this insight, inwardly rebelling against giving up control of her life to God. Finally, she told Him: "Anywhere You ask me to go, I'll go. Whatever You ask me to do, I'll do."

The next Sunday morning, the French girl passed a sign on a pole that pointed towards the "Evangelical Church." Despite her firm Catholic convictions, she decided to follow the arrow's direction. She sat at the back of the church, trying to absorb the strange service, but she understood little.

At the door, Pastor Dan shook her hand. Anne-Marie was surprised by his friendliness. She had never gone to a church where the priest had greeted her. "Hello," she responded. "My name is Anne-Marie, and I'm French."

"Really?" Pastor Dan mused. "My secretary speaks French. She'd love to talk with you."

In the kitchen, Anne-Marie met Anne, a Swiss woman who was the pastor's secretary. She had briefly returned from Geneva to be a translator at an international convention in Torremolinos. The two found an instant rapport.

"Why don't you come to lunch with me?" Anne asked spontaneously, and Anne-Marie soon found herself seated in a corner of a Chinese restaurant. Although she was usually shy, Anne-Marie felt very comfortable with the friendly Swiss woman, who talked about the Lord and what He had done for her. Anne-Marie could see that although she was a normal young secretary like herself, her life was full of miracles.

That's what I'm looking for, Anne-Marie thought to herself excitedly. *These people know God personally.*

On the way back from the restaurant, Anne pointed out the Youth with a Mission (YWAM) coffee house, located in an abandoned mansion with an overgrown garden in front. "If you want to know more, go see those Christians."

When her friend left for Switzerland shortly afterwards, Anne-Marie dropped into the YWAM coffee house and approached one of the girls. They talked for half an hour, and then the YWAM volunteer invited Anne-Marie into the kitchen to pray.

The YWAM team "camped" in the house. They had no water or electricity and lived in crude conditions. The girl and Anne-Marie sat down on two paint tins, which they used for chairs. As they prayed to God, Anne-Marie had a deep experience with the Lord. In that empty kitchen, she was spiritually born again.[25]

The next Sunday, Pastor Dan met Anne-Marie outside the front doors of the church. "Would you like to come to a baptism service tonight?" The service would be held in the nearby town of Málaga.

"Yeah," Anne-Marie shrugged, "I suppose so."

At the little Málaga church, Casa Ágape, Pastor Dan preached a sermon on the Ethiopian eunuch who said to Philip: "… here is water. What hinders me from being baptized?"[26] At the end of the service, Pastor Dan asked the congregation: "Who wants to be baptized?"

Anne-Marie was the first to respond. Afterwards, as she walked away from the baptismal tank, a dignified English woman with silver-blonde hair greeted her. "*Hija,*" she said simply, which in Spanish means "daughter." Anne-Marie was touched by the warm greeting from this stranger.

The next Sunday, Anne-Marie went with the YWAM team to this English woman's villa for the regular meatloaf lunch. She sat at the right side of Barbara, who presided over the meal from the head of the table. At one point, Anne-Marie lit a cigarette.

"Would you smoke outside from now on, dear?" Barbara asked her in a firm but loving tone. Anne-Marie consented. A few weeks later, she was delivered from her smoking habit altogether.

---

[25] Nicodemus, a ruler of the Jews, came to Jesus secretly at night. "*Jesus answered and said to him, 'Most assuredly, I say to you, unless one is born again, he cannot see the kingdom of God.'*"

[26] Acts 8:36: "*Now as they went down the road, they came to some water. And the eunuch said, "See, here is water. What hinders me from being baptized?"*"

In November, Anne-Marie was working at her job as a receptionist in a real estate agency when two blonde girls her own age dropped in, wanting to see the manager.

"Do you know of any work around here?" the French girl, Sylviane, asked with easy camaraderie when she discovered that Anne-Marie was also from France.

"No. As far as I know, there's nothing available," Anne-Marie answered. She sized up the two girls and, feeling sympathy for them, asked, "Have you had lunch yet?"

"No," they replied.

"See that building." Anne-Marie pointed to one visible through the window. "That's where I live. Why don't you go there and wait for me? When I finish working, we can go to a restaurant for lunch. Here are my keys." She opened her handbag and offered them to Sylviane.

Sylviane was shocked. She didn't know what to say to this young woman who was willing to hand her keys over to two total strangers. "Well, I really enjoy cooking," Sylviane responded hesitantly. "We could buy something and cook it for lunch."

"Sure, that would be fine," Anne-Marie smiled.

Sylviane and her South African friend, Pat, went to her apartment and prepared lunch. While they were waiting for Anne-Marie, they discussed their hostess' amazing display of trust. Sylviane looked around at the valuable objects in the apartment and shook her head in wonder. "Why did she do this?" she asked Pat, who was equally baffled.

As they later sat down to begin the meal, Anne-Marie bowed her head and prayed. Sylviane didn't like this one bit because it reminded her of the nuns who had prayed at meals when she was a child at summer camp. When Anne-Marie directed the conversation to her recent experience of meeting Jesus Christ, the two young women dutifully listened. Sylviane, who professed to be an atheist, politely remarked, "Well, if there is a God, there are many ways to get to Him."

"No," Anne-Marie declared firmly. "There's only one God, and Jesus said, "*No one comes to the Father except through Me.*"[27]

This girl is really narrow-minded, Sylviane decided.

Anne-Marie told the two girls about Barbara and how she might be willing to let them stay at her villa. When they expressed interest, Anne-Marie phoned Barbara and asked if she would like to meet them.

"Yes," Barbara affirmed. "Bring them for lunch tomorrow."

At lunch the next day, Barbara served tea and sandwiches. As they walked into her villa, Pat and Sylviane stared in astonishment at the "Jesus Saves" posters that decorated the walls, and at a table stacked with Bibles. They didn't know quite how to take the lively British woman who greeted them, with a very obvious five-inch wooden cross dangling from her neck.

"We've been in weird situations before," Pat whispered to Sylviane, "but this is the limit!"

The two apprehensive girls were introduced to Pastor Dan and his mother, whom Barbara had invited along to check the girls out. Barbara wanted to make sure this time that those she invited to stay in her villa were genuinely spiritually receptive and not just taking advantage of a free place to live. She wanted to have "sheep" and not "goats."[28]

Sylviane let Pat handle the conversation. As she sat by herself on the red sofa, Sylviane was suddenly overwhelmed by a wave of love. Embarrassed, she tried to hold back the tears. She didn't want anyone to see her vulnerability. It wasn't the Christians' words that so deeply touched her but what she was to later recognize as the

[27] John 14:6: "*Jesus said to him, 'I am the way, the truth, and the life. No one comes to the Father except through Me.'*"

[28] Matthew 25:32: "*All the nations will be gathered before Him, and He will separate them one from another, as a shepherd divides his sheep from the goats.*"

Presence of God. Before the girls left, Barbara invited them to move into her villa, adding the clinching point: "It's free."

Sylviane and Pat discussed the invitation as they returned to their *pension* in Málaga. Sylviane didn't want to stay at Barbara's villa. When she had left the church of her youth, she had closed the door on Christianity.

"Oh, but I'm interested," Pat declared strongly. "It's free, and I don't have that much money."

Sylviane and Pat moved into Barbara's villa, "The Way Inn," as she now called it. They shared one bedroom; a pregnant Malaysian girl occupied the second, and Barbara herself stayed in the third. The first night, the two girls met two handsome boys from South Africa, and from then on, they went out with them every evening to popular places in town.

Barbara hardly saw her two guests. During the day they were out job-hunting, and by the time they got back at night, she was already in bed. The only chance she had to speak to them about the Lord was at the supper table. The two girls listened politely, but as soon as their dates showed up, they lost all interest in anything spiritual, distracted by the more immediate lure of good times.

After a week, the girls were jubilant. Pat had been offered a marvelous job in a boutique in one of the best hotels in Marbella, with an apartment thrown in for free. "Freedom! Freedom!" Pat yelled to Sylviane as she joined her friend in the garden. The two young women wanted to move out of Barbara's villa as soon as they could.

Barbara prayed fervently for God to touch the two girls' lives, asking Him for a miracle: that they would be saved during the annual convention taking place the following week. One-hundred-and-fifty Christians from the United States would fill the church, raising their arms in worship and praise. Barbara knew that she could only try her best to keep the girls at her villa for this special time—the Holy Spirit would have to do the rest. She felt sure they would become "sheep," willing to follow the Good Shepherd.

Unknown to Barbara, Anne-Marie had encountered Sylviane, Pat, and the two South African boys on Calle San Miguel one evening and told them about the Christian coffee house. Sylviane, tired of their superficial night life, wanted to check the place out. At the YWAM coffee house, a clean-shaven boy welcomed them and led them into a large room made cozy by a fireplace and gas lamps. The others felt uncomfortable in the wholesome atmosphere and soon wanted to leave, but Sylviane admitted to herself, *I like this place. I'm coming back.*

During the next evenings, Sylviane returned alone to the Christian coffee house. A French fellow struck up a conversation with her. As he talked about the love of God, the same feeling she'd experienced at Barbara's villa came over her. She was very moved, struggling with tears because she'd never heard of God's love before.

"Would you like to pray?" Maurice asked her gently.

"Yes," Sylviane nodded. As the young man began, she panicked: *What am I going to pray? I've forgotten all my prayers.*

As Maurice continued to pray, he surprised the French girl by saying, "Lord Jesus, this is Sylviane."

Wow, that's so strange, Sylviane marveled to herself. *He really speaks to Jesus as his friend.*

She looked through the windows at the stars, so brilliant in the clear Spanish night, and she thought of the immenseness, the greatness, and the beauty of creation. All at once she had a question burning in her heart that she hadn't considered for years: "Is there a God?" The question haunted her with its intensity. It seemed her whole life now depended on the answer. She found herself crying out: "God, are You there?"

As she continued to gaze at the sky, it seemed an answer came clearly back from somewhere behind the stars to penetrate her heart: *Yes, I AM.* A deep conviction, a certainty gripped her. Sylviane knew that nobody could ever take this assurance away from her—it was an answer from God Himself.

Sylviane left the coffee house, not saying anything to Maurice. She could see he was disappointed; he had expected something to happen. And something had. As Sylviane made her way back to Barbara's villa, she danced with joy.

"There is a God! There is a God, and there is hope!" she laughed with happiness. After searching in so many directions and finding nothing but emptiness, she felt excitement surge up within her. Sylviane thought she was a "believer" now because she believed in God. *This is faith*, she thought, not realizing there was more for her to discover.

"Pat, there *is* a God!" Sylviane enthusiastically shared with her South African friend. Pat, however, didn't want to hear any more about it. Sylviane didn't tell Barbara about her new discovery—she thought her deep spiritual experience was too personal to share.

Barbara, after much prayer, asked the two girls if they would attend the coming convention. Sylviane wanted to, but Pat wasn't so sure. On their last Sunday at Barbara's, the girls attended church (which was a requirement for staying at the Way Inn). Pastor Dan preached a sermon on Peter denying Christ three times, which really convicted Pat. After lunch, she called the pastor, tearfully asking "What should I do?"

His reply was direct: "What is more important to you, God or money?" At that moment, it was clear to Pat that God was more important! The two young women decided to stay and learn more about the Christian faith. Despite looking forward to moving out on their own, they turned down the apartment and job in Marbella.

Sylviane and Pat attended the first morning meeting of the convention with Barbara. They were amazed at the way people hugged and greeted each other. They seemed so alive, so joyful, and so full of love. *If being a Christian means being like this*, Sylviane decided as she observed the unfeigned love flowing between the people around her, *then I want to be one.*

At lunchtime they returned to the villa. As Sylviane entered the kitchen, Barbara turned from stirring a pot of soup and studied her with her typically direct glance: "You're looking very happy today."

Sylviane walked straight over to her and, not feeling her usual reserve, gave her a big kiss.

"Oh my dear!" Barbara stepped back in surprise. "Has anything happened to you?"

Sylviane didn't know what she was referring to.

"Have you accepted the Lord?" Barbara persisted. Because she could see that the French girl was so radiant, she took it for granted that this had happened. As Barbara served lunch, she went around to the other guests and told them the good news.

"But what does she mean?" Sylviane whispered to Pat, who had no idea either. The other guests hugged the bewildered young woman and called her "sister."

On the third day of the convention, as she listened to the preaching, Sylviane, who was not familiar with Christian vocabulary, asked God to help her grasp the things she needed to understand. Christ was revealed to her, and she suddenly understood the responsibility of humanity in His death. *Why, why did He have to suffer?* she lamented inwardly. *He was so perfect, so pure and holy, so full of love*. As she thought of humanity's wickedness, she became angry. *Human beings are so cruel to do such a thing.*

Suddenly the finger she was pointing at them turned back on her. An inner voice told her: *You have a part in this.* Sylviane began to weep as she saw her guilt, her corruption, and her own sinful nature. Sometime later she realized the service had ended and people were leaving the church. Embarrassed, she got up to go with Pat. She could hardly walk because she was so overcome with her own guilt.

"What's the matter?" Pat asked her friend anxiously as she tried to comfort her.

Sylviane, however, knew her own condition—she had seen, in God's light, who she really was. After supper when the others had retired, the young woman crept into the villa's lounge. Under the heavy weight of conviction, she knelt on the carpet, and in tears before the Lord, asked for forgiveness. Nobody had told her to do this—the Holy Spirit sovereignly led her to confess her sins and ego-centric life. Sometime later a very happy girl tiptoed back to her room. *I feel so clean, so fresh—like after a storm when everything is washed by the rain*, Sylviane marveled to herself. *I have peace at last.*

Two days later, Pat also turned her heart to the Lord, and both girls were baptized in water by the end of the week. When Sylviane's turn came, she said simply, "Jesus, here I am." The brief statement summarized a whole change of life.

At the final service, they announced that anyone interested in receiving the baptism of the Holy Spirit could go for prayer in the side room. Sylviane was one of the first to respond. Pastor Dan went around praying for each of the people in turn. When he came to Sylviane, he lifted her arms above her head in a position of praise, and she simultaneously burst out into a new language.

"Lord, You know I'm not worthy to have anything like this." Sylviane's heart overflowed with thanksgiving to God, who would bless her with such a gift. She felt someone at her knee. Looking down, she saw that it was Anne-Marie, kneeling beside her and weeping with joy.

CHAPTER TEN
THE WAY INN

Twenty-one-year-old Mark walked doggedly along the shoulder of the road, a tall young man with longish hair and beard, his lanky frame easily supporting his backpack. The Canadian youth was feeling discouraged. He had intended to fly home from Málaga, but his return plane ticket had not been accepted. He needed to get his departure details changed by a travel agent. He was now so close to Torremolinos, he didn't even bother to hitchhike.

A car slowed down and pulled over to the side of the road in front of him. A friendly man with twinkling blue eyes rolled down the window. "Do you want a lift?" he called out in English.

"Sure." Mark shrugged and climbed into the back seat, throwing his pack in before him. The Spanish man with long sideburns in the front passenger seat nodded, "*Hola.*"

With seasoned eyes, the American driver studied the young traveler in the back seat and liked what he saw—the handsome youth, though dirty and scruffy, had an honest, open face.

"Do you have much money?" Pastor Dan asked bluntly.

Mark was surprised by his direct question. He fingered the meager twenty-five *pesetas* in his pocket self-consciously. "No."

"Do you have a place to stay?" the pastor persisted.

"No." Mark shrugged.

"Well, I know a place you can stay," Pastor Dan offered, smiling. "It's very cheap. In fact, it's free."

Mark's interest perked up. With only a few *pesetas* to his name, he was willing to take chances.

"I'm the pastor of the local evangelical church," Dan introduced himself. "And this is Benito, my helper. We run a Christian community made up of young people from different countries. You're welcome to stay there."

Mark was overwhelmed by the offer of free accommodation and gratefully accepted. Pastor Dan led the young man into Barbara's villa, "The Way Inn." He was immediately struck by a poster on the wall of the kitchen: "*Come to Me, all who are weary and heavy-laden, and I will give you rest.*"[29]

Sylviane and Pat had already finished their lunch and were in the lounge. Pastor Dan introduced the tall, easy-going Canadian to them, while Barbara prepared a meal tray for their new guest. When Barbara presented the hot meal to him, the hungry young man gobbled down his food. This unquestionable display of compassion at first alarmed the Canadian.

Why are they doing this for me? he asked himself as he took a welcomed hot shower, his first since leaving Canada.

Over the next few days, Mark observed Barbara and the young people and got to know them. He had many questions about their faith and lifestyle. He had come to Europe searching for answers, looking for a standard by which to live his life. The idea of backpacking around Europe, living without time restrictions or limitations, had greatly appealed to him.

As Mark observed Christianity in practice, he was very impressed by what he saw. These people genuinely loved one another,

[29] Matthew 11:28 (NASB1995).

and their love was put into action in daily living. They didn't need to tell him about Jesus's love—he could plainly see it. Two days before he was scheduled to fly home, Mark accepted Jesus Christ into his own life.

One evening on her way to the YWAM coffee house, Anne-Marie met another disheveled, long-haired youth from Canada—twenty-four-year-old Mo. She stopped to talk to him and found that he had an interest in spiritual things.

"I'm on my way to a Christian coffee house. Why don't you come along?" Anne-Marie invited him.

"Yeah, sure," Mo responded easily. "I already went last night. I met one of the guys from there at my campsite, and he invited me to play chess. Actually, I'm going there now."

As they walked up the street to the coffee house together, Mo explained to Anne-Marie that he had just come from Morocco. While there, he'd met some people who had encouraged him to examine his life. A Muslim had influenced him to try fasting.

At the coffee house that evening, Pastor Dan spoke about the grace of God. He referred to this grace as being inexhaustible. Mo listened to the message intently. Although he didn't believe in God, he realized that he was quite unworthy of the blessings he had received.

"You can't earn God's love," Pastor Dan stressed, and the words struck deeply into Mo's heart. He understood that God was apparently offering him something free.

You're trying to do it yourself, Mo's conscience accused him when he thought of his fasting and other religious exercises. *You're trying to earn your salvation.*

That evening when Mo returned to his campsite, he thought back over his life and his search for meaning and purpose. He had enrolled in university, thinking that education was the answer to life's problems, but this step had only increased his dissatisfaction and inner emptiness. Mo had then hit the road, trying every lifestyle imaginable, "dropping acid," and "going back to nature." The Canadian's search had eventually taken him to Europe and then to Morocco for "more dope, sun, and sand."

As he lay awake in his tent thinking, Mo realized that his search hadn't yielded a single answer to the enigma of life. It had been a futile process of exchanging one set of worthless values for another. He thought of the Christians he'd met and the hospitality he'd received at the coffee house. They had spoken of the Bible and had given him a gospel to read.

These people are sincere and serious about life ... and so joyful, he reflected enviously. He was most touched by the way they practiced their beliefs in daily living. That same evening, alone in his tent under a canopy of stars, Mo experienced a personal encounter with God. "I give control of my life to You," he offered a prayer in humility. Mo moved into The Way Inn.

That spring of 1974, the zealous young Christians spent most of their days on the streets witnessing to others. Pastor Dan believed that as soon as you were saved, the best way to grow in your faith was to share it. After breakfast and prayer, Barbara would drive everybody in her van down to Calle San Miguel, Torremolinos' busy pedestrian street lined with shops, bars, and discotheques. She returned to pick them up at five in the afternoon.

At the bottom of San Miguel, near the steps that led down to the beach, the enthusiastic group of young believers set up a portable wooden bar and served free cold drinks and biscuits to anyone walking by. It was a great location, directly beneath the crumbling old mill tower from which Torremolinos derived its name, with a beautiful panoramic view of the Mediterranean below.

"Would you like some lemonade?" they would eagerly ask the passing tourists, hoping for a chance to talk about Jesus. Many of the people they encountered were suspicious of their free offer and friendly faces, but others, especially young backpackers, stopped and listened.

The enthusiastic Christians would share their personal testimonies, give out tracts, and invite the tourists and backpackers to church. Street-witnessing proved to be a wonderful training ground in evangelism. The new believers learned to rely on the Holy Spirit for their words, and often when they were asked questions they couldn't answer, they'd be inspired to search the scriptures. In this way, they learned to fight with the "*sword of the Spirit.*"[30] As they testified of God's love and life-changing power, their own faith grew stronger.

Pastor Dan and Theo, an elderly Englishman, were taking turns holding daily Bible studies at the church during the week to nourish the hungry young converts. After the study, Sylviane prepared lunch for everyone in the tiny kitchen, usually an inspired vegetarian improvisation, and served the meal in the prayer room. With limited money to spend, Sylviane found the Lord gave her creative ideas for the meals. When she was worried that there wouldn't be enough for everybody, God supernaturally multiplied what they had.

At one of these Bible studies, Pastor Dan played a tape dealing with the subject of "High Places, " the "idols" a person holds in his or her heart. At the end of the study, everyone prayed. Anne-Marie

---

[30] Ephesians 6:14–17: "*Stand firm then, with the belt of truth buckled around your waist, with the breastplate of righteousness in place, and with your feet fitted with the readiness that comes from the gospel of peace. In addition to all this, take up the shield of faith, with which you can extinguish the flaming arrows of the evil one. Take the helmet of salvation and the sword of the Spirit, which is the word of God*" (NIV).

closed her eyes and suddenly had a vivid vision of the street where she worked and lived. An inner voice whispered: *High places.*

"Oh no," Anne-Marie cringed as the two words convicted her conscience. She knew the Lord was asking her to leave her job at the real estate agency and her comfortable apartment. After grappling with these issues for three days, she finally visited Pastor Dan at his office and unburdened her inner conflict.

"Pastor, I have no peace," Anne-Marie confessed. "I can't go on in my situation. It's terrible."

"That's wonderful!" Pastor Dan contradicted her, grinning. He then told her the story of Abraham and Isaac and how God had asked Abraham to give up his own son. As Anne-Marie listened to this story of sacrifice and obedience, she decided to commit her living and working conditions to the Lord. At once she felt peace and relief.

"Now remember," Pastor Dan said, "whenever you leave your job, you have a place here."

A few weeks later, Anne-Marie moved up to Barbara's villa, The Way Inn. The house was filled with five girls sleeping in the bedrooms, including Sylviane and Pat, and the guys, including Mark and Mo, sleeping in the garage, so Anne-Marie was forced to sleep on a couch in the lounge. Shortly afterwards, Anne-Marie's boss opened another hotel and asked her to be on reception. When she was on the evening shift, she would finish work at midnight and have to walk along the dark, deserted roads to Barbara's villa on the hill in El Pinar. In the mornings, rising early to pray, Anne-Marie found she was soon worn out. She realized she had to make a choice about her priorities, so she resigned from her job.

One Wednesday afternoon after the Bible study and lunch, Anne-Marie was leaving the church when Pastor Dan stopped her. "Where are you going?"

"Witnessing," Anne-Marie replied matter-of-factly.

Pastor Dan shook his head, his eyes twinkling, and pointed. "I can use your help in the office."

"Okay," Anne-Marie agreed, and so she became Pastor Dan's faithful secretary and organizer—a position she held for fourteen years.

In the fall of 1974, Sylviane and Mo were witnessing late one afternoon on Calle San Miguel. They stopped to talk to a wiry, bronzed Australian who was leaning nonchalantly against a wall, waiting for a friend to come out of a shop. With his long hair and beard, and an ornament in the shape of his country dangling from one ear, this easy-going surfer was definitely "anti-establishment." Undaunted by his outward appearance, Mo told the Australian backpacker about the love of God.

Barry maintained a cool aloofness, but inside the words had struck a responsive chord. "They were like rain," he later testified. "I was so hard against the world, but I longed for the love of God to get liberty from myself."

When Barry was nine years old, his mother had deserted his father, leaving him to take care of his siblings. With the break-up of his home, Barry had found something inside of him had crumbled. He had felt like everything was against him, but he'd promised himself that he was going to make it in life—nothing was going to keep him down. Barry had left Australia, and after traveling for a few years, had ended up in Europe. As Mo and Sylviane continued to share with him, Barry found himself crying out in his heart: *God, if this is true, I want it!*

"Why don't you come up with us to the villa?" Mo casually invited the Australian. The young evangelists were in the habit, when they found someone showing interest in the Christian way of life, of bringing them back to Barbara's for lunch.

Barry and his friend, who had rejoined him, agreed—a free meal proved irresistible, and they followed Mo and Sylviane up the hill to The Way Inn. As usual, Barbara served cucumber sandwiches, the regular lunch the community ate almost every day for the first few years. The other Christians talked to Barry and his friend all afternoon. In the evening, the two backpackers moved their gear into the garage and slept there for the night. Everyone was fervently praying for God to touch their hearts.

Sylviane came into the lounge for breakfast the next morning and met Barry's eyes. She had been praying for his salvation and felt a deep love and concern for him. Barry quickly turned his head, unable to stand her penetrating gaze. After breakfast, Barbara confronted the two young men. "You have to make a decision," she announced firmly. "You have to choose. Are you going to stay or are you going to leave?"

Both of the Australian lads had clearly heard the gospel by now. If they were interested in following it, they were free to stay, but if not, they would only be taking up valuable space. "Well," the friend replied first, "I'm leaving."

All eyes turned to Barry, waiting in suspense for his answer. Barry thought for a few minutes. "I'd like to stay," he finally answered.

The next day, Barry committed his life to Christ—just forty-eight hours after meeting Mo and Sylviane on the street. "Christ touched my heart and broke it wide open and filled it with His love," Barry testified in the Sunday evening youth meeting soon after.

CHAPTER ELEVEN
"FAITH, HOPE, AND LOVE"

By late 1974, the evangelical community was in desperate need of a coffee house. The one started by YWAM had been bulldozed to the ground six months earlier. Pastor Dan had temporarily opened the church prayer room and kitchen to serve as a coffee house on Wednesday nights, but already these facilities were becoming too small. A casual place where youth could drop in and discuss the Christian faith, apart from any established church connection, had proved to be an effective means of outreach.

One day when he was witnessing near the post office, Benito noticed an old abandoned mansion—just two doors down from the original YWAM site. As it was right in the center of town and perfect for a coffee house, Benito felt impressed to claim it for the Lord's work. Copying the YWAM method of taking over abandoned properties by faith, he started going there and cleaning it up by himself. Soon after, Pastor Dan tracked down the owner, a priest, who gave the church permission to use the house for six months.

All the boys helped Benito clean up the villa, which was in a terrible state of disrepair. They whitewashed the walls, replaced missing floor tiles, painted the doors, repaired the ceilings, collected the rubbish, and neatly cut the garden. Paul from England painted signs on the wall: "Jesus is the Way," and Max from Madagascar plastered the gaping hole in the kitchen ceiling. After he'd finished plastering it, he proudly stepped back to admire his handiwork. Two minutes later, the ceiling collapsed in a pile of rubble at his feet, and poor Max bravely started all over again.

In January of 1975, Pastor Dan officially opened the coffee house, "Ebenezer," with a simple prayer of dedication. By now, Barbara's villa was bulging at the seams with French, British, Canadian, American, Australian, and South African young people. While the girls occupied the bedrooms, the fellows were packed side by side on the garage floor. To the inquisitive neighbors, Barbara's place resembled a campsite—with a caravan trailer parked in the driveway, and two tents with three people sleeping in each set up in the garden.

"What about moving all the boys down to the coffee house?" Pastor Dan suggested to Barbara when he observed her crowded facilities.

Barbara looked at him, eyebrows raised, and replied at once, "Oh, but my dear, you're taking all the fun away!"

In deference to Barbara's wishes, a few boys were left at The Way Inn, but most were moved down to the freshly renovated premises of Ebenezer. As the coffee house was right in the heart of Torremolinos, it was a perfect location for holding the Wednesday night outreach meetings. In one way, however, it wasn't so ideal. Whenever it rained, the roof leaked and water dripped through the ceiling—despite Max's valiant efforts—splashing down on the assembled youth. Even this inconvenience couldn't dampen the spirits of the zealous young Christians as they pressed on with their outreach.

The house also proved to be important for the beginning of the Spanish youth outreach. Benito had moved into his own large room in the main house, which was separate from the internationals. Here he spent a great deal of time on his knees, fasting and travailing in prayer for his own people. Then all by himself, he would pound the streets of Torremolinos, seeking for lost Spanish souls.

The previous year, after living, working, and being discipled under Pastor Dan for two years, Benito suffered through a very dark period in his life and became discouraged. Despite all the sincere efforts to reach his fellow countrymen, his labor among the Spaniards was reaping dismal results. He began to doubt his call to the ministry. One night as he lay in bed, attacked by doubts, the Lord spoke to Benito's heart. He felt the literal physical hand of the Lord on his shoulder, and power surged right through his body. After this strengthening touch of the Lord, Benito continued to preach the gospel on the streets, boldly witnessing to those passing by. Even the lack of tangible results failed to discourage him now, for he knew the Lord was with him. Benito also knew that his responsibility was to testify about Jesus. The results were in God's hands.

The Lord honored Benito's earnestness and gave him souls. The first was a Spaniard named Juan, who would later be in charge of an inner-city work in Villafranca de los Barros. Jorge, a drug addict and delinquent, was also saved at this time and would eventually pastor the Spanish church in Torremolinos. These young men moved into Benito's room at the Ebenezer house. With day-to-day contact and close personal relationships, Benito discipled them, firmly establishing them in the Christian way of life.

After six months, in May of 1975, the coffee house was returned to its owners, and the occupants, which by now had grown to thirty young men, split up. The international young men moved to Barbara's villa, which once again became extremely overcrowded. Benito and his young Spanish disciples moved to the basement of the church that had been established in Málaga, Casa Ágape.

At Barbara's villa, ten guys slept on the garage floor, three more in a pup tent erected in the tangled, overgrown garden, while the overflow slept on the flat roof under the summer stars. The girls were crammed in bunk beds in the bedrooms, the lounge, and the living room, while outside, two New Zealand nurses shared a caravan trailer parked in the driveway. The neighbors marveled at the eccentric Barbara's strange assortment of guests.

The Spanish joined the internationals for Tuesday and Thursday Bible studies at the church and came to the Friday "family night" at Barbara's. Anne-Marie, who had already been translating for Benito, now found herself surrounded by a small group of Spanish young men—most of whom were long-haired hippies, and one or two who were drug addicts. Anne-Marie didn't feel a natural affinity for this motley, unkempt group; in fact, she was repulsed by their appearance.

Anne-Marie admitted the state of her own hard heart to God. In desperation one Friday night, she gave the Lord an ultimatum: "Lord, You're going to have to give me love for these people, because I just can't go on like this," she confessed frankly. "Either You give me love for them or send someone else to translate."

That same evening, the Holy Spirit fell upon Anne-Marie in an extraordinary way, like a "baptism of love." She was surprised by the tremendous love she suddenly felt for the Spanish. From then on, she felt truly united in spirit with them.

At the Torremolinos church services, the handful of Spaniards were relegated to the back pews in order that the translation didn't disturb the English meeting. Anne-Marie sat in the pew behind the group, and with her limited Spanish, translated Pastor Dan's sermons for them. Years later, the Spanish members confessed to her that they hardly understood anything she said, but they had listened patiently. Yet despite the language barrier, the Holy Spirit moved among the Spaniards, and the believers began to multiply at a phenomenal rate.

In the summer of 1975, Pastor Dan had his eye on an abandoned property at the end of the road from the church. It consisted of a large villa and two small bungalows, with a courtyard in the middle—a perfect place to accommodate the overflow needs of the expanding community, which now numbered twenty-six people. Pastor Dan knew the owner, a lawyer from Córdoba, and he asked the man if in exchange for a small rental fee, the Christian young people could move into his place and keep it free from squatters. Surprisingly, the lawyer agreed.

Pastor Dan dispatched Anne-Marie to the house to live in it by herself for a few days. She was pleased to find that this new place, unlike the old coffee house that had been dirty, dilapidated, and in desperate need of repair, was a real home—complete with comfortable furniture. When a visiting group of Dutch Christians from The Hague arrived soon after, Pastor Dan allowed them to stay in the large villa, while Anne-Marie moved into one of the smaller bungalows. Sylviane joined her for company.

In the fall, more girls joined Anne-Marie and Sylviane in their modest bungalow, and a few boys moved into the corner bungalow. Inspired by scripture, Pastor Dan christened the boys' bungalow "Faith," the girls' bungalow "Hope," and the largest villa "Love"—and "*the greatest of these is love.*"[31]

Eventually a dozen young men lived in Faith, the three-bedroom, one-bathroom house with its infamous triple bunk bed. The

[31] 1 Corinthians 13:13: "*And now these three remain: faith, hope and love. But the greatest of these is love*" (NIV).

unfortunate fellow who slept on the top bunk would often wake up with a bump on his head. It became a community joke that the Faith, Hope, and Love houses were used as training grounds "*to comfort the afflicted and afflict the comfortable.*"

Through the summer of 1975, Barry and Mo took their tent to the Málaga campground to reach the backpacking radical youth. One backpacker reached through this kind of "tent mission" was an Australian in his early twenties named Gus. Two community members spoke to him one night at his campground in Los Alamos, on the outskirts of Torremolinos. Gus had been on the road for four months and had never heard much about the gospel in his native land. He politely listened to the Christians and expressed a casual interest in what they had to say. He may not have pursued this interest much farther if a sudden change in his circumstances hadn't occurred.

The next day while Gus was at the beach, his backpack was stolen. The chagrined young Australian dropped by Faith to find someone to translate for him at the police station. Mike, who had talked to him the day before, offered to accompany him to the station, where they filed a report.

"What are you going to do now?" Mike asked.

"Guess I'll hang around for a few days," Gus shrugged. "Maybe the police will find my backpack, or someone will turn it in."

"Why don't you come back to the community and stay with us?" Mike smiled, suspecting that Gus's backpack had not been stolen by "chance." "We'll help you all we can."

Mike took Gus to the church office and introduced him to Pastor Dan. "So you're Australian?" The pastor shook Gus's hand and then turned to introduce him to the grinning young man seated on the couch. "This is Barry. He's from Australia too."

"You're welcome to stay with us," Pastor Dan continued. "Barry will take you up to Barbara's place."

At The Way Inn, Gus was given the privilege of the best bed in the garage—the one nearest the door and, therefore, the fresh air. He couldn't foresee himself putting up with such crowded and uncomfortable circumstances for very long.

"This is a pretty rugged existence," Gus muttered as he confronted his breakfast the next morning. The milk that was passed to him was greyish in color. Later he found out that this was alfalfa milk, normally fed only to calves.

"These people *must* be committed," Gus quipped, marveling that no one seemed to notice or complain about their impoverished existence. After four days of living at Barbara's villa, Gus was overwhelmed with the sincerity and dedication he saw evidenced in the daily lives of the Christians around him.

This Christianity is a huge commitment, Gus thought to himself with fearful sobriety. The Australian was convicted of his need for a Savior, but the cost of following Him seemed too big a price to pay.

Can I afford to give my life to Christ? Gus agonized. He had gone forward the night before in response to an altar call, but he knew in his heart he was resisting a full commitment to Christ. After a lot of inner struggling, Gus made up his mind to leave the community. *If I stay here much longer, I'm going to be trapped*, he reasoned. *My friends from the campground are leaving for Morocco today. I'm going to join them.*

"Are you going down to the church for the prayer meeting?" Barry called out cheerfully.

"You go on ahead," Gus replied evasively. "I have some things to do first."

When he was alone, Gus packed his few remaining clothes in a small bag—his stolen backpack had not been returned. He stopped by the church and met Dory at the door. "I just want to say goodbye," Gus said gruffly, kicking the gravel nervously. "Will you say goodbye to Barry and Pastor Dan for me?"

Gus couldn't bear to face the pastor, and especially not Barry. The energetic Australian, so on fire for God, had tremendously impacted his life. In Barry he saw a person similar to himself; he could relate to Barry's former lifestyle. The fellow Australian had spent many hours patiently talking to him.

Gus left for Morocco, knowing that he was running away from God, and in his heart, deceiving himself. *Someday I'll give my whole heart to Christ, but not now*, Gus thought stubbornly. *I've got lots of plans, and I want to spend many years traveling before I settle down.*

When Barry discovered that Gus had fooled him and slipped away, he felt bad. Heavy with a heart-burden for his fellow countryman, Barry sought a quiet place to pray. "Lord, I've made a mistake," Barry pleaded earnestly. "But You know where Gus is. You'll keep your hand on him and save him. I claim his salvation for Your glory in the name of Jesus!"

Four months later, Barry's prayer was answered. Gus, after traveling down through Africa, had ended up in Rhodesia (present-day Zimbabwe). As an electrician, he had found work in an electricity commission housing estate. One of the first homes he had serviced belonged to a pastor, and as he worked, Gus chatted with the friendly man. On Christmas Day, the pastor and his wife invited the Australian over for lunch and gave him a Bible as a present. Deeply touched, Gus opened up his heart to the pastor and prayed with him, accepting Jesus as His Lord and Savior. Beaming, Gus knew he had finally made a whole-hearted surrender to Christ, a decision he hadn't been ready to make earlier in Spain. He wrote to Barry to share the good news, and one year after leaving the Christian community, he returned.

Over the decades, visitors from almost every nation in the world have passed through the doors of the Torremolinos church, receiving a touch from God. Thousands have been impacted through the international outreach that began there. Transformed, these people have returned to their own countries, bearing precious seed to spread to others. Pastor Dan found he didn't have to go out into all the world—the whole world came to Torremolinos! Even famous Christians like "God's Smuggler" Brother Andrew, who smuggled Bibles into the former Soviet Union, and the great Bible teacher, Derek Prince, participated in conferences held at the church.

The world-renowned *People* magazine found out about the community and its impact on backpacking youth passing through Torremolinos. The magazine published a positive two-page article, "Troubled Young Travelers in Southern Spain Find Help from an Evangelical American," in its July 1976 issue:

> …in nearby Torremolinos, Del Vecchio and his wife Rhoda, have established a church, a halfway house and a thriving religious community aimed at salvaging young dropouts and druggies…The Del Vecchios' 85 young charges drifted into Spain from all nations—"99 per cent of them," he says, "are the products of broken or unhappy homes." As they "receive Jesus into their hearts," in Del Vecchio's words, they trim their hair, wash themselves and their clothes, stop drinking and taking drugs. [32]

The magazine photographs show Pastor Dan preaching in the sanctuary, community members gathered around an outdoor table, where "up to 70 converts meet Tuesdays for a festive but frugal

[32] Maurice F. Petrie, "Troubled Young Travelers in Southern Spain Find Help from an Evangelical American," *People* magazine, July 19, 1976, 53.

lunch,"[33] and Rhoda and daughters Deborah, eleven, and Rebecca, nine, sharing "their lives with a pet collie and youngsters from all over the world."[34]

The growing "community was filled with young people from many countries: Canada, USA, England, France, Germany, Australia, New Zealand, Italy, Colombia, Denmark, Sweden, Switzerland, Scotland, Ireland, Finland, and South Africa and other places in Africa. Some had been hippies in Morocco smoking hashish; others had been robbed and found themselves without documentation or money; and others were seeking for a reason to live"[35] before they ended up at the community. Pastor Dan observed that the church was acting like "Jonah's whale," scooping them up and rescuing them from their rebellious lives. These Christians, now "full of the Holy Spirit and fire, went out two by two to evangelize. Their joy was contagious, and there was such love and power from God that when new youth came in from the street, they were soon converted and filled with the Holy Spirit."[36]

"You see the wind that's blowing these trees," Pastor Dan told the *People* magazine reporter, pointing through the church window. "When you look at this community, I want you to see the wind and not the trees. The reason those trees are moving is because there is a wind blowing them, and the reason people are being delivered and helped here is because of the Holy Spirit. We're just a visible manifestation, but He is here working with us, and that's the picture we want to get of God—the Cause behind it all."

---

[33] Ibid.
[34] Ibid, 52.
[35] Del Vecchio, *El Manto de José,* 125
[36] Ibid.

The author and her sister with backpacks

The author and her sister on the beach in Torremolinos

Torremolinos Church postcard (Del Vecchio family in upper right)

Del Vecchio family (Deborah and Daniel Jr.)

Malaga Tabernacle (Domed Geodesic Wonder)

Interior of Malaga Church

House on the Rock

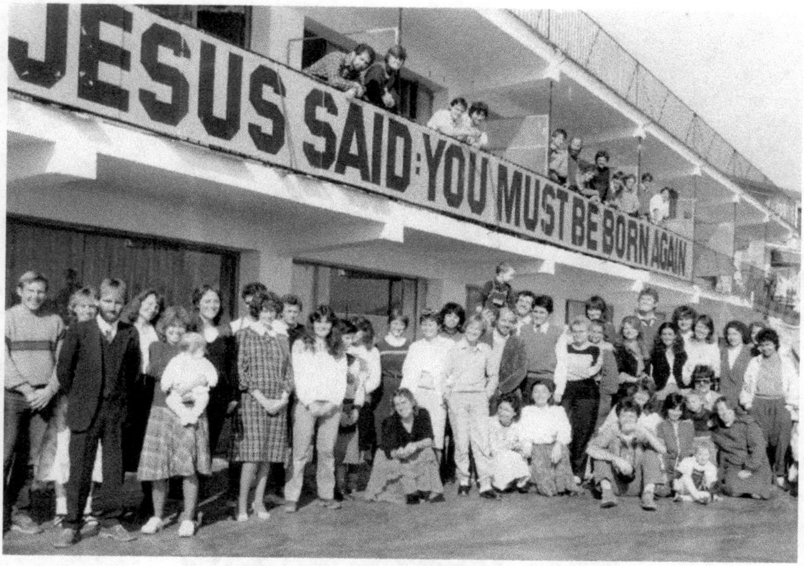

Panorama Hotel

Conference with former drug addicts (on platform)

Leslie, former heroin addict

Dan and Rhoda

Dan and Rhoda with daughter Deborah

Seville meeting

Antequera Farm with dome structures

Aerial view of Antequera farm

Daniel Lucero and Pastor Dan on the farm

Antequera church

Community 1985

2014 Reunion in front of Torremolinos church

CHAPTER TWELVE

HIS FARM AND HIS SCHOOL

At a family evening in March of 1976, Pastor Dan shared his vision of having a farm on which to raise crops to supply the community's dietary needs. Barbara was now serving over seventy guests for family night dinners—6,500 meals each month. Also, as some of the former long-haired youths knew nothing about manual labor, Dan believed that the physically-demanding farm work could prove therapeutic. He wanted a place where he could train young people, teach them to work and to become self-sufficient. In the prayer meeting that followed, the idea was presented before the Lord. They asked God to open the doors and to do it according to His will.

The first day that Pastor Dan began seriously searching for a farm, the Lord showed him the place of His choice—a property near the village of Alhaurin El Grande, a half-hour drive from Torremolinos. Dan and his children held hands on the brow of the hill overlooking the farm and "by faith" claimed it for Jesus.

After that, everything seemed to go wrong. For many weeks, Dan and his lawyer tried to reach an agreement with the owner and his lawyer over the property. Twice they all came together in the lawyer's office to settle the legal entanglements involved, but each time the negotiations broke down. Finally, Dan, confused and clouded with doubts, decided not to pursue this particular site. He began to search for another farm with no results.

During this uncertain period, one of the community young people received a word from the Lord, from Numbers 14:8: "*If the Lord delights in us, then He will bring us into this land and give it to us, 'a land which flows with milk and honey.'*"

Dan believed this word applied to their present situation, so receiving new confidence and hope, he resumed negotiations with the owner. Although from the beginning the Holy Spirit had impressed upon him not to pay more than $14,000 for the property, during the former bargaining, Dan had unwillingly agreed to go higher. Now for the third time, with three lawyers and the owner, he tried to reach an agreement. No one, however, could resolve a legal technicality that had surfaced: apparently the landowners whose fields surrounded the Alhaurin farm, had first rights to purchase the property.

"I'm sorry." the owner told Dan. "You may have the money, but you can't have the land unless all the other landowners forfeit their first claim rights."

Discouraged, Dan left the meeting and drove home. On the way, however, God dropped a word of wisdom into his heart and showed him what to do. The next day, a determined Dan rode on his motorbike in the pouring rain and visited all the neighboring farmers. He presented a document he'd drawn up to each one, stating that they would be willing to renounce all their purchasing rights to the property in question. Miraculously, all the landowners signed it. A jubilant Dan rejoiced before the Lord. The legal impediments had been resolved. Once again, he offered the owner the original amount that God had shown him, and it was accepted.

The whole community visited the property, which hadn't been worked for several years. They prayed over it and then celebrated with a picnic. They christened the new farm "His Farm." Within its borders, His Farm had eight varieties of fruit trees, including lemon and orange groves. Dan hoped that much of this fruit could be canned and kept for winter use. With the shortage of food and rising prices, he believed that this would be an essential part of God's plan for the future direction of the community—enabling it to be eventually self-supporting.

The first thing that Dan turned his attention to was the problem of irrigation. If the farm was to produce vegetables to supply the community's needs, a substantial source of water had to be located. In this region of Spain, the summers were dry, with sometimes no rain for six months, but with a sufficient water supply, two crops a year could be produced.

Dan chose a spot to begin digging a well near the small river at the bottom of the property, but they found no underground water. Next they tried a location at the top of the property. The crew began to shovel the earth, hitting a green layer of clay beneath. As they dug deeper, the ground became harder and harder until a jackhammer and compressor were needed. At thirty feet down, they unearthed a fish fossil.

"It's probably been there since the Flood," Dan remarked dryly, unable to hide his terrible disappointment at the waterless well. All their hard labor had yielded nothing. And to make matters worse, the neighboring farmers were shaking their heads at this display of foolishness, declaring there would be no water at this location.

"Lord, please give me a word," Dan pleaded in frustration. The entire Christian community was seeking the Lord in prayer about the dismal situation. After another day of striking nothing but rocky ground, a discouraged Dan opened his Bible to Isaiah 35. Verses six and seven jumped from the pages:

Then the lame shall leap like a deer,
And the tongue of the dumb sing.
For waters shall burst forth in the wilderness,
And streams in the desert.
The parched ground shall become a pool,
And the thirsty land springs of water …

Dan knew that God had spoken, and he shared the good news with the community: "We'll have water shortly." Instead of digging deeper, Dan decided to drill a small hole in the center of the well. The drill penetrated another twenty-five feet, striking even harder clay than before. Finally, they gave up digging. Despite the apparent failure, Dan didn't lose the confidence that God had placed within his heart.

Many weeks passed by and then some light showers came. The well began filling up with the water, and strangely, even after the rain had stopped, it remained nearly full. Dan examined the well with some of the boys. "Where's all the water coming from?" he asked them, perplexed by the odd phenomenon.

Dan pumped all the water out of the hole. As the level receded, water flowed in to replenish the supply and continued pouring into the well to a level of twelve meters deep. Later they discovered that this water was not in fact coming from the well but from their neighbor's irrigation channel!

Years later, Dan and Rhoda visited the farm, now operating as a rehabilitation center under Betel, a sister Christian organization based in Madrid. They were surprised to see a large swimming pool on the property.

"How did you get water?" Dan asked in wonder.

"We decided to build a home not far from your well. We hit an underground stream that broke through the foundation, so we made a swimming pool instead!"

Although not discovered until years later, God had indeed provided "*streams in the desert.*"

For a long time, Dan and Rhoda had been grieved over the poor education that their three children, Daniel Jr., Debbie, and Becky, were receiving. The costs of English-speaking private schools were exorbitant, and immorality plagued the local public schools. They were at a loss about what to do. Then two teachers, Carol and Barbara, came to Dan in consternation. Both had been tentatively hired to teach the children of a group of parents in Mijas, a mountain village about a half-hour's drive inland from Torremolinos. When the parents discovered that the two teachers were Christians, the director of the school hastily drew up a charter that stated no religious instruction could be given and no mention of Jesus Christ could be made.

"Pastor Dan, what should we do?" the teachers asked. "We can't agree to not speak of Christ."

Dan agreed that they shouldn't accept positions with that school. Then, with two unemployed but qualified professional American school teachers standing before him, an idea occurred to him: *Why don't we start our own school for our kids?*

As it was nearly August, they began a frantic search for a building to rent for a school. Although they looked in the villages of Mijas and Arroyo de la Miel, they couldn't find anything suitable. All doors closed. Then during a Wednesday morning prayer meeting, eleven-year-old Debbie Del Vecchio approached her father. "Daddy, why don't we start the school at the farm?" she whispered.

"Yeah, why not?" Dan mused, marveling that "*out of the mouth of babes*"[37] wisdom had come.

---

[37] Matthew 21:16b: "*And Jesus said to them, 'Yes. Have you never read, "Out of the mouth of babes and nursing infants You have perfected praise"'?*"

His Farm, however, had no facility in which to house a school. To build a structure seemed out of the question. There was not time to hire an architect to draw up plans, and besides, the whole process was too costly. Then Dan discovered that wooden edifices didn't require building permits because they were considered temporary dwellings. No Spaniard in his right mind would build with wood because it rots so easily in this country's climate, but Dan knew that with proper treatment, it could be made to last.

"We'll build wood cabins," Dan announced to the community, "and each cabin will be a classroom."

Inexperienced but willing, the young men all pitched in to help with the construction. With only primitive means at their disposal, they rolled the earth by hand using large poles. As they couldn't afford a cement mixer, even the concrete needed for the foundations was mixed by hand. When the school term started in September, the cabins were not yet completed. Undaunted, the four teachers (Carol, Barbara, Beth, and Sue) each chose their own orange tree, arranged a few chairs under the fragrant boughs, and proceeded to teach their classes. The children loved their unique outdoor "classroom."

Pastor Dan and a few community helpers continued on their grueling schedule, frustrated often by the inferior wood they were forced to use. By the time the rains started in October, Dan and his able young assistants had erected the first two cabins. The first they named "Patience," for its construction had been a real test of their patience. The second Dan called "Perseverance," for he had been tempted to quit and hire help. The third cabin, which went up in less than half the time of the others, was aptly christened "Peace." Eventually five other cabins were completed: Prudence, Providence, Prosperity, Promise, and Praise.

Even with no advertising, the Lord sent seventeen children to the school, ranging in age from pre-school to the first-year high school. The teachers, who soon numbered eight, gave of their time sacrificially and received no salary. In turn, no tuition was charged to the students.

From the beginning, the uncompromising emphasis of this Christian school was on worship first and then study and work. Dan christened it "His School." Each morning began with prayer. After four years, His School reached a steady enrollment of around sixty-five students, staffed with fourteen full-time and part-time teachers. The students were from Finland, Sweden, England, America, and Germany, and from mixed Spanish-expatriate homes. In the eight years that this Christian school was open to the general public, literally hundreds of children had an opportunity to hear the gospel, and many accepted Christ.

To meet the growing needs of the community, Barbara had generously exchanged her car for a nine-seater van, which was promptly nicknamed "The Bug." The van soon became well-known throughout Torremolinos. In fact, it was hard not to notice, as Jesus references were painted all over it. Across the front hood, Barbara had written "Jesus is Comming" in bold red letters. By mistake, she had misspelled "coming" with two "mms."

"My dear, what shall I do?" she fretted after discovering that the paint couldn't be scraped off. Then she had the brilliant idea of modifying one of the "mms" into a great yellow and red flame. "That's either the flame of the Holy Spirit or hellfire," she explained to curious observers. "Take your choice."

Once a week, Barbara would take along two boys to the market to buy food for "His School" (which now boasted fifty children), for the coffee house (which slept thirty), and for the inhabitants of her own villa. She bought everything in bulk and piled it all in: sacks of potatoes, onions, and tomatoes. Eventually the inevitable happened: the floor of the van caved in. The poor "Bug" also had a broken axle, which Stuart, the community mechanic, patched up as best as he could.

Barbara decided it was time to buy a bigger van. She had her eye on a green Ebro, a top of the line, very expensive van. In order to purchase it, Barbara sold the studio apartment she owned in town. Although she lost money on the deal, she received the exact amount needed to buy the van. Barbara took great pride in driving "God's Chariot," as she fondly referred to it. The Ebro proved to be a blessing to the community.

"We need your van today, Barbara," Pastor Dan would often phone her. "Thanks."

Although she knew her attitude was wrong, Barbara began to resent these requests. When she was told her van would be needed to transport the teachers to His School every day during the term, Barbara fumed. "Now I'll have to take the bus everywhere."

Once a week, Barbara visited a hospital in Málaga. As soon as she'd become a Christian, she had started visiting the sick. Because she'd spent so much time in hospitals when she had contracted tuberculosis, she felt very accustomed to their corridors. This hospital was filled with middle-aged tourists who had developed health problems on their holidays, usually pneumonia, heart attacks, or broken bones. Wearing her prominent "Jesus is Lord" badge, Barbara prayed with as many English-speaking tourists as she could find. Now without her van, she realized her hospital visits would require five bus changes there and back. She wasn't looking forward to this particular "sacrifice."

Strangely, after two months of traveling by bus, Barbara discovered that she was enjoying the rides. Almost as soon as she'd experienced this change of heart, a church member loaned her a car. After that, Barbara never minded when her van was used—with or without her.

Barbara had more lessons to learn in the "School of Humility," as the community wryly referred to their training by the Holy Spirit in Christian obedience. The Friday family night dinners, now serving eighty people, were traditionally held at Barbara's villa before the evening service. This was always a special day for Barbara. She would spend her morning in the fields collecting flowers to decorate the dining tables. As even the weeds appeared beautiful, she sometimes found it hard to tell the difference between the two.

"Well, what does it matter?" Barbara decided cheerily. "I'll just gather them all and dedicate them to Jesus."

One Friday morning, Pastor Dan informed Barbara that dinner would be served after the service instead of before. Apparently, the large meals were making some people sleepy, and a few girls had complained that the generous portions were making them fat. Everyone would now serve themselves. Barbara was upset by this new arrangement. The crowning thorn was that she wouldn't be at her usual place at the head of the table. For three days she snapped at everybody. Finally, entering her bedroom closet, she sank to her knees and asked God to forgive her anger. Later Barbara, who had done what she wanted all her life, confessed to Pastor Dan, "Actually, if you really want to know, I'm the most rebellious person in the whole community!"

Pastor Dan laughed. "I believe you are!"[38]

When Barbara's van was no longer sufficient to meet His School's transportation needs, Dan decided to purchase a large school bus. To Rhoda, he suggested using the money they had received from the sale of their "honeymoon cottage" to purchase this expensive vehicle—money they had been saving as a "nest egg."

[38] Fletcher, 43–44.

Years earlier, when the Del Vecchios had been ministering in Mexico, Dan had suggested selling their "honeymoon cottage." Rhoda had lifted this matter, which had weighed so heavily on her heart, up to God: "Father, You know this home is a place we can always come back to. But if You want us to sell, then take the love and concern out of my heart for this house and give me faith to release it."

As Rhoda had read her Bible, a scripture from Mark 10:29–30 leaped from the pages, and she took it as God's special promise to her:

> *So Jesus answered and said, "Assuredly, I say to you, there is no one who has left house or brothers or sisters or father or mother or wife or children or lands, for My sake and the gospel's, who shall not receive a hundredfold now in this time—houses and brothers and sisters and mothers and children and lands, with persecutions—and in the age to come, eternal life."*

The joy of sacrificial giving had flooded Rhoda's heart. She had been willing then to give up her home and use the money they received from its sale for the furtherance of the gospel. Now Dan was suggesting to Rhoda that they use this lump sum of cash, their "nest egg," for the immediate need of a school bus. She was again willing to give this sacrificial offering. The Lord would indeed prove faithful in multiplying their costly gift.

CHAPTER THIRTEEN
CASA ÁGAPE

The main outreach among the Spanish centered in the busy seaport of Málaga, the capital of the province of Andalusia. There in the basement cellar of the Casa Ágape church, Benito faithfully persevered in discipling new converts for five years. He passed on to them all that Pastor Dan had taught him about the Bible and practical Christian living. Many of these converts, who had been drug addicts and delinquents, would eventually become pastors, leaders, and teachers of their own churches. Some later ran drug rehabilitation centers throughout Spain.

Every day Benito and his youthful band of disciples handed out tracts on a crowded street in Málaga called Calle Sanchez Pastor. By now, these unusual young men were recognized by the regular pedestrians of this street. One of those who frequently passed by and stopped to chat was a twenty-five-year-old drug addict by the name of Luis.

For the last eight years, Luis had been heavily involved in the world of drugs and rock music. He played in a rock group well-known all over the province of Andalusia. Even though he had everything he could desire—fame, drugs, money, and girls—the young Spaniard found that his life was quite empty and unsatisfying.

Whenever Luis sauntered down the street "stoned" as usual, Benito would greet him and talk to him about Jesus. Luis would pretend to scoff and try to offer him drugs, but something in Benito's eyes and voice drew Luis' attention. He was captivated by the love and compassion he saw. For two years, Luis continued to bump into Benito and his motley band of converts. They fervently preached the gospel to him, and he would always shrug: "Yes, all right, but it's not my time."

Then one day when he and his rock band were in Seville, Luis experienced excruciating pain at the back of his head. He felt sick and rushed to the bathroom, where he vomited an ugly black fluid. Terrified, he got his friends to drive him to the hospital, where he blacked out. When he regained consciousness, he was in intensive care, hooked up to all sorts of tubes and surrounded by masked doctors.

"At last, you have opened your eyes," one of the doctors leaned over, concern evident in his voice. "You've been in a coma for two days. Do you know what you have?"

"No," Luis answered hesitantly.

"You have meningitis—the most dangerous and contagious form."

After eleven days in the hospital, Luis regained his strength, amazing even the doctors, who scheduled his release. The next morning, however, Luis felt the same overwhelming pain return. As he was about to call for the doctor in charge, an inner voice stopped him: *Remember when you called out to God when you were a child? Do it now.*

Luis remembered Benito and the God he was always talking about. Some of his own friends had already turned from their old life of drugs to follow this God. Could he take the same step? *Is it my time now?* Luis questioned himself, wondering if the hand of God was somehow involved in his illness. "God, if You exist, if You are true," Luis prayed, "then heal me, free me, get me out of here. And I promise I'll leave my music, drugs, and friendships and follow You."

A few minutes later, the pain vanished completely. Luis forgot all about his promise to God. He left the hospital and took a bus to Málaga, where he went in search of drugs and his friends at their usual hangout, a bar called *La Buena Sombra* (The Good Shadow). Strangely, none of his pals were there. Disappointed, he walked out of the bar and found himself suddenly surrounded by four Christians—Benito, Felipe, Paco, and Vicente. Vicente was an old friend of Luis' from Algeciras. A month before, he had given his life to Jesus.

"We've really been praying for you," Vicente hugged him. "We even fasted for you so that God would heal you and you would be able to get saved."

At that moment, Luis felt the conviction of the Holy Spirit saying to him: *Remember your promise. You told Me that if I healed you, you would follow Me. Here I am. These people are My disciples. Follow Me.*

Two days later, Luis attended their church in Málaga, Casa Ágape. After Felipe finished preaching, he invited those who wanted to accept Jesus as their Lord and Savior to come forward. Deeply aware of his own sin, Luis walked to the front of the altar, and Felipe prayed with him. Luis asked the Lord to forgive him and to free him from drugs. From that time on, he never smoked cigarettes, drank, or took drugs again. He left his friends and the world of rock music behind. Shortly after, Luis moved into the basement cellar of Casa Ágape, joining Benito and six other zealous converts. Here his discipleship in the Christian way of life began in earnest.

Under Benito's firm leadership and steadfast example, Luis grew rapidly in the Christian faith. Every morning at half past seven, he rose with the others to begin the day with prayer. This was an especially hard form of discipline for Luis, who was used to going to bed at six thirty in the morning and rising some time past noon. His old lifestyle had to change radically.

The day after he was converted, Luis was out on the street witnessing with the other Christians, giving out tracts and sharing his newfound faith. Either Benito or Felipe was always at his side to support and encourage him. Some of Luis' old street friends were amazed at the change in him, and they were afraid.

"You believe what these guys preach?" they would taunt. "You're crazy! You'll come back to your senses soon. And then you'll come back to us."

The grace of the Lord, however, strengthened Luis, and he remained at Casa Ágape for two-and-a-half years undergoing intense Christian training and discipleship. A real bond of love grew amongst the eight young men living in the basement of the church. Although the sun didn't touch their damp, dingy quarters, the light of the Lord scattered the darkness, uniting the young men in true brotherhood. Most of the future leaders of the Spanish work were to come out of this cellar basement, committed to a fellowship forged in poverty, hardship, and self-denial.

Often for breakfast the young men ate only a flour and milk paste, and when there was no money, even that meager meal was reduced to flour and water. Many times they could only afford one meal a day, usually a spinach and potato soup, but their meals were always consumed in the almost tangible Presence of the Lord.

The young Spaniards lived on the barest of budgets. Benito would regularly go down to the docks and collect the day-old fish that hadn't been sold to the markets. Once he was given so many fish that he had to hang them on a clothesline to dry so that they'd last longer. That afternoon, every cat in the neighborhood sat under the clothesline, drooling at such a feast.

During this time, Benito and the others learned to scrounge and scrape and survive. This simple, rugged life formed in the young men an immense dedication, perseverance, and zeal for the Lord. They were willing to give up everything—comfortable, self-indulgent lifestyles—to serve Christ. To win a soul became their supreme goal—to be a true disciple of Christ became their burning desire.

Every morning at Casa Ágape, the young men, full of fervor, would rise to pray. After their scant breakfast, they'd walk the many miles to the busy pedestrian street Sanchez Pastor in downtown Málaga. On the pavement they would spread a blanket and display Christian books, and there they would preach and witness to the passing crowds. Often they would pray: "Lord, give us a soul today. Give us a soul."

One particular day, Diego[39] handed out a tract to two young women. Although he didn't know it at the time, they were nurses, and one of them, Sofia,[40] was taking morphine. Her girlfriend had tried everything to get her to quit. With a guarded openness, the two nurses listened as Diego spoke to them about how Jesus had changed his life.

"Come to our meeting on Saturday night," Diego urged them. "We have a music festival." As far as music festivals go, the "music" was somewhat lacking. Benito was the only one who could play the guitar, and even he only knew three chords.

"*Sí*, maybe we'll go," the girls half-promised.

On Saturday night, Diego was waiting by the bus stop in eager anticipation of meeting the people he'd invited to the meeting. He wasn't sure if the two girls would come, but he rejoiced when he saw them step off the bus. The two nurses sat at the back of the church. As Benito preached, Diego silently prayed that the Lord

---

[39] Not his real name.

[40] Not her real name.

would touch their hearts. Before the service ended, his prayers were answered as both of them broke down in tears. After that evening, they started to attend the services regularly.

Shortly afterwards, Diego realized that he was falling in love with Sofia. This really worried him because he only wanted to serve the Lord and nothing else. He wasn't sure if he could share his heart with Jesus and a girlfriend too. In those days, Benito used to preach constantly on the theme of being "Eunuchs for the Lord"—that was, of course, until he met his future wife. Every time Diego's thoughts drifted in the direction of Sofia, he rebuked them.

One day, Diego read a Proverb in his Bible: "*Better is open rebuke than hidden love*."[41] With this in mind, he approached Sofia at a meeting and took her aside, confessing his feelings for her. He was delighted when she admitted, "I've noticed you too." For the next two years, Diego went through intense suffering with their on-and-off relationship. Sofia, who had experienced traumas in her childhood, was finding it difficult to kick her morphine habit.

In the fall of 1977, Anne-Marie noticed Sofia at the church and felt a burden for the young woman. It was obvious she was drugged and in bad shape. "Would you mind if I took Sofia in to live with me at the coffee house?" Anne-Marie asked Pastor Dan, who nodded his approval.

From the beginning, Anne-Marie realized that she had no idea whatsoever of how to care for a drug abuser. Sofia was one of the first addicts the Torremolinos community had taken in, so nobody had much experience in this area. Because she was working as a nurse, Sofia had easy access to morphine. She would bring the drug back to the coffee house and inject herself with a needle, leaving her blood-soaked cotton batten around on purpose. This deliberate provocation drove Anne-Marie crazy.

[41] Proverbs 27:5 (NIV).

"You're destroying yourself!" Anne-Marie confronted her angrily.

Often Anne-Marie searched Sofia for the drugs she concealed on her body. On one occasion, suspecting the nurse had smuggled in drugs, she stormed up to her room and wrestled the young woman to the floor. While one of the boys held Sofia down, Anne-Marie thoroughly searched her. Sofia had plastic bags of liquid morphine wrapped around her waist and stuffed inside her jeans' pockets. One by one, Anne-Marie furiously pulled the plastic bags out of her pockets while the nurse struggled and twisted wildly.

The pressure of living with an addict humbled Anne-Marie. Reaching her limit, she collapsed to the floor in the prayer room. She felt a tremendous burden for Sofia and sensed the Lord was asking her: *Do you accept Sofia?*

Anne-Marie immediately answered: "No!"

Will you accept her? the gentle inner voice continued to plead.

Anne-Marie fiercely resisted this quiet voice but finally she gave in. "Yes, I will." She knew that this was the only response that would please the Lord. In a tiny way, she felt like Jesus must have felt at Gethsemane, sweating drops of blood and wrestling in agonizing prayer when he realized that the "cup" he must drink meant taking the sin of the world upon Himself and being marred by it. For Anne-Marie, this experience led to a deeper identification with Christ and His sufferings.

Later that same day, after Anne-Marie had yielded to the Lord, Pastor Dan told her that he was moving Sofia to his family's house. Anne-Marie sighed in relief. In retrospect, she realized that God hadn't allowed Sofia to be taken away from her care until He had completed His work in her own heart by changing her attitude and making her willing to do His will—*whatever the cost.*

"Are you still in love with Sofia?" Pastor Dan asked Diego on one of his visits to Casa Ágape. Diego blushed and nodded, afraid that somehow he might be blamed for her rebellious behavior. Surprisingly, the pastor's countenance softened. "Then I think it'll be good if you come to see her from time to time. If she has a friend, someone who loves her—like you—it will help her."

Two months after she had moved into the Del Vecchios' house, Sofia committed herself totally to the Lordship of Jesus. The Christian brothers at Casa Ágape prayed for her, and she was finally and completely delivered from her drug addiction. Diego and Sofia were married.

The Spanish people were hungry for the Good News. Churches were started in Córdoba, Seville, Fuengirola, Madrid, and many other locations.

CHAPTER FOURTEEN
MIJAS

At a Tuesday morning Bible study, His School teachers Carole and Barbara informed the assembled group of the great need for evangelization in Mijas, the town where they lived. Although only 12,000 people inhabited the village, over 300,000 tourists visited it annually.

"Hundreds of English-speaking people have bought villas there," the teachers enthused. "And there's no gospel witness whatsoever. These people need to hear about Jesus!"

In the spring, Barry and Sylviane took the bus up to Mijas, a whitewashed village perched high in the mountains overlooking the Mediterranean, about a half hour's drive from Torremolinos. Their mission was to "spy out the land" and explore the possibilities for evangelism. After that, for the following two years, evangelical teams were sent regularly to witness in the quaint tourist town and establish home Bible study groups.

This mountain village proved to be rocky ground for the planting of the Word of God. Ironically, although the early Christians of the first century had found refuge from persecution in the caves around Mijas, the region had long since become a stronghold for "religious" tradition that was more pagan than it was genuinely spiritual. The opposition against the new Spanish believers was intense. The whole village mocked them, and recruits were even paid to hound them. Although quite a number of Spaniards were eventually won to Christ, under this heavy pressure most would either backslide or go underground.

Finally, after two years of perseverance, the community established a small bilingual church in Mijas. They met in a woefully inadequate one-room shed. Whenever it rained, the worshipers had to endure water dripping through the roof, leaving them damp and cold. It became increasingly obvious that a more suitable, permanent place for a church was desperately needed.

Eventually a lovely panoramic site overlooking the sweeping Mediterranean coast was chosen to be the ideal location for a church building. The cost of the land, however, seemed astronomical: $11,500. On top of that amount, Pastor Dan estimated that the cost of constructing a church building, even with the help of volunteer labor, would be roughly an additional $30,000. To believe God to supply this enormous sum required a great test of faith for the community—still a group of relatively young believers.

During a Sunday morning service in February of 1979, Pastor Dan felt compelled to speak about the financial needs for the purchase of this property. Normally he never made appeals for money, but in this case, he felt he should ask for the entire amount. At the end of his sermon, the Holy Spirit impressed upon him the words *eight loaves.* He was reminded of the loaves and fishes that Jesus had blessed, broken, and multiplied.

"The eight loaves represent the 800,000 pesetas we need to purchase this property," Pastor Dan told the congregation. "Each loaf represents 100,000 pesetas." He led the church in prayer and asked for pledges or promises to give the required amount within one month.

Incredibly, within a few minutes, as fast as the pledge cards could be counted, 800,004 pesetas were promised. The visiting tourists in the congregation were thunderstruck. Much of the money was donated by the community's young people who had sacrificially given all they possessed. This was the *spirit of sacrifice* in operation—the spirit that had earmarked this community from its birth.

By April 1979, Pastor Dan had paid 825,000 pesetas in cash for the property. In preparation for the foundation of the new church, he then hired a bulldozer, and 220 huge truckloads of earth were removed from the site.

The Mijas church was built on solid rock. As the young men from the community painstakingly chipped away at the rock with their pick axes, they often found that their physical labor was accompanied by an inner breaking of their attitudes.

One person who made this discovery was twenty-seven-year-old Gordon, a tough, feisty truck driver from Scotland. The first day that he worked on the foundation of the church, he had to dig a one-square-meter hole with nothing but a pick axe. As he pounded away at the rock, he found himself comparing, by a revelation of the Holy Spirit, the hard ground beneath his feet with his own hard heart.

I guess the Lord is trying to break me down, Gordon thought with a sudden flash of insight. *Just like I'm chipping bits off this rock, He's chipping away at the hard exterior of my heart, trying to get inside …*

Although Gordon had given his life to the Lord a few months before, there were many poor attitudes that the Holy Spirit had yet to deal with. For Gordon, that first year of hard labor building the church was accompanied by an inner softening. For twelve years, Gordon had been a truck driver in Scotland—the last five of which he'd been hooked on drugs, including cocaine, and his life had taken a downhill slide. His longstanding relationship with his girlfriend, Mairi, had disintegrated. After he'd been busted for drugs, he'd wanted nothing more than to get away from the town of Dumfries.

At this point, a friend who had just returned from the Torremolinos Evangelical Community Church had dropped by to see him. Excited by his newfound faith, the friend had eagerly shared with Gordon. Within a month, Gordon had also accepted Christ and was on his way to Spain.

"I'll stop on the way to see Mairi," Gordon planned. "I want to tell her what has happened."

Twenty-five-year-old Mairi was teaching English at a private school in Zaragoza in the north of Spain. When Gordon arrived in November with a sleeping bag in one hand and a Bible in the other, she was shocked. "This is just another phase he's going through," Mairi scoffed. "I'll get some friends to get him drunk, and that'll get him out of this ridiculous mindset about Christianity!"

But instead, Gordon persuaded Mairi to go with him to Torremolinos on her Christmas vacation. At the community, she saw the dramatic change in George and Lyn and in other friends from Dumfries, and she was deeply convicted. After a week, a stubborn Mairi finally gave in and accepted the Lord. Five days later, when her vacation ended, she returned to Zaragoza—minus Gordon.

Gordon knew that he had to stay in the community; he'd been a Christian for only two months and had already slipped back into his old habits. He realized that if he were to grow in his faith, he needed the support and fellowship, the teaching and training of a strong group of believers. For the first week, the wiry Scot, with the shoulder-length blond hair and red beard, slept on the church floor with three other guys. By his second week, however, an extra bed had been moved into Barbara's garage, and he slept there with eight other young men.

From the beginning, Gordon was impressed that the community's leadership confronted him directly with his problems. He'd always thought Christians were just pleasant people with nice smiles, but at this community, they corrected and challenged him, all in sincerity of love. For the first time in his life, he was forced to honestly face himself.

Five months later, Mairi quit her teaching position in Zaragoza, packed her bags, and returned to Torremolinos. She arrived at the church with her suitcases and knocked at the pastor's office door. "Well, I've come back," Mairi announced airily. "Can I stay here in the community?"

Pastor Dan studied the pretty Scottish lass whom he'd considered to be very rebellious and stubborn when he'd met her at Christmas. "Well, I don't know if we want you in the community," he commented frankly.

"What?" Mairi gasped in shock. "But I've left everything to come here!" She couldn't believe that the pastor might actually turn her away.

"Well," Pastor Dan relented, "you can live up at Barbara's and we'll see how it works out."

Mairi moved into The Way Inn and shared the studio with two other girls. At first, she was terrified of the proper, upper-class British woman, with her erect posture and forthright manner. Barbara maintained strict order and discipline in her household. Mairi walked with "fear and trembling" around her. As time progressed, Barbara amused Mairi with humorous stories, and gradually Mairi found herself warming up to her.

In early 1980, on a palm tree-lined walkway in Málaga, a young Swiss fellow named Bernard swung peacefully in the hammock he'd strung between two palm trees. A notice he had pinned to one palm announced in four languages: "Hammock for sale." Every now and then, an interested passerby stopped to inquire about the price of the large Mexican hammock. As he wasn't in a hurry to sell, Bernard quoted a high figure. He was content to spend a few days swinging in the shade, passing the time by strumming on his classical guitar.

"Ah, this is the life," Bernard sighed happily, proud that he was able to combine business with pleasure.

After graduating from business school in Switzerland, Bernard had decided to fulfill his dreams of world travel. For the last six months he'd been traveling around the Mediterranean, spending idyllic months sunning in the Greek Islands, touring the pyramids of Egypt, and working in Israel. He had loved the freedom that traveling with a hammock afforded—sleeping on beaches, swimming, and doing whatever he pleased.

Why don't I start a hammock business? he thought with excitement. *I could travel to South America and buy hammocks for ten dollars and then sell them in Switzerland for fifty dollars. I'll sell this hammock and then return to Switzerland to do a market study.*

When business in Málaga proved to be slow, Bernard packed up and moved along the coast to nearby Torremolinos. He immediately found an ideal spot to spread his hammock in front of a closed bar off the main walking street of San Miguel. He hung up his advertisement and lay down in the hammock to await prospective customers. Late in the afternoon, a passing Belgian couple decided the hammock would be the perfect addition to their sailboat. They agreed on a price, which they would pay on Monday.

Happy with the arrangement, Bernard packed up his hammock and strolled down San Miguel, where he bought an ice cream cone to celebrate. As he rested on the rock pillar at the top of the street, licking his ice cream, an Australian girl and an English fellow approached him.

"We're from the Christian community," Anita began. "We have a music night this evening and we'd like to invite you. There's a lot of singing and good music, guitars—"

"Guitars?" Bernard's interest perked up.

When Bernard agreed to go to the music night, Anita gave him a map with directions to the coffee house. As Bernard continued to sit on the pillar licking his ice cream, George and Lyn, a married couple from Scotland, came up to talk to him. They'd been making and selling puppets on the street before they had joined the community over a year before.

"Yeah, I know all about the music night," Bernard groaned. He felt embarrassed because his ice cream was dribbling down the side of his cone, and also because the couple were talking to him about God, a subject he didn't feel very comfortable with. "I'll be there," he said, cutting the conversation short.

At the informal music night held inside the coffee house, Bernard listened to the truck driver with a red beard and thick Scottish accent, named Gordon, giving his testimony for the first time. The next morning, Bernard attended a Bible study at the church. Pastor Dan talked about the "pruning process" that takes place in a Christian's life. Bernard didn't understand a word of what he said. At the end of the study, as everyone was leaving, Sylviane and two other girls sat at the piano, playing a song with a classical sound. Bernard drew close to listen.

Sylviane looked up at the handsome dark-haired youth and smiled. "Are you a Christian?" she asked in French.

"No, I'm not," Bernard admitted frankly. But her question had made him realize that he wanted to become one.

At the Friday family night at Barbara's villa, Bernard became convinced that God was in their midst. At first, he had adopted a superior attitude to these Christians. He believed that all of them had deep problems, such as drug or alcohol addiction, which had brought them to Christ. After talking with several people, however, he realized that they hailed from a wide range of backgrounds, varying in age, education, nationality, and experience. Yet they all had one thing in common: they professed to have found the truth.

There's something I don't understand here, Bernard marveled, recognizing a certain peace that filled their lives. *I want that too, but not now. First I'm going to start up my business.*

Bernard determined to avoid the Christians after that. At the *pensión* where he was staying, however, the concierge asked him to talk to a German guest who had tuberculosis. Feeling sorry for the sick old man, Bernard told him about the church and then agreed to accompany him to the door. When they arrived at the church, Bernard spotted five other Swiss people going into the meeting.

I'll stay to the end of the service so I can talk with them afterwards, Bernard decided. Ironically, halfway through the meeting, the old German slipped out the door, and Bernard was left alone. At the end of his message, Barry asked, "Who wants to become a Christian?"

Bernard carefully raised his arm only halfway up, bent at the elbow, signifying that he wanted to become a Christian—but not now.

"Whoever wants to receive Jesus Christ tonight," Barry continued, "come forward."

Bernard found himself walking to the front. Barry began to lay his hands on the shoulders or the top of the heads of those gathered by the altar and to pray for each individually. When he came to Bernard, Barry didn't say anything except to give him two scriptures: "… *whoever comes to me, I will never cast out*" (John

6:37b, ESV) and "… *if you confess with your mouth that Jesus is Lord and believe in your heart that God raised him from the dead, you will be saved*" (Romans 10:9, ESV). When Bernard finished praying to accept Christ, he knew with absolute assurance that Jesus was in his heart.

That night as he lay awake in his bed, he wondered what he should do about his hammock. He was supposed to meet the Belgian buyer the next morning. *I promised myself that if I sold the hammock, I was leaving Torremolinos.*

There is a way around that, the Holy Spirit impressed upon him. *Give your hammock away. Give it to this man. In this way, you are not tied to the word of your own mouth.*

The following day, Bernard visited the Belgian man's home. The man wasn't in, so Bernard left the hammock by the door with a tract and a note explaining that he'd become a Christian and inviting him to church.

For the next three months, Bernard slept on the church floor with as many as twelve other young men. Barbara's villa and the coffee house were filled to capacity. During the day, mattresses were stored in the prayer room, but at night, the guys would spread them out and make their beds. One chose to sleep by the altar, another under the cross. Bernard slept under the organ, and Big André, a six-foot-five fellow also from Switzerland, slept in the aisle—the only place large enough for his body. Sometimes Pastor Dan would arrive early at the church to pray, and he'd have to tiptoe over the mattresses on the way to his office.

Bernard was saved on Sunday, and on Wednesday, Big André finally gave in and accepted Jesus as his Savior. "Lord, take my life! Take everything I have!" André sincerely cried out at the front of the church. "I want to follow you." That morning after he put away his mattress, André went to get some clothes from his backpack and found that it had disappeared. All of his belongings had been stolen. "I guess the Lord answered my prayer," André laughed good-naturedly.

Within the space of fifteen days, six French-speaking Swiss people were saved—four others besides Bernard and André. It was the beginning of a healthy French-speaking community, which would eventually number twenty-five. In time, Bernard would become their pastor, but before that took place, the Lord worked a "breaking" in him, bringing his will to submit completely to Him.

Bernard, who had grown accustomed to an easy-going lifestyle, found the first months of hard labor at the Mijas church and the Alhaurin farm very difficult. At the Mijas site, he helped erect the church walls, spending hours in the hot sun mixing the cement by hand and assisting Pastor Dan in laying the heavy blocks. At the end of the day, he was totally exhausted.

The main "breaking," however, took place on the farm. There Bernard had to carry heavy boxes loaded with fruit to the top of the hill, till the ground, and push wheelbarrows filled with dirt. Bernard, who had a weak back, found this work extremely painful. "Lord, I'm willing to do this work," he prayed. "But You have to heal me." On Bernard's second trip, he took the shovel and by faith started loading the wheelbarrow. After that, his back gave him no pain.

The boys on His Farm worked out in the fields from early in the morning and often late into the evening. When it got too dark to see, the boys wanted to quit, but inevitably Mike would appear with a gas lamp and hook it to a tree. "Here you are, guys. Keep going."

When they were on irrigation duty, the young men would have to do night shifts. All of the farms in the area were assigned six hours each in which to channel the water flowing from the mountain onto their land. Usually His Farm received its supply of water at night. After Mike was informed when to expect their turn, he'd wake up his sleeping crew, including a very groggy Bernard.

In March, less than three months after Bernard had become a Christian, Lyn, one of the women who had invited him to the music night, died in a tragic accident. Her death shook the entire community, especially her husband, George, and those who had known her from Scotland.

Shattered by the terrible news, Barbara gathered everyone staying in her villa into the living room. "I have something sad to tell you," Barbara began, fighting back the tears as she related what she'd heard from Rhoda in an early-morning phone call. "Last night after the meeting here, George and Lyn walked back to the coffee house. As they were crossing the main highway, hand in hand, they hesitated in the middle of the road."

Barbara cleared her throat and continued, with every eye in the room riveted on her. "George pulled Lyn to cross over with him, but for some reason, she let go of his hand, and he ran across alone. As Lyn waited for the car on her right to pass, a car on her left struck her, throwing her straight into the path of an oncoming car." Barbara paused until she regained control of her emotions. "When George rushed over, she opened her eyes for a fleeting instant to look at him and then died."

Everyone in the room wept. "The Lord must have His reasons for cutting off her life," Barbara added consolingly. "One minute she's alive, and the next she's in the arms of Jesus."

That night during the Saturday prayer meeting, everyone sat quietly in the church. Some were finding it hard to understand why this tragedy had happened. Then suddenly George, who was up at the front, on his knees in prayer, lifted his arms in worship and started praising the Lord. With that, the Spirit of joy seemed to descend on the grieving group, and everyone burst into spontaneous singing, which soared upwards to the Heavenly Throne.

"I see Lyn standing in front of Jesus," Barry softly related the vision he was receiving. "Both Jesus and Lyn are dressed in white robes. Jesus is holding in His hands something that looks like delicate rainbows studded with precious jewels. It's absolutely beautiful in His hands. He's now placing it as a crown upon Lyn's head. She is bowed down with reverence, awe, and wonder. Then with a wave of His hand toward God the Father, the Lord Jesus is saying: 'Father, behold Your daughter. She is My precious Jewel, My Bride.' Jesus is now presenting Lyn to Father God. She's dressed in her robe of righteousness and wearing her crown of life and victory."[42]

At the same time, Pastor Dan was at his house working on his sermon for the next day's memorial service for Lyn. The Holy Spirit impressed upon him the words of Stephen recorded in Acts 7:

> *But he, being full of the Holy Ghost, looked up steadfastly into heaven, and saw the glory of God, and Jesus standing at the right hand of God, and he said, "Behold I see the heavens opened, and the Son of Man standing at the right hand of God."*[43]

Lyn's parents flew down from Scotland to Torremolinos for the funeral. They weren't Christians, but their hearts were touched by the Lord during the service. After returning to Scotland, they

[42] Barry was encouraged to keep yielding to the Holy Spirit in the area of visions, dreams, and revelations from the Lord through scripture, such as, "'*Eye has not seen, nor ear heard, nor have entered into the heart of man the things which God has prepared for those who love Him.' But God has revealed them to us through His Spirit. For the Spirit searches all things, yes, the deep things of God*" (1 Corinthians 2:9–10).
[43] Acts 7:55–56 (KJ21).

passed a church that their daughter had often urged them to attend, but they had always made excuses. This time, however, when they passed this church, they both could hear Lyn's almost audible voice calling them to go in. They entered and were saved. After that, they opened up their home for young people's meetings. Lyn had once remarked to friends in the community that she had two main desires: to be nearer to Jesus and to see her parents become Christians. Both of her prayers were answered.

In September 1981, Barbara left Spain to return to England. Two years before, the Lord had spoken to her during the night: *I am sending you back to your country—not for worship only, but to proclaim Me as Lord and King.*

Barbara rallied the community members to paint her villa. "You can go on living here until it's sold," she wistfully told the six girls who were sleeping in her house.

Barbara felt sad at leaving this "refuge" that the Lord had given her. The Way Inn was charged with memories. Hundreds of young people from many nations had passed through her villa's doors in the past eight years, and she had proudly served thousands of meals. For Barbara, those years had been rich with abundant gifts from God, rare times of sorrow (as at Lyn's funeral), and countless times of joy, including seven weddings. It would be especially hard to part with certain community members with whom she'd shared a special bond.

Everyone wept as they kissed Barbara goodbye. They'd grown to love this no-nonsense mistress of The Way Inn, now in her mid-sixties, with her upper-crust manner and noble bearing. The community recognized the debt of gratitude they owed to this eccentric British lady for her years of dedicated service and sacrifice. If Barbara hadn't so generously opened up her own home to hordes of strangers and scruffy youth, many of the community members wouldn't be there. They would dearly miss her.

> *To everything there is a season,*
> *A time for every purpose under heaven:*
> *A time to be born,*
> *And a time to die;*
> *A time to plant,*
> *And a time to pluck what is planted …* [44]

[44] Ecclesiastes 3:1–2.

CHAPTER FIFTEEN
HOUSE ON THE ROCK

While one evangelical team was sent up to the mountain village of Mijas, another one was directed to the neighboring coastal town of Fuengirola. There in the main plaza, the Christian group sang and performed street dramas. By the spring of 1979, the Fuengirola team was so heavily involved in evangelism that they were spending six days a week there, either in street witnessing or in house-to-house visitation.

The spiritual ground was proving to be so fertile that Pastor Dan decided a base should be started in Fuengirola. Mo had spied a large abandoned facility surrounded by an acre of overgrown fields on the edge of town. This former restaurant-hostel was in a terrible state of disrepair and needed a tremendous amount of labor to get it anywhere near habitable. Dan placed Mo in charge of this formidable task.

At the Tuesday afternoon Fuengirola team prayer meeting, Mo announced, "Today we're not going to pray. Pastor Dan and I have seen this abandoned place. We're going to claim it for the Lord and we're going to clean it up and move in there. Here's a mop and bucket for you. And a broom for you," Mo said, distributing the assorted cleaning items to the eight team members. "David, take the shears. You can trim the hedge."

David, a young Englishman and former rock musician, looked up at Mo in astonishment. "Mo, is this the one on the bus route?"

"Yeah, that's right."

"Hallelujah!" David shouted in amazement. "On my way here as I passed by that place, I had a strong impression of the Lord saying to me, '*You're going to be trimming the hedge there this afternoon,*' and now you've just handed me the shears!"

As an act of faith, the work party of eight trooped down the road with their mops, buckets, and brooms to the crumbling property. All the windows and doors were bricked up except the main door—its rusted padlock had been broken long ago by vandals. As they entered the house, the work crew stared around them in disgust. It was absolutely filthy. The vandals had cleared out anything of value, leaving nothing behind but broken furniture. The stench of urine was unbearable. Upstairs, the rooms were filled with dirt and piles of rubble, the air thick with clouds of dust.

"Okay, let's get started," Mo urged the work team, whose enthusiasm had diminished considerably after entering the deserted building. That first day, he killed a snake, but he kept it quiet or the girls would have run a mile!

While the others scrubbed and cleaned inside, David surveyed the yard. "It's a jungle," he declared woefully. "I should have a machete to cut through this lot."

While the team cleaned up the abandoned facility, Pastor Dan finally tracked down its owner and asked permission to occupy the premises, guarding it from further vandalization. The man agreed to discuss the request with his four brothers, co-owners of the property.

"I'm sorry," the man reported back to Pastor Dan. "My brothers are totally against you living in the place. I'd like to allow you to, but I don't want to argue with my brothers."

Not accepting defeat, Pastor Dan rallied the whole community to pray and fast over the use of the villa. They had a time of praise and prayer, simply committing it to the Lord and trusting Him to glorify His name.

"Okay," the owner relented when Dan contacted him once more, "you can stay until the end of September—but then you must leave."

The community christened their new home *La Casa en La Roca*, or "The House on the Rock," inspired by the wise builder of Matthew 7. The building was enormous: twenty-one rooms, including a living and dining room, which could accommodate one hundred people. Although the community knew they would have the facility for only two short months, they decided to fix it up and give it everything they had.

Bits and pieces to furnish House on the Rock came from a variety of sources. Somebody gave the group a door, and someone else donated three armchairs and a two-burner stove. A woman who ran a delicatessen donated a fridge, a shower curtain, some towels, and seat-covers. The young people scrounged through the garbage piles and collected a bed, four mattresses, electric heaters, and a television from this unlikely source.

One Saturday as they worked in the house, an Australian woman, whose children attended His School, came frantically running through the front door. "I need to clear out my second-hand shop by seven tonight! Could any of you help me please?"

David accompanied the woman to her shop and helped load the entire contents of her store into a hired van. They drove the vanload of furniture to another second-hand shop in Torreblanca, where they were met by an elegant woman dressed in black and sipping a martini. She appraised the contents of the van with a critical eye.

"Oh my dear, that's broken," the woman declared scornfully. She pointed to another piece. "And this is scratched. And oh, I wouldn't have that in my shop!" She snubbed her nose at everything in the van.

The Australian woman bristled with anger. "Well, if you don't like it, I'll give it away!" Defiantly, she turned to David. "You can have it all! I'd rather give it to you than sell it to this woman!" Offended that this posh woman regarded her furniture as "junk," she stormed out of the shop and instructed the van driver, "Take it to the House on the Rock!"

Before the day was over, the House on the Rock had acquired three vanloads of furniture and appliances for a token twenty-three hundred pesetas, or twenty-five dollars. Although some of it was indeed junk, most of it proved quite useable.

After three weeks of hard labor, the House on the Rock finally appeared semi-habitable, and David and John moved in. They chose one of the twelve bedrooms upstairs and cleaned it out. Next they bought a huge chain and padlock to lock themselves in at night—they were not keen to share their newly renovated quarters with tramps or other sinister strangers. After a few sleepless nights in stifling heat, David and John knocked out the bricks that boarded up their bedroom window. Soon they not only got a refreshing breeze but a balcony with a view.

The young people who eventually lived at House on the Rock were to see God provide for their needs, sometimes in miraculous ways. In the first week, David and John discovered that they only had enough money to pay the train fare to the Friday night meeting, with nothing remaining to buy food. They realized that unless the Lord intervened, they'd have to go on a fast. In a way, they were excited to see how the Lord would provide—this was a chance to develop their faith.

An hour later, an Englishman came to their villa. "I've just been to St. Anthony's," the man said, referring to the private English school next door, "but nobody's there. I wonder if someone from the school lives here?"

John and David shook their heads. "Maybe we can help you," they offered.

"I have a letter from a Spanish lawyer that I need translated into English," the man explained.

"I speak Spanish," John volunteered. "I'll translate it for you."

For this translation work, the man paid three hundred pesetas—enough for the young men to purchase several meals. David and John celebrated and praised the Lord for His goodness. Afterwards, John went for a swim in the Mediterranean. On his way back from the beach, he spotted a ball rolled up in the gutter: another three hundred pesetas! John[45] and David rejoiced over the Lord's provision and lived like kings for the next few days.

In the beginning, the House on the Rock had no running water. For showers, David and John took a bar of soap down to the beach and used the temporary shower units that had been installed for the summer tourist season. Sadly, the plumbing fixtures in the House had been stripped by vandals. Everything that could be stolen had been stolen: toilets, sinks, bathtubs, and tank systems. Pipes protruded from the walls; gaping holes and broken bricks testified that bathtubs had once been installed.

Feeling like Moses, Mo walked around the house with a stick striking every pipe, toilet, and plumbing fixture. "Let there be water!" he commanded.

---

[45] John and his future wife, Agnes, would later open an outreach in the strategic port city of Algeciras.

Fortunately, a Danish plumber volunteered to help fix House on the Rock's piping system. Through scavenging the dumps, the community acquired some sinks and toilets. When a building was being demolished across the road, they received permission to take anything of use, including a bathtub.

In September, when the community was supposed to vacate the House on the Rock, Pastor Dan presented a beautiful smoked ham from Granada to the landlord as a token of his appreciation. "We're very grateful for what you have done for us," Dan told him. "Do you want us out now?"

The landlord smiled. "You can stay until December. If the villa isn't sold by then, I'll bulldoze it to the ground. Then I won't have to pay taxes on the building, just on the land."

When December came around, however, the landlord allowed the community to continue living in his villa. In fact, this arrangement carried on for another five years.

"One man's garbage is another man's treasure" became a popular slogan around the community. As a regular routine, the House on the Rock members scavenged the garbage dumps around Fuengirola, retrieving items that others considered worthless and transforming them into pieces of value. They rated the garbage dump sites "one-star" through to "five-star." One day at a "five-star" dump, they found a bathroom suite, a folding table, and a double sink.

They also practiced the "waste not, want not" principle. By buying provisions in bulk, using houses and vehicles to the utmost, and sharing talents and skills, they were able to cut down on unnecessary expenses. Vendors at the local market gave them scraps of ham, sausage, fish, bread, and fruit for free. They became masters of economy, maximizing their resources.

Whether it was finding abandoned furniture, abandoned houses, or even "abandoned" people, the Christian community sought out and salvaged those which others had cast away or neglected. Through Jesus Christ, they restored destroyed human lives and developed their unrealized potential—for His glory.

For a long time, the young people at House on the Rock had been praying for a piano. One day, somebody noticed a large sign propped up against two pianos in the yard of St. Anthony's School next door: "Take away for firewood." Upon closer inspection, the pianos proved to be absolute wrecks, but the community had hopes of salvaging them.

"C'mon, you can fix them, David," one fellow urged.

"You must be joking," David replied scornfully. As a professional musician, he had a certain distain for the pathetic instruments that were now stored in the House on the Rock.

Before coming to the community, David had worked for eight years as a keyboard player, traveling with various bands all over Europe. While performing with his band at the American naval base in Rota, he had attended church and given his life to Christ. Some months later, the Rota church pastor and a visiting evangelist invited David along for the four-and-a-half-hour drive to Torremolinos to see Pastor Dan.

Although Pastor Dan was at the farm in Alhaurin, the three visitors stayed for dinner at the coffee house. David eyed the meal before him with uncertainty; it appeared to be a red slop of tomatoes and rice. He pecked at his plate politely, but he was thankful that the men stopped later for a proper meal on the way back to Rota.

"The Lord has spoken to me clearly," David told the two men as they drove along. "I'm supposed to go back to Torremolinos and live in the community."

The Rota pastor laughed. "Well then, we'll have to send you rations of hamburgers and peanut butter to keep you alive!"

David returned to the Christian community in October. The first thing Pastor Dan told him was to get a haircut. David was not pleased; he had sported long hair since the age of thirteen, and his whole identity, especially as a band member, had been tied up in his appearance. But even though he hated to cut his hair, David submitted to the pastor's suggestion.

"That's not short enough," Pastor Dan frowned when he saw David. "Cut it again."

Another area that the Lord dealt with was David's pride in his musical ability. The first time that he played the piano during the music night, Pastor Dan took David aside. "What do you think you're doing? Putting on a performance?"

David stared at him in surprise.

"Stop squirming around," the pastor admonished. "You're drawing too much attention to yourself."

David was genuinely mystified. While playing in bands, he was accustomed to bopping up and down to the beat of the music, looking like he was enjoying himself. He thought he had toned down his stage mannerisms considerably—but apparently not enough.

Should I just sit there like a dummy? David wondered, perplexed.

After that, David consciously tried to sit still at the piano, which at the start made him look stiff, bored, and serious. Later, as he matured, he became very gifted in leading a congregation in worship, directing their attention to the presence of the Lord and not to himself.

The two pianos collected dust for many years at the House on the Rock, until a third one was salvaged from a Swedish school. This last instrument was in fairly good condition—only the hammers of the last three octaves were broken off. David used the parts from the worst piano to repair it and then fixed the remaining piano. The House on the Rock now proudly possessed two very playable pianos. Soon after, a professional Spanish pianist brought a beautiful medium grand piano to the House on the Rock. "Can I leave my piano with you for a year?" he asked David hopefully. "I've no other place to store it."

As David ran his fingers lightly over the keys, delighting in the grand's perfect tone, he smiled to himself, quoting the Scripture: "*as having nothing, yet possessing all things*." [46]

In 1981, when David sought Pastor Dan's blessing to marry Ullie, the pastor asked him how he was going to support his bride. "Oh, the Lord will provide," he mumbled, thinking he sounded very "spiritual."

"Why don't you advertise your piano-tuning services in the local newspaper?" Pastor Dan advised him in his usual practical manner. This action resulted in paying jobs, which helped David to provide for Ullie and their growing family.

Another significant event occurred at the House on the Rock. One day while Pastor Dan was eating there with community members, the Holy Spirit fell upon him in such a way that he collapsed on the table. The others present thought he was having a heart attack, but God was speaking to him very clearly, His words reverberating through him like thunder: *I want dance to be added to My worship.* After this direction, the community introduced dancing into the worship services—not wild dancing, but graceful and choreographed Hebrew-style dancing.

Over a five-year period, the House on the Rock community branched into many ministries (including a Christian literature table, a street-theater group, and a dance group), along with micro-businesses that helped the young people support themselves

[46] 2 Corinthians 6:10b.

(piano-tuning, book-binding, ceramics, a bench factory, a bakery, and farming). Before the House on the Rock was bulldozed to the ground in the fall of 1984, it had become home for twenty-seven community members and almost three hundred animals: one-hundred-and-fifty rabbits, one hundred chickens, eighteen pigs, sixteen goats, and a cow.

CHAPTER SIXTEEN
HOTEL PANORAMA

"Pastor, there's this abandoned hotel right in the center of town," Anita, a perky Australian who lived with the Del Vecchio family and helped to take care of their children, informed Dan. "Nobody is living in it. It's in a state of total disrepair."

By now the community had taken over several properties, renovating them with little money, and had moved in. Dan had asked Anita for her opinion on another hotel that the community was excited about, but instead she now drew his attention to the "El Panorama" hotel. Earlier in the afternoon as she'd been walking by this empty hotel, she'd felt a strong witness in her spirit that *this* was the one for the community and *not* the other site. "I really feel in my spirit that the Lord is in this," she enthused. "It's ours!"

Pastor Dan was used to his "kids" wanting to step out in faith and claim this or that for the Lord. They were all eager to grow in faith but often lacked the discernment that only came from exercising their spiritual "muscles." He had to maintain a balance between encouraging the new believers and firmly channeling their growth in wisdom and sound judgment.

"Well, maybe, but I doubt it." It seemed too much to expect that this six-story hotel located just fifty yards away from the main walking street of Calle San Miguel in the heart of Torremolinos would be available. "I'll check it out anyway," he promised her.

Dan walked through the iron gates at the entrance of the abandoned hotel, past an empty swimming pool, to the broad terrace. Leaning against the wrought iron railing, he surveyed the *playa* (beach) beneath him and the distant snow-capped Sierra Nevada Mountains along the coast. The terrace had the grandest view of the Mediterranean in all of Torremolinos—living up to the hotel's name, "El Panorama." He pressed his face against the dirty glass windows of what had once been its restaurant. Even in its filthy, unkempt state, the pastor could see that the hotel had potential. It was certainly in an ideal location, perfect for reaching the hordes of tourists and backpackers who passed by on their way to the beach. Dan jotted down the yellowed phone number that was posted on the window.

"I'm sorry, I sold it quite a while ago," the former owner told the pastor when he dialed the number. Dan decided not to pursue the matter any further.

"But I really believe this place is from the Lord," Anita insisted with unwavering conviction. Because of the young Australian's unabated persistence, Dan reluctantly began to search for the hotel's owner once again. The current owner, Dan discovered, actually turned out to be an association of three brothers. Feeling foolish, he dropped in to see one of the brothers, a prosperous businessman who owned several leather and clothing shops.

"We're having a national conference," Pastor Dan explained to the owner, who met his eyes with coolness. "People will be coming from all over Spain, and we need a place to house them."

The Spaniard regarded him impassively.

"If we could use your hotel to put them up for a few days, we'd be very grateful. In exchange," Dan offered, "we'd clean up the place to get it in some kind of living condition."

"No, I'm not interested." The man shrugged and started to rise, signaling an abrupt end to the conversation. But Dan, who was not one to give up without a fight, couldn't be dismissed so easily; the owner's attitude of indifference irritated him.

"This could be to your benefit as well as ours. We're willing to spend three months cleaning up your hotel, and we'll only use it for a few days. We're involved in drug rehabilitation, and a lot of the people coming to this conference are former drug addicts. If you let us have this facility, it would be a great help to our work."

"I'm sorry," the owner interrupted him, "but the answer is no."

"No?" Dan repeated, suddenly angry with "divine" indignation. "Here we are, people coming from many different countries to help the Spanish people—your people! And you, a Spanish citizen, with a hotel sitting empty—you do nothing! Just let us repair it and use it for a few days and then we'll give it back to you."

The man lowered his eyes. Dan's thunderous outburst must have touched his conscience, because he muttered, "Go see my brother."

The man's brother turned out to be head of the electric company. Calmly, Dan explained once again why he wanted the hotel.

"Well, as long as it's just for three months," the brother relented cautiously. "I'll give you temporary light, and you can pay a flat rate for the electricity. But make sure that you don't put any people in it except for those few days."

"We'll just maintain a skeleton staff to keep squatters out," Dan replied, knowing that it would be convenient to the owner to have trustworthy people preventing vagrants from occupying the premises. Already one squatter had been making the empty hotel his home for many months.

With the owner's consent, Pastor Dan dispatched a team of workers to clean up and repair the unkempt property. "Why don't you go live in the hotel and fix it up?" he suggested to Gus, George, and Tom.

After touring the premises, Gus, who would be in charge of the electrical wiring and plumbing, was aghast. "Fifty bathrooms!" he moaned. To the Australian, the prospect of getting the Hotel Panorama's fifty bathrooms in running order was staggering. In addition, Pastor Dan had warned him that everything needed to be fixed up for the pastors' conference in three months' time. Gus shook his head in disbelief. "Look at all the work!"

Gus, who was an electrician by trade, had also become the community plumber. While working on the House on the Rock and Ebenezer, Gus had assisted a Danish plumber and gained useful experience, but most of his knowledge had been acquired through trial and error. With minimal experience in soldering and joining pipes, Gus went from bathroom to bathroom in the hotel, trying to diagnose the problem in each case. Many toilets, tubs, and taps had to be replaced or were missing altogether. Scrounging all over town for these necessary items, Gus found perfectly good toilets and tubs in garbage piles. At the scrapyard, he bought taps—ironically, these taps were the original ones that thieves had stolen from the hotel and sold to the scrapyard.

As Gus labored on the plumbing and wiring of the hotel, he sometimes got discouraged. As an electrician, he felt reasonably confident replacing old wiring with new, but the plumbing was a real test of perseverance for him. He was often confronted with problems he had no idea how to solve, but he knew that Pastor Dan was counting on him to solve them anyway.

"We're putting in all this effort and most likely we'll be moving out next month," Gus grumbled after a particularly trying day.

"Surely you can't keep a hotel in the heart of Torremolinos for very long. It's prime real estate!"

Despite his lack of faith that they would be allowed to remain in the hotel, Gus doggedly persisted with the plumbing. At last, when he had checked and double-checked the pipes, Gus turned the flow of water on, fervently praying that none of the pipes would burst. The three young men rushed from room to room checking for leaks, but amazingly, they only found a few.

"Praise the Lord!" they sighed thankfully.

For the fourth annual pastors' conference in September of 1982, the community was able to accommodate three hundred people in the newly renovated premises. In each room of the six-story hotel, community members had packed as many bunk beds as they could fit, stacking them three beds high. They had scrounged old sheets, beds, and mattresses from donor hotels, dinnerware from donor restaurants, and furniture from garbage dumps—collecting anything and everything they could find. Gus, a master at scrounging, had even been able to repair the hotel's rusted commercial washer and dryer from scraps of old washing machines he'd found. In this way, the community had repaired, fitted, and furnished the hotel, using little money and a lot of ingenuity.

Much time and labor had been poured into the Hotel Panorama's restoration, but even for just the few days of the conference, compared to the exorbitant costs of rented accommodation, it was worth all the trouble. During the conference, the community daily fed over 650 people at tables on the hotel's scenic terrace. Pastor Dan was so pleased with the hotel facilities that at the conference's conclusion, he approached the owner again. "We're so happy with the hotel, we'd like to continue using it. Is that possible?"

The owner had been impressed with the industrious efforts of the Christian community. "I'll give you another three months."

After the three months had passed, Dan visited the owner, this time with a freshly baked chocolate cake to show the community's appreciation and gratitude.

"Okay," the owner smiled between mouthfuls. "Another three months."

With each subsequent visit and extension, a fond rapport grew between the pastor and the businessman. After three years, the owner finally told Dan, "Listen, I don't foresee us using the hotel for the next two-and-a-half years. You can have it until then."

The community kept the Hotel Panorama for six years almost free of charge, paying nothing for water and only a minimum monthly fee for electricity. On the premises they had a dining room, a fully equipped kitchen, a swimming pool, a school, a supermarket, and 280 beds. The community used the hotel to hold national conferences, to house team members, and to disciple new Christians. In all of this, they saw God's miraculous provision.

As the El Panorama was situated near Torremolinos' busy pedestrian street of San Miguel, thousands of tourists passed by daily on their way to the beach promenade below. To reach out to these vacationers, the community set up a "coffee house" where they offered refreshments and desserts. The young people sang and testified to those who dropped in.

Overlooking the crowded beach on Spain's famous Costa Del Sol, a fifty-foot-long sign on the Hotel Panorama's terrace boldly proclaimed to the sun-worshipers below: "JESUS SAID: YOU MUST BE BORN AGAIN."[47] In the heart of this hedonistic

---

[47] John 3:7: "*Do not marvel that I said to you, 'You must be born again.'*"

playground, the evangelical community dared to uphold the standard of Jesus Christ. It's the last place one would expect to find such a strong witness, but "*where sin increased, grace increased all the more.*"[48]

[48] Romans 5:20b (NIV).

PART THREE

GRANARIES FOR THE HARVEST

CHAPTER SEVENTEEN
A GEODESIC WONDER

God, how can we build a church that won't cost much money or take a long time to build? This was the constant unspoken prayer on Pastor Dan's heart. The Spanish work was multiplying so quickly that the need for a large meeting place was acute.

The Evangelical Community Church in Torremolinos was now packed to capacity with Spanish people sitting in the windows, spilling out the front doors, and filling the side prayer room and kitchen. Whenever Dan preached in the Málaga church, Casa Ágape, he thought the floor was going to cave in. Two-hundred-and-fifty people were jammed into the suffocating space. The windows had to be kept closed because, otherwise, the neighborhood children would throw shoes, balls, and tomatoes through them.

It was obvious that the Spanish church had outgrown its Casa Ágape quarters. Pastor Dan recognized that they needed a larger facility—but how could a building be provided? Although Spain was now enjoying greater religious liberty, the country was still not so open that schools or halls could be used on a regular basis for church services, so renting a facility wasn't a practical consideration. The prospect of building a church similar to the one in

Torremolinos or Mijas, with so much time, money, and labor involved, wasn't feasible.

"We need more space, but we have no land or money." Frustrated, Dan kept coming back to these facts.

Pastor Dan wanted a structure that could be erected by nonprofessionals, be economically feasible, and be considered temporary and therefore not requiring architect's fees or building permits, which were notoriously difficult to obtain in Spain. It needed to be built on rented land and, in the event that the congregation was forced to move, be dismantled and raised again in another location. He asked God to give him an idea so that he could build without money, without builders, and without building permits—a pure miracle!

As he pondered the problem, Dan began scribbling on scraps of paper. "How can I build a structure without pillars?" he asked himself, drawing on all his building expertise to tackle the problem. He sketched various rough designs but always ended up tossing the unsatisfactory drawings into the waste bin.

One day an idea occurred to Dan. He folded two sheets of paper together to conform to the image he had drawn, an image that resembled an elongated barn. As he examined his paper model, he began to get enthused. "These flanges on the side will give the necessary structural strength," he calculated as he analyzed his model, excitement mounting at his discovery. "Now what would be the best material to build with?"

His first thought was fiberglass. A member of his congregation had a solar energy panel factory that worked with this medium. When Dan paid the young man a visit, the Dutch Canadian dissuaded him. "Don't use fiberglass. It's very expensive and impractical. Why don't you try fiber cement?"

Pastor Dan and some of the community boys constructed a mold and took it over to a factory to have it sprayed. Using a special gun, cement mixed with pieces of fiberglass was sprayed on the mold to form a matte. The mold became very heavy and awkward, and it took six men to pick it up. As they attempted to lift it, the mold cracked because of the tremendous weight.

Undaunted, Dan experimented with all kinds of mixtures: any kind of powder, glue, or paste he could find. As a builder, Dan knew the materials needed to have equal elasticity and contraction-expansion ratios; if they didn't, the structure would buckle. In the end, he returned to his original vision of fiberglass but reinforced with polyester resin. After nearly a year had passed, Dan and his assistants (notably Helmut from Germany) had also designed new molds, overcoming the problem of ninety-degree angles by removable ends.

In a factory they had rented in Málaga, Dan and his community helpers erected the first two molded pieces, bolting them together at the top. Dan was overjoyed at this achievement—until they removed the scaffold and the pieces sagged, the flanges bending under the weight. Without a word to anyone, Dan turned and walked away. After almost a year of exhausting experimentation, the design was a total failure.

Deeply disappointed, Pastor Dan returned to his church office and fell to his knees. He wasn't praying—his heart was too heavy to form words. For a whole year, he'd been obsessed with one relentlessly driving thought: *What materials can I use to build these churches?* And now, just when he thought they had finally discovered the right combination, the experiment had been a disastrous flop. As he knelt by the couch, he suddenly remembered a bag of powdery material resembling asbestos that had been lying around on the factory floor.

What would happen if this substance was mixed with polyester? Dan wondered. *Would it reinforce the flanges?*

The next day, Dan hurried back to the factory and mixed polyester resin with the mysterious powdery substance he had found in the abandoned bag. It formed a very lightweight but bulky paste. Not taking too much time or care, Dan splashed the mixture sloppily on the mold. In a few hours, he returned to find the substance had hardened like steel.

"Hallelujah!" Dan exclaimed, rejoicing that at last God had led him to the key missing ingredient.

In June of 1981, the first prefabricated church building made of the unusual combination of fiberglass, polyester resin, and lightweight powder was erected in Palma del Rio. It had a brick face and tiled floor and could comfortably seat 250 people. And it only cost around $10,000! In September, the second prefabricated church was erected in Alhaurin El Grande on the way to His Farm, the men's drug rehabilitation center. The Lord was adding so many souls to their Spanish churches that the need for larger meeting places continued to grow.

Prefabricated churches were inexpensive and quick and easy to erect. Theoretically, Dan figured that a church seating two hundred people could be molded at the factory in two months and then be erected on rented land in two weeks. Although the construction price was a fraction of the cost of a regular brick and mortar church, Dan wasn't satisfied. To cut building costs, Dan once again turned his attention to the lightweight powder. At seven hundred pesetas a kilo, it was a very expensive element.

"There must be a similar material that's cheaper," Dan persisted. He asked the company that sold him the powder to ask their scientific advisors if an equivalent substance existed.

"No," the answer came back. "There is no substitute."

There is, an inner voice in Dan's mind would not be silenced. *Find it.*

Dan contacted a friend in Barcelona who worked at a chemical company. Miraculously, after an exhaustive search, he discovered a material imported from Germany called K-3, a waste product from a metal factory. Dan mixed this new substance with polyester, and to his amazement and joy, he found it worked identically to the first substance. Thankfully it cost only a hundred pesetas—a fraction of the cost of the other!

Dan now became even more ambitious. He'd heard about a geodesic dome in China that Christians had built, and he decided that was just what the Málaga church should have—a geodesic dome! With his artist's mind, he sketched a dome with elongated structures radiating out from it like spokes on a wheel. This structure required octagonal, pentagonal, and hexagonal pieces joining together.

"The only trouble is," Dan puzzled, "who can work out the complicated mathematical equations?"

He turned the problem over to Mo, who had experience working with computers. "The idea is to build a church that seats a thousand people, using a geodesic dome as the hub, and the originally designed church structures spreading out as spokes," Dan informed a surprised Mo. "I'm leaving it up to you to work out the mathematical details."

With courage and faith, Mo took on the enormously perplexing and challenging task. He had two main problems: the first, to work out the pattern of pieces over the dome surface, and the second, to find the method of joining the geodesic dome to the already designed church structure. He began to experiment with various designs, toiling away on the problem alone. At last, in desperate need of help and inspiration, he approached a fellow community member, Bob.[49] He led Bob to his desk, which was covered with cardboard model domes of all shapes and sizes.

[49] Bob and his wife, Julie, would eventually pastor the Torremolinos Church.

"What are these for?" Bob's eyes opened wide in amazement. The sight was too much for his curiosity and hooked him into a long-term commitment to the "dome project."

Mo and Bob, who turned out to possess amazing mathematical ability, began to seriously calculate the dome construction, spending months crouched over a pocket calculator and reading figures to each other. Finally, they made their first fiberglass model. To their embarrassment, they had made some awful calculation errors. They prayed for the Lord's wisdom, and their second model was a success. They erected the mini six-foot structure in the garden behind House on the Rock, which caused quite a stir amongst the inhabitants of Fuengirola.

In the spring, Paul, the community carpenter, began the grand task of making the wooden pre-molds for these peculiar hexagonal and pentagonal shapes. It was a carpenter's nightmare: not one right angle to be found anywhere. Before long, the finished pieces were sent to the factory to construct the fiberglass molds.

As the parts for the prefabricated geodesic dome were being molded in the factory, Dan was searching for suitable property on which to erect the church. He realized that a lot of the land in Spanish cities was designated for green zones such as parks, but usually for lack of funds, these "green zones" ended up as garbage dumps.

"Málaga must have zones such as these," Dan reasoned. He drew up a petition requesting 2,500 square meters for a church and 6,000 square meters for a park, which he presented to the mayor of Málaga. The Málaga City Council approved his project to erect a removable building that could be used for meetings, weddings, and other social events.

The mayor ordered a councilor to find suitable land. The official, however, had little enthusiasm for the project and shoved the petition under a pile of government documents. Every time

Dan paid him a visit to ask if he had found property, the official shook his head lazily. "Come back next month," he'd say in his best *mañana, mañana* (tomorrow) attitude. After this fruitless exchange had carried on for several months, Dan finally pinned the man to a specific date. "Come back in September," the official said. "We'll have property for you by then."

But when Dan showed up at the designated time, the official shrugged. "Sorry, we still haven't found anything."

Dan was outraged. After a year of delays, he vented his frustration in explosive Spanish. Paradoxically, the official showed a new respect for the angry pastor. "Go see this man," he advised, giving him the name of another government official.

When he met with this official, Dan asked to see the city's plans. Málaga had recently been newly zoned: orange indicated areas zoned for social concerns, and green, areas zoned for parks. As Dan examined the plans for the city, he knew he was searching for the impossible—a section of land earmarked with orange and green zones side by side.

"Here, this is it!" Dan circled a spot on the map with his pencil. Remarkably, it was zoned exactly as he had requested in the petition: 2,500 meters for social needs and 6,000 meters for park land. It was also the area that Dan had felt God had been speaking to him about—only a five-minute walk away from the old church, Casa Ágape. The location was ideal.

"That's the place!" he declared, firmly convinced that God had chosen and reserved this particular property for Himself. Dan presented a formal request for these 9,600 square meters to the Málaga City Council, and it was approved. The church would be allowed to use the land on the condition that it created a park, including a playground and tennis court, and maintained it for ten years.

As construction of the Málaga Tabernacle got under way, another miracle happened. Dan hadn't been able to get a building permit at first because no one had ever seen a structure like this. But without a building permit, they couldn't get access to electricity or water. God gave Dan favor with the director of the electric company, who allowed them to break up fifty yards of sidewalk with a jackhammer to connect their electric cables to city power. They got water in a similar fashion, through a city councilor who was sympathetic to their work.

Then another obstacle arose. Málaga was hit by one of the worst droughts it had experienced in years, and the city's water table was very low. Water was severely rationed. This created a considerable problem for the volunteer workers, who needed a large quantity of water to mix concrete for the slab floors and the tennis courts. Under the direction of the landscaper, John, community members had just planted thousands of pesetas' worth of grass seed, trees, and shrubs in the park. If these weren't constantly watered, they would die.

"If you use the water, we'll fine you up to a million pesetas!" the police warned.

"What can we do?" Dan agonized. "We desperately need water!" As always when faced with impossible issues, he took it to the Lord. He felt impressed to start digging for water on the property. "Try that low spot over there." Dan directed his volunteers to a place near the drainage ditch. The boys started digging in faith, despite the drought and having no idea where the water table would be.

Within one meter, the earth was becoming moist. At two meters, they struck water! After digging a little more and installing a sub-pump, they had enough water to irrigate the garden and finish all of the construction. In fact, they had so much water they were able to generously pipe it to an adjacent school building site. Neighbors from nearby apartments lined up with their buckets to get water to wash their dishes and flush their toilets. The sharing of their abundant natural water supply became a tremendous testimony of His blessing to the surrounding community.

The neighbors watched in awed fascination as the strange "outer space" geodesic dome was erected piece by piece. They had seen nothing like it. Each prefabricated piece was screwed to the adjoining piece, leaving the bottom pieces loose so they could be re-screwed when all the parts were finally fitted together.

What happens when we get to the top? What if the last piece doesn't fit? Dan worried, spending many sleepless nights turning potentially disastrous scenarios over in his mind. He feared that even if the piece fit, its own weight would pull it down.

Piece by piece the dome-shaped church was erected, until at last it was ready for the crowning piece. With suspense, Dan watched as the final piece was pushed up to the ceiling and dropped into place. Miraculously, it fit the gap perfectly. "It fits to the millimeter!" he exclaimed joyfully.

After a year of experimenting, and another seven months of labor, the grand one-thousand seat *El Tabernáculo* was finally a reality. "We'll erect these churches all over the country!" Dan enthused, his vision ever-expanding.

In addition to its unusual futuristic shape, it's noteworthy that the Málaga Tabernacle was built to a large degree by society's misfits: former drug addicts, convicts, and others on the "margin" of normal society. Besides issues involving the breaking or stealing of tools, Pastor Dan had faced the extra challenge of working with people who weren't accustomed to manual labor. Often he had rolled up his sleeves and shown them the proper way of doing things.

"Here's how you handle a hoe." The pastor had pitched right in with the work, directing his volunteer laborers by his industrious example. "This is the way you use a trowel." He took the tool from a bewildered ex-heroin addict's hand, patiently showing him the correct way. When he had felt frustrated because of his unskilled labor force, Dan had to remind himself: "I'm not building churches ... I'm *building* men!"

Pastor Dan was far more interested in building true followers of Jesus Christ than in erecting religious monuments.

On August 30, 1983, the Mayor of Málaga and other official dignitaries came to inaugurate the new Tabernacle. As the mayor tried to get out of his limousine, an angry mob blocked his entry into the facility, ferociously denouncing the city for ceding the land to a Protestant church. When Dan tried to show the park to the mayor, the crowd screamed and shouted their protests at him. Despite the yelling and swearing, this noble man, a devout Catholic, gave an excellent speech, welcoming them to the city.

On Sunday at the newly inaugurated *El Tabernáculo*, six hundred people participated in the Lord's Table, forming the largest communion service in the history of the nation. The Tabernacle could accommodate one thousand people and was large enough to hold national conferences. Through these conferences and Dan's powerful cassette ministry, spiritual revival spread to many parts of Spain.

Today the Tabernacle in Málaga occupies prime real estate, which has increased tremendously in value. The city council maintains the park, tennis courts, and children's playground. In addition to a rehabilitation center, an RKM station is installed in the facility, which broadcasts the Good News throughout the region.

CHAPTER EIGHTEEN
SHADOWS

"*... the word of the Lord grew mightily and prevailed.*" (Acts 19:20)

The work among the Spanish was multiplying at a phenomenal rate, far surpassing the growth among the internationals. While the international community had once provided the necessary "scaffolding" for the "infant" Spanish church, challenging them by their fervent example, the Spanish Christians had now matured into spiritual "adulthood." They were striking out on their own and opening up new mission outreaches in various cities throughout the nation. Prefabricated churches had already been erected in Palma del Rio and Alhaurin El Grande on the way to His Farm.

As a missionary, Dan had always worked towards his goal of seeing the Spanish church become self-propagating, self-governing, and self-supporting, and he was now watching this take place. Most of the emerging Spanish leaders had been discipled by Benito in the basement cellar of Casa Ágape. Dan encouraged these young men to step out in faith and pastor churches and open drug rehabilitation centers on their own.

In 1981, Benito and his wife moved to the picturesque city of Granada, famous for its Moorish castle, the Alhambra. In their small apartment, they began holding informal services, and soon their home was so overflowing with people that they were forced to meet in a rented hall.

Because of the vision Pastor Dan had imparted to the Spanish pastors of opening drug rehabilitation centers throughout the nation, Benito began seeking a suitable place for such a venture. For a year and a half he searched fruitlessly, but during this frustrating time he always felt led back to a particular location: an abandoned olive oil factory. Two old ladies and their collection of cats occupied the premises. When these eccentric women finally vacated the property, Benito and his wife moved in, claiming the factory by faith.

Several months later, the director of the bank who owned the property contacted Benito. When Benito explained the purpose of their ministry, the rehabilitation of Granada's drug addicts and dropouts, the bank director granted him permission to occupy the building until it was needed.

Benito called his new center *El Buen Samaritano* (the Good Samaritan) and soon had many recovering drug addicts under his care. Benito and his wife devoted their time and attention to the needs of these addicts, "living simply so that others can simply live." They believed that Christians are called to be conformed to Christ, not only in their inner attitudes of heart, but in an outward radical lifestyle as well.

For two-and-a-half years, Luis trained in the Casa Ágape cellar, becoming increasingly aware of an intense desire to preach the gospel. Always before his mind's eye he held the dedicated examples of Pastor Dan and Benito. He wanted to follow in their footsteps to become a servant of the Lord.

One day Luis was invited to give his testimony at a church in Asturias in the north of Spain. When he returned, to his surprise, he had a burden to pray for both Asturias and a certain young Christian woman who worshiped there. Finally, he spoke to Pastor Dan about this burden.

"I'm sure your place is there," Pastor Dan counseled him. "Why don't you go?"

Luis stared at his pastor, taken aback. "How?"

"Well, by faith of course," Pastor Dan grinned.

"But I don't have any money," Luis replied lamely.

"Then ask your Father … your Heavenly Father."

Luis decided that he could live for three months without any wages. "If in three months God doesn't show me anything in Asturias, I'll come back here."

Luis went to Oviedo, the capital of the province of Asturias, and slept every night on a pew in the church. Although he started preaching in the universities and showing evangelical films, nothing much happened. He was also getting frustrated and tired because he drove thirty kilometers almost every day to visit his girlfriend in the port city of Gijón.

"I've heard you're sleeping on a church pew," a Christian brother approached him one day.

"*Sí. Claro*," Luis replied.

"Well, I've got an apartment you can live in."

"Where is it?" Luis asked with interest.

"Gijón."

"Hallelujah!" Luis shouted enthusiastically, believing that God's will had indeed been confirmed. So Luis moved to Gijón, and shared with this same brother his desire to open up the apartment to drug addicts who wanted freedom from their substance abuse.

"I've something even better," the man offered generously. "I've got a room in a commercial building you can fix up and use for a rehabilitation center."

Although not much work with drug addicts was in fact carried on in this place, a healthy church was born on the premises. Two years later, Luis and his group of believers moved to a larger facility. The vision of a drug rehabilitation center hadn't been forgotten; in fact, it was growing stronger. Luis knew it would be best if it were located in the country, and he always kept a keen eye on lookout for a suitable place. One day while he was driving, a certain villa caught his attention.

Ask whose it is, an inner voice urged him.

But that's such a nice modern house, Luis protested silently. *No one is going to give it to me.*

Luis had no peace, however, until he sought out the owner. The landlord turned out to be a client of the factory he was working in. To support his wife and child, Luis had to work half-days. He knew this client and decided to approach him.

"I'm interested in this house you own," Luis began. "I'd like to put some recovering drug addicts in it. Would you consider giving it to me for free?"

The man shrugged. "Okay. Okay."

Luis was dumbfounded.

Luis' dream of a drug rehabilitation center came to pass. It became well-known in Asturias—the only rehabilitation center in the whole north of Spain, from Santander to Galicia. On the tranquil farm far away from the frantic city, the former addicts kept busy doing chores and tending the cows, pigs, chickens, and rabbits. Within two years, the center housed eleven young men—four of which Luis was convinced had a deep, sincere desire to serve God.

When the center started, Luis resigned from his factory job. He realized he couldn't carry the workload of the center, guiding it to its full potential, and hold down a secular job, so by faith he quit. When Pastor Dan had sent Luis to Asturias, he had passed on some wise counsel Luis would never forget: "When you receive wages," Pastor Dan had advised the young pastor, "then you're limited by those wages. But when you live by faith, you can have everything—*according to your faith.*"

The work continued to spread rapidly all over Spain. When Dan wasn't meeting with those who knocked on his door, pastors seeking counsel or substance abusers seeking deliverance, he traveled throughout the country. In Seville, he baptized new believers and encouraged the work at *La Puerta* (The Door). He ministered at a conference in Córdoba, where fifteen Spaniards were baptized in the Holy Spirit, and he preached in Valencia, where thirty received Christ. He made several trips to Madrid, teaching on the ministry of deliverance. The Lord was opening doors, especially among the student population. In Gijón, three meetings were held in one day; many Roma were hungry for God. When "Christ Is the Answer" arrived in Spain with a two-thousand-seat tent, the Spanish communities worked together with this ministry in tremendous evangelistic outreaches in Coín, Alhaurin, Mijas, Fuengirola, Marbella, and Málaga. Street meetings, with theater and Hebrew-dancing, attracted large crowds all summer.[50]

While Dan was away visiting the Spanish churches, others held the fort in Torremolinos and other nearby towns on the coast. Paul and Janet, parents of three-month-old baby Sarah, watched over the international community. Paul (from England) and Tom worked in the radio room late into the night, sending out more than five thousand cassette tapes a year. Jack, the principal of "His School," oversaw fifteen teachers and sixty pupils. In Marbella,

[50] Rick Medrington, "La Obra," *The Standard*, January 1982, 2.

Mark and Jeff ran a small coffee house community in "The Gospel House," miraculously loaned to them rent-free. They held seven children's meetings a week in the streets, with more than a hundred children and parents turning out for a single meeting.[51]

By 1982, the international community had renovated seven properties, including the six-story Hotel Panorama and the luxurious two-story, four-bathroom villa El Pinillo. The community was taking over abandoned mansions and turning them into rehabilitation centers to care for those with drug or alcohol dependency. Wherever possible, they returned the houses to the owners in better condition than when they had found them.

Dan had contacted the owners of El Pinillo, who were living in Morocco, and informed them that the community was looking after their house, but they didn't reply. The property had a beautiful garden and a swimming pool. On the third floor was a space like an "upper room," where they could pray. Bernard was in charge of the twenty males living in "Father's House," as they called the palatial mansion. The huge lounge easily accommodated the Friday night "family" gatherings.

"Why don't we get the guys out of El Pinillo and move the girls in?" Pastor Dan suggested to Anne-Marie one day in the church office. Lately, so many young women had been arriving at the community that there was a crucial shortage of accommodations for them. They were also taking in more and more female drug addicts.

"We could have a half-Spanish and half-international group," Dan mused out loud. "The only question is—who's going to lead such a house?"

Anne-Marie stopped her typing and looked up at the pastor. From his expression, she knew who he was thinking of. "I suppose it's me," she commented dryly.

---

[51] Medrington, "Community News," *The Standard*, January, 1982, 4–5.

"Well, I don't really see anyone else," Pastor Dan grinned. "After all, you speak French, English, and Spanish."

During Easter, Anne-Marie and her team of Spanish and international young women moved into the luxurious quarters of El Pinillo, the huge, sprawling villa that had previously been an elegant restaurant. Before long, they were also taking in drug addicts and alcoholics who wanted freedom from their habits.

After working all day at the church office, Anne-Marie then had to deal with the problems that had developed during the day at El Pinillo. The girls fought amongst themselves, and she was often called on to settle their disputes. As if that wasn't enough, she was also trying to spend time with Paul, the Englishman to whom she was engaged.

One of the toughest cases to test Anne-Marie's leadership was a Spanish alcoholic and drug abuser in her late-twenties, Maria Eugenia. She assigned Mara, a Spanish girl from Madrid, to be her "shadow," a responsibility that entailed being with the needy woman around the clock while she suffered through withdrawal. In time, Maria Eugenia grew into a mature Christian believer.

In Los Boliches near Fuengirola, the community had discovered another large abandoned mansion—the sprawling, marble-floored Torreblanca villa. The Torreblanca villa had belonged to a corrupt government official who had fled the country, leaving everything behind, including a car in the garage.[52] The mansion was incredibly luxurious, with bathrooms made of solid marble. Vandals had begun to strip it, removing the doors and copper pipes. After first notifying the owner's family in Madrid, Dan bought used doors

---

[52] Ironically, the former owner had been the Director of Information and Tourism, the same department that so many hotels had feared would shut them down if they allowed a church to meet on their premises.

and installed locks. Neighbors who were watching over the property were glad to have the Christians clean, repair, and occupy the villa.

At first, Dan turned the Torreblanca mansion into a retirement home for senior citizens and placed Dr. Pablo, a surgeon from Cuba, and his wife, Isabel, a nurse, in charge. While they were waiting for documentation to enter the United States as political refugees, the pastor invited the couple and their three children to live in the mansion and take care of the elderly people. With the contribution of the seniors' pensions, the retirement home became self-sufficient. Both Pablo and his wife received the baptism of the Holy Spirit and were formed as strong workers for the Lord before they left for America.

"We're going to move the old folks out of Torreblanca into the Hotel Panorama," Pastor Dan told Mara one day. The location of the retirement home had proved to be too remote for the seniors living in it, who wished to be more involved with the community. The pastor decided it would be perfect for the needs of recovering drug addicts.

"We're going to start a drug rehabilitation center for girls in the Torreblanca villa," Pastor Dan told Mara, "and I want you to be in charge."

The young Spanish girl was overwhelmed at being chosen for such a responsibility, but having gained invaluable experience as a "shadow" in El Pinillo, she rose to meet the challenge. Armed with a broom, mop, and bucket, she moved in by herself and spent a week cleaning up the recently vacated villa, with its red marble floors, white-plastered walls, and high beamed ceilings. At the end of the week, Mara received an addict from Barcelona, who moved into the freshly scrubbed premises to be "shadowed" while she went through the difficult process of getting off drugs.

At first, Mara was the only Christian in the house, shadowing between one and four young women herself. In June, Maria Eugenia and Nuri moved into Torreblanca, and Mara was glad for their company and support. By now, Maria Eugenia, a former alcoholic and drug addict, had matured so much spiritually that she was ready to be a prayer warrior and shadow herself.[53] Nuri, also an ex-addict, had been living in the community for a year, and everyone thought she'd been rehabilitated. Sadly, a few weeks later, while visiting her daughter, she was tempted to try heroin again and died of an overdose.

After a few months, Torreblanca was established as a functioning drug rehabilitation center and close-knit girls' community. Rising at seven, everyone ate breakfast and then attended a prayer meeting at eight. This was the highlight of the day—a time of sharing, renewing relationships, praying for healing, and asking forgiveness from one another. Then the young women busied themselves with their household duties, sewed cushions and curtains, and painted furniture. After lunch, they were required to read their Bibles for an hour and a half and then finish their chores.

The Rehabilitation Center in Torreblanca grew to accommodate an average of eighteen women, including both drug addicts and their shadows. While some of the addicts stayed only long enough to go through withdrawal, others remained for months, receiving a firm grounding in the gospel. Ideally, the addicts were encouraged to stay in the community for two years.

At that time, the pastor of the church in Fuengirola, Pacha, was pastoring the Torreblanca women too. Every Sunday morning and some evenings, worship services were held in the Torreblanca villa with the residents and the Spanish congregation, who were always helpful and supportive of the rehabilitation work. The living room

[53] Maria Eugenia eventually became a stalwart of the church in Antequera.

was huge and could hold 150 people. The community had use of the Torreblanca villa for six years.

One young woman who came to the Christian community to be freed from the slavery of drug dependency was a young Irish heroin addict named Leslie …

In a villa in Mijas, the twenty-four-year-old girl lay in bed, shooting heroin into her veins. Needle marks scarred her elbows, wrists, and ankles. When she heard her name called, she yanked the needle out of her hand and threw both it and the spoon frantically under the sheet. "Come in," she answered as casually as possible.

Gene, a family friend, opened the door. With troubled eyes he studied the gaunt young woman, tangled blonde hair piled on top of her head, her skin a sickly yellow from hepatitis. His gaze dropped to her wrist; in horror, he saw the blood streaming out of her vein.

Gene spent the rest of the day in shock. *This has nothing to do with me*, he thought. But his conscience kept arguing, *You've got to do something!* Many times while driving to Coín, he'd noticed a sign that read "Help for Drug Addicts," not knowing that it referred to the Christian rehabilitation center based at His Farm in Alhaurin. Now this sign kept reappearing in his mind. *Perhaps Leslie can get help there*, he thought hopefully.

He drove back to the villa to confront Leslie's mother with the truth about her daughter's addiction. "But Leslie's been off heroin for a year," her mother insisted indignantly. She had no idea that her daughter, although sick in bed with hepatitis, was sneaking out of the house at night to purchase the drug from nearby gypsies.[54]

[54] Now called Roma, an "ethnic group of traditionally itinerant people who originated in northern India, but live in modern times worldwide, principally in Europe" (britannica.com/topic/Rom).

"Leslie, come here!" Gene commanded as the disheveled girl emerged from the bathroom. "You're still shooting up, aren't you?"

"What do you mean?" Leslie stalled, but she knew her deception had ended.

"C'mon, Leslie, look at your hand!" Gene pleaded. "I can see the needle marks. They're fresh."

Leslie burst into tears, and then her mother knew it was true. "Why didn't you tell me?"

"Mummy, I've been crying out to tell somebody, but there's nothing anybody can do!" Then Leslie sobered up immediately. "There's no hope for me, no hope for heroin addicts at all!"

After Gene told them about the sign he had seen by the highway, Leslie shrugged. "As far as I'm concerned, I'm a lost cause. I'm just waiting for the moment when I die of an overdose like everybody else."

"We've got to try this place," her mother insisted. "You can't give up!"

Leslie knew that they both were aware of the numerous times she had sincerely attempted to kick her habit … and failed. That afternoon, Gene contacted Pastor Del Vecchio.

"I'm sorry," Pastor Dan sighed, "but we have no room." As the dejected man turned to leave, the pastor relented. "Bring her here; we'll have a chat anyway."

"C'mon, get dressed," a happy Gene instructed Leslie. "We're going to see this pastor." Weak from hepatitis, the young addict obeyed.

Born in Dublin, Leslie was the tenth of twelve children and grew up on a large estate. After her parents split up, she moved with her mother to Spain.

"At the age of fourteen, I was introduced to drugs: hashish, speed, and acid," Leslie recounted her story. "At sixteen, I sampled cocaine and dropped out of school. At eighteen, I tried heroin for the first time. I fell very much in love with this Spanish man, a drug dealer, and we both became addicted to heroin. Eventually I moved to the Caribbean and worked for a clothes and necklace designing company. I was given a free place to live, a free car, and a completely new wardrobe every three months. There was so much luxury, but I didn't have the one thing I truly wanted: love."

Leslie returned to Europe to search for "love." Instead of finding love, however, she found heroin again. After living for more than a year with her mother in Fuengirola, she had a bad car accident, one of six in a period of two years. Her pelvis was smashed, her ribs broken, and she was hemorrhaging internally. As she lay in the hospital bed, she wondered if she would ever walk again. For the first time she cried out to God, asking Him to heal her, and she promised that if He let her walk, she'd never take heroin again. After being released from the hospital, however, some junky friends came to visit Leslie and shot her up.

"As soon as I could walk, I threw my crutches away and once more became totally addicted to heroin. I knew I had made a promise to God, but I knew in my own strength I was incapable of keeping it. This time I really dived headfirst into destruction. I was injecting heroin into my veins five or six times a day, and I was hooked twice as bad as before.

"I was leading a completely double life. In the morning before even washing my face, I'd drive off to the gypsies and wake them up, pleading for heroin so I wouldn't feel any withdrawal I can remember moments of great torment and an emptiness of all consciousness except for the need of my dose—an animal-like desperation to find that drug, with an absolute ruthless and exhaustive search for anything that could be sold, pawned, or traded for the drug."

Leslie's habit was becoming harder to hide, and it was becoming impossible to pay for the amount of heroin she was using, even from stealing. She was eaten up by guilt and shame.

"When I came down with hepatitis, I knew once again the end was near, and I was willing it with my whole being—but my heart was pleading for deliverance. While my mother slept, I would sneak out of the house and literally crawl to the gypsies for heroin. I'd shoot it right there with whatever needle I could find—usually a broken one from the rubbage heap."

Pastor Dan agreed to accept Leslie into the community. He looked the dejected heroin addict with the tangled blonde hair in the eye and said, "Within three weeks, you'll be a different person."

Leslie arrived at the Hotel Panorama yellow from hepatitis and so underweight she could tuck three sweaters into her skirt. She was just skin and bones. She shared a room with a young English girl, Jan, who was assigned to be her "shadow."

For the first seven days and seven nights as she suffered through withdrawal, Leslie didn't sleep. In order not to wake the other girls up, she sat on the bathroom floor, chain-smoking and writing. She didn't believe in God, but she was aware that everybody in the community seemed very conscious of her needs. The drug addict knew that something was different, so she began to ask people questions. Their testimonies fascinated her. Everyone said the same thing: she had to "open her heart" to Jesus, but she had no idea what that meant.

Finally, on Christmas Eve, as she sat on the bathroom floor, she cried out, "Oh Jesus, if You are there, I open my heart up. I open it up in whatever way one has to open it up, and I ask You to please come in. Please show me You are alive!" Leslie felt a love flowing over her and suddenly knew she was loved by God.

For the first two weeks at the community, Leslie had been taking codeine and sleeping pills because of the excruciating pain in her back and her deformed hip and knee. Then Pastor Dan instructed that all her medication be taken away, explaining to the girl that she was psychologically addicted to the pills. "Now you *have* to pray," he told her.

That night in bed, Leslie prayed silently, *God, I'm sorry that You have to pull me this low to get my full attention, because now I really need You. I'm willing to let You show me who You really are.*

In that second, God revealed Himself to Leslie. He showed her the vastness of His power and glory, and right beside that, an insignificant tiny white pill she had been crying out for. Leslie was in terrible agony: "I hate to threaten You, God, but I have to be honest. If tomorrow I wake up with the pain, You know I won't be able to stay here. I'll run away and find drugs and pills, because I can't exist without something."

When Leslie woke up the next morning, she immediately knew one miracle had occurred: for the first time in three years, she hadn't taken anything to get to sleep. Her first thought was *Oh, the pain*, but then she realized that she wasn't feeling any pain. She got dressed and made a cup of tea, and then she stopped in the middle of the room. A silly grin crossed her face. "No, it's not possible." She touched her back and then kicked her leg up in the air. "No, it can't be true!"

Leslie walked back and forth across the room, amazed that she felt no pain. In awe, she climbed up the stairs to the hotel's terrace overlooking the Mediterranean and jumped up and down with glee. After two years of walking with a limp, the twenty-five-year-old Irish woman could now walk normally.

As Pastor Dan had prophesied, within three weeks of living in the community, Leslie was indeed a different person. Jesus Christ had freed her from her need for heroin and drugs. He had begun a very long but real journey with her, a process of healing Leslie's broken spirit, delivering her from sadness, shame, and despair.

Jesus Christ indeed sets captives free.

CHAPTER NINETEEN
ANTEQUERA

"I am Joseph your brother, whom you sold into Egypt. But now, do not therefore be grieved or angry with yourselves because you sold me here; for God sent me before you to preserve life." (Genesis 45:4b–5)

In the late 1970s, God through His Spirit impressed upon Dan that he would have a ministry in Spain similar to that of Joseph's in the preserving of life. The Lord had said it very clearly: *Prepare granaries for the time of famine to come.* Dan had taken this to be both a natural and spiritual directive. In the natural realm, he had encouraged farms and food distribution centers in order to feed the hungry through the fruit of the land. But he also believed a spiritual "famine" of not being fed the Word of God was coming.

Dan has been called to disciple men and women who would be faithful to the Word of God—who wouldn't be deceived by false doctrines or the ideas of men. The "granaries" are these men and women who are trained and able to retain the seed of the Word to teach others. The fields are white and ready for harvest, but storm clouds are gathering on the horizon.

Pastor Dan drove along the twisting mountain road until he came to a panoramic vista overlooking the valley of Antequera. In the lush valley below, he could see miles of fertile farmland, and in the distance, the city of Antequera. For many years now, he had believed that the community should buy another farm for the purpose of a drug rehabilitation center. They already had their first rehabilitation center in Alhaurin el Grande, which formerly had been His School. There the addicts followed a disciplined routine, rising early to take care of the farm animals or to work in the orchard with its twelve types of fruit trees. In the peaceful country atmosphere, surrounded by rolling hills and fragrant blossoming groves, the drug addicts learned to live with each other and learned about God. In the morning they attended a Bible study, and in the evening, they listened to a teaching tape or attended a service. Many became Christians, and after a period of three or four months, often became "shadows" themselves. Their newfound faith, daily work, and increasing responsibility all served to promote their rehabilitation and recovery.

Dan thought a larger farm would take the community one step further towards fulfilling the goal of becoming self-sufficient and self-supporting. As he drove down into the valley, he noted happily that the land around him appeared promising indeed. He hadn't thought of looking around the Antequera region, but a community member had told him that the Lord had given him a vision of an arrow shooting from Torremolinos to Antequera.

I have a farm in Antequera. Warwick had shared with Pastor Dan what he believed the Lord had clearly impressed upon him. *A farm with a well.*

The community members had often passed through Antequera on their way to Portugal, where they had to go every three months to get their passports stamped and their tourist visas renewed. In faith, Pastor Dan drove out to Antequera to investigate, trusting the Lord to lead him to the farm of His choosing. He pulled over to the shoulder of the road and asked a couple of men who were working in the field in front of a big dairy farm. "Do you know of any farm for sale around here?"

"*Sí.*" They nodded their heads. "There's one just down the road. We'll show you."

The two men got into their car, and Dan followed them to a farm two kilometers away. Dan couldn't get over how kind and friendly the Spaniards were. They were going out of their way to help him, a total stranger, and they had nothing to gain from it. As he was driving, the Holy Spirit came down upon Dan with power, and he struggled to keep back the tears. He heard the inner voice of God: *My angels are leading you.* Dan had clear confirmation in his spirit that God was indeed guiding him to the exact farm He had prepared for them.

As Dan surveyed the forty-one-acre farm with its large white-washed *hacienda*[55] and enclosed inner courtyard, he felt an excitement growing in his spirit. He could envision drug addicts working with their hands in the fields as they went through the jumpy, hyperactive stage of drug withdrawal, or *mono*, as the Spanish call it. Here in the peaceful country, they would be far away from the pressures and temptations of the city, far away from their junky friends and dealers. Dan thought this farm would be perfect to grow crops and raise domestic animals to make the drug rehabilitation center self-supporting and to supply the community's dietary needs. Antequera itself was ideally situated between the cities of Córdoba, Palma del Rio, Granada, Málaga, and Sevilla, where the other churches and drug rehabilitation centers were located.

---

[55] Farmhouse building.

Dan noted that the name of the farm seemed significant *Casería Realenga*, meaning "belonging to the crown."

The farm was in ruins; the farmhouse was over two hundred years old and there were rats everywhere. Undaunted, Dan met with the four owners and started negotiating the purchase price. When he discovered the amount they were asking, however, he felt dismayed.

"Twenty million pesetas!" Dan groaned. "Where are we going to get the money?" The sum was a colossal figure for the community—its greatest test of faith for God's provision yet. For the next four years, Dan kept the vision of the farm burning in his heart. To raise the necessary funds to buy the farm in Antequera, Dan preached in England, America, Germany, and France, and he received eight million pesetas in gifts and offerings towards its purchase. *But this amount was less than half of what was needed!*

"Rhoda, we're going to have to sell our house," Dan concluded. It wasn't an easy decision. After much prayer and soul-searching, Dan and Rhoda were in perfect agreement that the sacrificial offering for the farm had to be the home they'd been living in.

The Del Vecchio family had been thankful for their Spanish-style house in Churriana, with its arches, patio, garden, and panoramic view. From the southeast side, they could see the Mediterranean in one direction and the mountains in the other. They had subdivided the large lot attached to their property into four sections: growing fruit trees in one section and grapevines in another, and raising chickens in the third and calves in the fourth. Often Rhoda had been asked to choose between buying something new for their own family or buying another community cow—with the result usually being a new cow!

For Rhoda, the decision to sell their home to help pay for the Antequera drug rehabilitation farm had been a painful struggle. For thirteen years she and Dan had lived in that house, raising their four children and seven collies; she had grown extremely attached to it. With Dan being away so often visiting the churches throughout Spain that had grown out of their ministry, she'd found a certain comfort in the security of their home. For Rhoda especially, the loss of their beloved home with its treasured memories was a costly sacrifice.

"Before we sell this house," Rhoda determined, "we must be reunited again as a family."

Rhoda phoned her two eldest children who were now living in the United States and asked them to come home the following year. Twenty-one-year-old Dan Jr. worked in New York City and hadn't been to Spain for two years, while twenty-year-old Deborah was a freshman at a southern Christian university. Rhoda longed to see them both. To her, selling their house marked a definite end to their childhood.

"It would be a great injustice to sell their home from under their feet," Rhoda surmised. "They should be here to help me pack their belongings."

At the end of May, Deborah surprised her parents with a visit and had a great time catching up with her younger sister, Becky, who still lived at home. A week later, Rhoda heard a taxi stop and a figure flew through the gate and slapped a dozen red roses under her nose. She was suddenly wrapped in the arms of her son, Daniel Jr. As the children cleaned out their closets and packed up their belongings, they all had a wonderful time laughing and reminiscing.

The Del Vecchios sold their home and sacrificially gave the eight million pesetas they received from it to the farm fund. They had a great peace about moving into the basement of the church in Mijas. Located high on a mountain overlooking a valley below and the Mediterranean, their new abode offered a spectacular view, fresh air, solitude, and best of all—the absence of traffic.

By August 1984, the price of the Antequera farm had dropped enough to enable Dan to buy it in cash, for the equivalent of $100,000. Community members, already existing on bare-bones budgets, had also sacrificially donated to the cause. Dan had observed that it's not usually the wealthy who support God's work but, more often than not, the ordinary, even poor, people who give sacrificially. It's the "widows' mites" [56] that add up.

In the first stage of rehabilitation, drug addicts were admitted to the community's rehabilitation center at His Farm in Alhaurin El Grande. There they were helped off heroin "cold turkey" by those who had themselves been freed. These "shadows" supervised their withdrawal, supporting them and interceding for them in prayer. Before a drug addict can be successfully re-integrated into society, however, a second stage of rehabilitation is often necessary—learning a useful skill or trade. Because many drug addicts didn't have job training when they left the centers, they had difficulty finding employment. From experience, Pastor Dan had observed that in such cases, these young people were likely to fall back into their former habits.

Dan envisioned that this new farm in Antequera would provide the second stage of rehabilitation for drug addicts—a place where heroin addicts could be taught useful occupations and skills. Here, not only could they learn agricultural skills but other trades such as plumbing, welding, carpentry, mechanics, and electrical work.

The Antequera farm became a thriving hub of activity. A deep artesian well on the property poured out thousands of gallons of

[56] Luke 21:1-4 "*And He looked up and saw the rich putting their gifts into the treasury, and He saw also a certain poor widow putting in two mites. So He said, 'Truly I say to you that this poor widow has put in more than all; for all these out of their abundance have put in offerings for God, but she out of her poverty put in all the livelihood that she had.'*"

clear, cold water to irrigate the land. The young people of the community built a large reservoir to retain water, installed a solar water heater, and laid a pipeline from the well to the house, a distance of over seven hundred yards. At first, they had to use the ancient method of flooding to water the fields, but later they were able to purchase a modern irrigation system. Eventually the old farmhouse was renovated and new buildings constructed. Fifty people lived on the farm, some with their families.

The Scottish couple, Gordon and Mairi, moved with their young family to the farm in Antequera, where Gordon supervised the rehabilitation work. Raising children in Spain presented special challenges. The birth of their daughter in a Málaga clinic had been complicated by a breach delivery, not covered by their insurance. Fortunately, Pastor Dan had given Gordon a calf when he'd been looking after the mini-farm at their house, and the young father had sold this calf in order to pay for the anesthetic. They'd been required to provide all their own medical supplies for the birth, including swaddling bands, iodine, and even a peg to clamp the cord!

When their second child was born, Mairi had been out picking corn in the fields earlier in the day. To check that her infant son was gaining weight, Mairi regularly weighed him on the farm's rabbit scales. Their young daughter loved the farm and often sat on a bale of hay, watching the pigs furrowing, the kid goats head-butting, or her father milking the cows.

The community set up a geodesic dome on the farm, like the one erected for the Málaga church, to use for straw storage. As the dome was made of panels that could be dismantled, Dan didn't think too much about where it was placed. After the storage facility was already assembled, a public works inspector visited the farm.

"Nothing can be built within fifty meters from the center of the road," he informed Dan sternly, referring to a building code by-law.

The inspector took out his tape and measured the distance from the center of the road to the storage dome. Tension filled the air. If the location of the structure was found to be even a few centimeters less than what was legal, they'd have to tear it down. When the inspector reached the dome, he was astounded to find that it was exactly fifty meters and two centimeters away from the center of the road! Breathing a collective sigh of relief, the community gave God glory for this miracle. Later they turned this straw-storage dome into a church!

At first, the financial burden of the rehabilitation center in Antequera was partly shouldered by stipends from the government, which supported some of the former addicts by offering them work off the farm. One young man, who worked for the city and was in charge of setting up platforms and sound systems for rock groups, confided to Dan, "I just can't take it anymore. I'm forced to do too many things that go against my conscience."

The pastor couldn't sleep for a few nights, inwardly wrestling over this concern. Even though the government stipends were helping to keep the farm going, Dan made a firm decision. He went to the mayor. "Is there anything else these men can do that won't defile their conscience or deny their beliefs?"

"When they get the job, they have to do everything that's required."

After that, Dan gave up partnering with the governmental social system. The community sought creative ideas from God to sustain the farm's operation.

"God will give us ideas if we're willing to step outside of the box and risk doing something different," Dan encouraged the community. He believed that instead of asking for money, they should seek innovative ideas from God.

Years earlier, Dan had brought in sweet corn seeds from the United States to grow crops. At that time in Spain, corn had only been regarded as animal fodder for hogs and chickens, not edible for human consumption. Community members had sold the sweet corn at traffic light stops and to fruit shops, gradually introducing it to commercial markets. Eventually God opened doors to supermarket chains, and refrigerated trucks arrived to transport the corn to national distribution centers. Sweet corn became a strong annual source of income for the support of the Antequera farm.

With a $15,000 offering received from a lady at the Torremolinos church, Dan had purchased ten purebred Holstein "Frisian" cows, imported from Germany, which were wonderful milk cows. The farm's herd eventually multiplied into 150 heads of cattle. Its herd was among the best in Spain because its cows received artificial insemination from the most highly-prized bulls in the world. Fifty dairy cows produced one thousand liters of milk daily. Profit from milk sales helped to cut down the enormous operational expenses of running the rehabilitation center. The community was "swimming" in milk for the next twenty years!

Dan frequently visited the farm in Antequera to check that everything was running smoothly. An ex-alcoholic was busy renovating the main living quarters of the *hacienda*. When Dan first gave permission for this man to stay, he had no idea that he was such a fine builder. Pastor Dan was equally impressed with another Spaniard, an ex-heroin addict, who was being trained to take over the daily operation of the farm. He was in charge of the milking, injections, and breeding of the cows. Pastor Dan firmly believed that one of the ways to rehabilitate these addicts was to give them confidence in themselves by showing confidence in them. As they were trusted with increasing responsibilities, they gradually learned to trust and believe in themselves.

The former addicts who had been rehabilitated were tremendous witnesses to the citizens of Antequera. They had amazing opportunities to share their testimonies at the nearby military and pilot-training bases and to the schools in the region, ministering to three thousand young people between the ages of twelve and twenty-five.

At the 1985 Pastors' Conference, the nine-hundred-seat auditorium of the Palacio del Congreso was jammed with excited participants. Spanish Christians from all over the nation had arrived in Torremolinos for a time of teaching and fellowship. Pastor Dan, now in his mid-fifties, walked with dignity across the platform to the head table, followed by Benito, Felipe, Luis, and other Spanish pastors who had matured under his ministry. With quiet authority he addressed the crowd before him, preaching about the "Glory of God," the theme of the five-day conference. As always, he challenged the Christians to total consecration, to give their lives in whole-hearted service to the Lord of Lords.

Near the end of the conference, Pastor Dan called all those who had been freed from drug addiction for six months or longer to come to the platform. Almost two hundred young people flooded the front of the auditorium to the sound of thunderous applause. Faith in Jesus Christ had set these drug addicts free and changed their lives, and all the glory was given to God.

By the late 1980s, the work in Spain had grown to forty-two churches, various mission outreaches, and several drug rehabilitation centers throughout the nations, involving more than two thousand people. The original Evangelical Community Church in Torremolinos, with its international congregation, had multiplied to sister Spanish churches in Alhaurin El Grande, Fuengirola, Riogordo, Granada, Gijón, Seville, Huelva, Vitoria, Palma del Rio, Barcelona, and of course Málaga, with its unusual geodesic dome. Mission stations had sprouted up in Algeciras, Arroyo de la Miel, and Villafranca de los Barros.

Drug rehabilitation farms and centers had been established in Alhaurin El Grande, Fuengirola ("Torreblanca"), Torremolinos, Málaga, Granada ("El Buen Samaritano"), Antequera ("Asociación Remar" later called "Asociación Real Rehabilitación de Marginados"), Gijón, and Vitoria. Treatment centers were also started in Barcelona and in Amposta.

After years of opposition and intimidation, Pastor Dan found that his ministry, especially among the drug addicts, received favor with the socialist government of Spain. Heroin addiction had become a horrible scourge among the Spanish youth, and the authorities were desperately searching for solutions. Twelve senators from Madrid toured the Christian treatment centers for three days, and Dan testified to them about God's work in the young people. On a weekly basis, dozens of drug addicts had to be turned away from the rehabilitation centers. There simply wasn't enough space or workers to accommodate the overwhelming demand.

One drug addict who came to the Antequera farm for rehabilitation was a violent criminal and drug dealer. He and his brother had terrorized their hometown, entering nightclubs, smashing bottles, and stabbing people with broken shards of glass. For his crimes, Antonio should have spent eight years in prison, but Dan had written a letter on his behalf, asking for his sentence to be commuted. The court had agreed not to send him to prison while he was being rehabilitated. After a month of living on the farm, however, Antonio was tired of the strict discipline and wanted to leave.

I'm going to start a fight, he decided. *Then they'll kick me out of here!*

Before he could carry out his plan, Dan noticed that the man's front teeth were rotten. The pastor took him aside, reaching out to the twenty-three-year-old with a fatherly instinct. "Antonio, you're just a young man. We have to get your teeth fixed. Go to the dentist. I'll pay for whatever needs to be done."

Antonio's own father had abandoned him when he was five years old. He had survived by sleeping in deserted buildings, pushing drugs, and thieving. Dan recognized that the young man needed not only rehabilitation but a father figure in his life—so important to the young men and women who came to the farm.

After experiencing this fatherly compassion, Antonio started to change. On the farm, he got saved and filled with the Holy Spirit, and later Dan officiated at his wedding to Cristina. Antonio now pastors a church in Huétor, a town of ten thousand, leading the second-fastest growing church affiliated with the evangelical communities in Spain.

Pastor Dan is so encouraged by witnessing God's transformational power in action and the miracles He performs in people's lives. The heroin addicts who arrive at the Antequera rehabilitation center, emaciated and weak from years of addiction, grow strong in body and spirit on the farm. They're taught new skills and trained to be disciples of Christ. The hard work, fresh air, sunshine, and the warm fellowship in the Spirit renews and reforms broken lives. The farm is also used every year for youth camps, prayer retreats, and leaders' retreats, as well as providing a church for the community and residents of the town of Antequera.

Dan's vision for the farm in Antequera (where the community could be both self-sufficient and supply food in times of need or persecution) inspired his revolutionary teaching on "The Four Seasons of the Church." He taught that churches pass through cycles or seasons. The first season is spring, evangelism; the second is summer, discipleship; and the third is fall, social work. After believers are discipled, they can go into every kind of social work imaginable, serving in hospitals, schools, prisons, feeding programs, and drug rehabilitation programs. The fourth season is winter: becoming self-supporting. Trained and committed Christians form a tremendous labor force, equipped with all kinds of talent and vocational skills. By opening community businesses, a church body can become self-supporting.

Dan finds it truly miraculous how God blesses a seed (an idea) and multiplies it to feed a dying world, which needs both natural nourishment and God's Word, the Bread of Life.[57]

[57] "God gives an idea, a seed, and blesses it and multiplies it to bless the world … He will use it to feed a dying world that needs the bread of life as well as natural seeds," (Daniel Del Vecchio, *El Manto de José* , 144–145).

CHAPTER TWENTY
THE ANOINTING

"The Spirit of the Sovereign Lord is on me, because the Lord has anointed me to proclaim good news to the poor. He has sent me to bind up the brokenhearted, to proclaim freedom for the captives and release from darkness for the prisoners, to proclaim the year of the Lord's favor." (Isaiah 61:1-2a, NIV)

Due to the increase in drug and alcohol abuse in Spain, the community opened nine rehabilitation centers over the years. Most of the young people arriving at the rehabilitation centers bring with them a tragic history of substance abuse and other self-destructive behaviors. Their journey to wholeness includes attention to their spiritual needs. These therapeutic communities are not only for the treatment of addictions but also for Christian formation and training for ministry. The centers provide a home in which Christian life principles and practices can be taught in an atmosphere of love, and where those who have surrendered their lives to the Lord can be truly discipled.

Living together in community, members learn the disciplines of the Christian life: prayer, reading the Word, submission to authority, self-discipline, time management, and diligence. They learn how to be considerate, to bear one another's burdens, to work for the love of God and neighbor without salary, and to develop talents and vocations. Attitudes are corrected and Christian character formed. In these centers, spiritual growth can accelerate.

Under the supervision of tested leaders, former substance abusers learn how to conduct healthy, wholesome relationships. Living together with spiritual fathers, mothers, brothers, and sisters, they learn to love and respect one another. This is a vital time of preparation for marriage and ministry, and for reconciliation with biological parents, spouses, siblings, and others. The emotional security and stability of being with people who really care for them is truly transformative.

Caring for addicts who struggled with intense emotional needs and personal problems thrust the community into ministering to the "whole" person—addressing the need for emotional healing and the healing of memories. Many of those who come to the rehabilitation centers for help have suffered childhood traumas, including verbal and sexual abuse.

In the earlier years of his ministry, Pastor Dan had prayed for physical healings and had witnessed many miracles. After his facial operation and the birth of his son David, a new avenue of ministry began to emerge: emotional healing. This ministry gifting came to Dan unexpectedly, but he believed it was somehow related to the emotional pain and trauma he had experienced after his operation and the birth of his son, who has Down Syndrome.

Dan realized that when Jesus described His ministry, He read from Isaiah 61: "*He has sent Me to heal the brokenhearted, to proclaim liberty to the captives and recovery of sight to the blind, to set at liberty those who are oppressed*" (Luke 4:18b).

Jesus had come to heal the brokenhearted. To Dan, "brokenhearted" spoke of experiences that break people's hearts—crushing disappointments, hurts, and traumas. As a pastor, he found many people suffered from disturbing childhood memories and poor relationships with their parents, especially their fathers. They carried a deep pain inside of them. Dan's ministry of healing the emotions seemed to just evolve naturally. One day while he'd been praying with a community member, the fellow fell to the floor, crying and talking to his father as if he was a seven-year-old boy. He was reliving a memory of a time when his father had wanted him to fight a class bully and stand up for his rights.

"No, Daddy, I can't do that!"

Dan watched as the Holy Spirit moved on the young man, revealing a traumatic memory and then healing this area of his life. It was a sovereign work of the Lord. Dan had nothing to do with what was happening.

Another time he witnessed the Holy Spirit coming upon a young woman and revealing the hurtful memory of her father holding her under a cold-water faucet, demanding that she apologize for lying.

"No, Daddy, I didn't lie!"

"I won't turn off the water until you confess you lied."

By now, Dan had learned to stand in "place" of the father or mother and speak words of healing: "It's okay, dear, I believe you." The Holy Spirit worked in this woman's heart to heal her painful memory.

While studying the Bible, Dan observed that before Jesus healed the cripple at the pool of Bethesda, He first asked him if he wanted to be "made whole."[58]

"*When Jesus saw him lying there, and knew that he had already been in that condition a long time, He said to him, 'Do you want to be made well?*'" (John 5:6)

Many pastors think that when someone receives Jesus Christ as their Savior, their salvation is complete. But although spiritually

[58] John 5:6 "*When Jesus saw him lie, and knew that he had been now a long time in that case, he saith unto him, Wilt thou be made whole?*" (KJV)

reborn, a person isn't necessarily *instantly* made "whole" in their physical body and their soul (their mind and heart), or healed of past traumas. Emotional healing requires special ministry. Dan taught his pastors how to minister in this area, and those who have lived in communities associated with his work in Spain have especially understood its importance. The healing of memories can begin with experiences as early as six months in the womb, when the developing human being receives impressions, such as feelings of acceptance or rejection.

"What's your first memory?" he would often ask when praying with an individual. Then he would invite Christ's healing presence into that scene. When praying with a group, he would sometimes call out years, beginning at age three and then continuing up year by year. As they regressed back to painful recollections experienced during those ages, some people would cry, scream, or become violent.

When ministering in emotional healing, pastors may have to deal with demons that have entered a person's life because of trauma. One of the names for the devil is Beelzebub,[59] or "lord of the flies." Where there is a soul-wound, demons can be involved like "flies attracted to infection." In addition to normal emotional responses, extreme traumatic experiences can open the door for demonic spirits to enter, such as a "spirit of fear" or a "spirit of anger."

Dan has seen hundreds delivered from the bondage of evil spirits through the power of the Holy Spirit in the name of Jesus. He Himself said, "*But if I cast out demons by the Spirit of God, surely the kingdom of God has come upon you*" (Matthew 12:28). Jesus came "*healing all who were oppressed by the devil, for God was with Him*" (Acts 10:38b). He came to destroy the works of the devil and deliver the captives of Satan.

---

[59] Luke 11:15: "*But some of them said, 'He casts out demons by Beelzebub, the ruler of the demons.'*"

Through experience, Pastor Dan and his ministers have learned to discern the difference between healing of emotions and demonic activity. In Madrid, Dan observed four men holding down a man who was acting like he was demon-possessed, banging his head on the floor. As Dan watched the commotion, he discerned that the man didn't have a demon but rather an emotional problem. Above the uproar, Dan shouted in the ear of the tormented man: "I forgive my father! I forgive my father!"

The man immediately became peaceful and calm. Dan discovered that forgiveness is of vital importance for emotional healing to take place. He has written a book about this crucial subject, which is available in Spanish.

"God's purpose in redemption is not only to restore us to fellowship with Himself, but to restore our fallen personalities," Dan teaches. Like the Good Samaritan[60] who poured oil and wine over the beaten-up traveler's wounds, God has compassion for believers: the wine of Jesus's blood that cleanses souls from sin, and the oil of the Holy Spirit that comforts and restores them. Like the inn in Jesus's parable, the Church provides a place of protection and rehabilitation. "The healing power of the cross does not stop at man's spiritual healing, but must penetrate into the body driving out disease, and into the soul, healing emotions and memories." [61]

"Is emotional healing scriptural?" Dan had his own doubts at first, until his attention was drawn to a clear case of the healing of the emotions and memories in the Gospel of John. After Jesus had been arrested by the authorities, Peter, while warming himself by a charcoal fire in the high priest's courtyard, betrayed Jesus in order to protect himself: "I don't know the man!" Three times, when

[60] Luke 10:30–34.

[61] "The Pastor's Message," *The Standard*, January 1982, 6.

questioned, he had denied being one of Jesus's disciples.[62] (Jesus had previously forewarned him that before the cock crowed, Peter would deny Him three times.)[63] Realizing what he had done, a wave of guilt overwhelmed Peter.

"Weeping profusely, Peter fled into the night, a broken man deeply ashamed, deeply wounded by his failure ... And every time he heard the simple crowing of a rooster or glimpsed people huddled around their charcoal fires, he would hear his own voice denying and cursing ..."[64]

After Jesus's death, Peter and some of the other disciples returned to fishing. By the shores of Galilee, the risen Jesus appeared to them while they were out in their boat. "*It is the Lord!*" John cried.[65] Peter threw himself into the sea and swam to shore, where Jesus was standing beside a charcoal fire. Dan notes that a "charcoal fire" is mentioned only twice in the New Testament: here, and once before outside the palace of the high priest where Peter had warmed himself and denied knowing Jesus.

"As Peter saw the fire and felt its warmth, he was again transported back to the scene that was so indelibly imprinted on his memory ... Jesus asked him three times: 'Do you love Me?' Jesus was giving him an opportunity to redeem himself. For every curse and blistering denial, Jesus was drawing from him a simple confession of love. Every painful emotion was erased and replaced by a deeper and more powerful positive emotion. The wounds began to heal, the horrific memory was soothed by the beautiful experience of true fellowship with the living Jesus.

"How many of us can say that we don't have memories that come back to us over and over again, bringing with them pain or remorse? ... We must allow Jesus to make His way into our past.

---

[62] John 18:15–27.
[63] John 13:38.
[64] "The Pastor's Message," *The Standard*, January 1982, 6.
[65] John 21:7.

We must bring Him into the painful areas of our memories and ask Him, in prayer, to be with us there. Perhaps it will help us to visualize Him standing there, suffering with us, or if we were the ones inflicting pain, to see Him forgiving us because of His love.

"Emotional healing is effected by having strong emotions of love and forgiveness, under the power and direction of the Holy Spirit, erasing the gaping wounds that have been left in the mind and the heart. If, as if often the case, we have been bruised by rejection, what we need to do is forgive and accept the person who has rejected us …"[66]

"When Jesus told us to love our enemies, it was more for us than for them. When we are willing to forgive those who have judged us, accept those who have rejected us, and love those who have hurt us, God can begin to heal us emotionally.

"One of the deepest and most damaging emotions is guilt. This can only be cured by knowing the power of the blood of Christ to forgive and cleanse us. Sometimes the counsel of a spiritual leader is helpful. If we are under condemnation, we need someone who can administer the medicine of comfort through the promises of the Word. 'Neither do I condemn thee, go and sin no more.'

"All healing stems from the cross for it was there that the curse was lifted from humanity and placed upon the sinless substitute …" [67]

Jesus proclaimed: "*The thief comes only to steal and kill and destroy; I have come that they may have life, and have it to the full.*" [68]

---

[66] "The Pastor's Message," *The Standard*, January 1982, 6

[67] "The Pastor's Message," *The Standard*, January 1982, 8.

[68] John 10:10 (NIV).

CHAPTER TWENTY-ONE
SOUTH AMERICA

"Religion that God our Father accepts as pure and faultless is this: to look after orphans and widows in their distress and to keep oneself from being polluted by the world." (James 1:27, NIV)

Many years ago, God had spoken to Dan in Spain: *I will make you a father of many nations.* God had not told him that he was already a father; He had said: "*I will make you a father.*" Dan discovered that this was a process, sometimes a heart-breaking one. Through his decades of ministry, he has suffered through many soul-wrenching experiences and painful struggles with those in the communities he pastored, and even with his own children.

When David was born with Down Syndrome in the early 1970s, Dan had struggled at first to accept him, but God had reminded him: "*Whoever receives one little child like this in My name receives Me*" (Matthew 18:5). Those words had changed Dan's perspective. From that moment on he received his son as an *envoy of Christ.* God helped Dan to feel love and compassion for his own son and for other children. Every child is special.

God burdened Dan's heart for abandoned, needy, and orphaned street children around the world. In the 1960s while ministering in Mexico, he'd seen thousands of children sleeping on the streets, using cardboard for beds and newspapers for blankets. At the time he'd experienced some compassion for them, but he hadn't *seen* them as he began to *see* them now.

The Lord showed Dan that the purest gospel is to help widows and orphans. The Holy Spirit impressed Proverbs 31:8–9 on his heart:

> *Speak up for those who cannot speak for themselves,*
> *For the rights of all who are destitute* (vs. 8, NIV).
>
> *Open your mouth, judge righteously,*
> *And plead the cause of the poor and needy* (vs. 9)

To defend the cause of the poor and needy became Dan's clarion call. He received it as a command from God to speak up for those who have no voice, who are unable to advocate for themselves. In the 1990s, he became driven with a passion to help street children, his heart breaking for these destitute urchins. The Lord opened doors for ministering to such children in Central and South America.

In Buenos Aires, the capital of Argentina, seven thousand children were living on the streets, lost and starving. Dan was aghast to see kids, some as young as five years old, sniffing glue from plastic bags and running around as if they were crazy. He saw kids eating out of garbage cans, trying to fill the hunger in their stomachs and the gaping hole in their hearts. Some turned to drugs. No one cared for them. No one loved them.

Dan became burdened for these kids who were struggling to survive on the streets and desperate to forget their troubles and the terrible pain in their hearts. They were despised, rejected, abandoned. He discovered that they were often abused, raped, and murdered by the sexually depraved. Sometimes, particularly in Colombia, these street children were hunted and killed.

Pastor Dan was invited by some pastors to speak in Buenos Aires in a service he will never forget. Dan shared his burden for neglected street children with 1,200 leaders gathered from all over Central and South America. He cried out to God with one of the most heart-wrenching prayers of his life:

"Oh God, cause them to hear the cry of these millions of children living in danger!"

The Spirit of the Lord fell with power upon these leaders. They united in prayer. A wail rose up and then sobbing—and this wailing rose up to heaven. The Lord touched these pastors' hearts, and many returned to their own countries to open works of mercy. As a consequence of this gathering, other ministries to help street children were birthed, especially in Brazil.

Pastors in Buenos Aires loaned Dan a farm to use to meet the needs of street children. He brought over two young men from Spain to help with the ministry and started taking in abandoned children. They couldn't take them directly from the streets to the farm. First, they had to go through a legal process. Often it could take his lawyers a month to be sure that these children didn't have a home. Dan asked the pastors to find families in their churches who would be willing to take in a child while the paperwork was being processed. One pastor, who later visited Dan in Spain, shared that receiving these homeless children transformed his church.

Dan took one street-boy out to a restaurant to eat.

"Do you believe in God?" the young boy asked him, not knowing that Dan was a pastor.

Surprised, Dan responded, "I sure do."

"If it wasn't for God, I would be dead by now," the boy confided soberly.

Dan was all too aware that these street children were subject to early death. Very few of them lived beyond the age of fifteen. At night they slept in public places like bus or train stations for safety. In Argentina they're not killed by the police but by sexual predators.

Eventually Dan bought a beautiful forty-acre farm in Argentina and built a home for street-boys. During this period, he was spending six months in Spain and six months in the States. While living in America, he would fly to Argentina for a time, leaving Rhoda to take care of their cows on their own farm in Georgia. This arrangement carried on for about five years until Dan handed over the Argentinian work to the national churches.

The situation for street children in Colombia was even worse. In Bogotá, Dan learned about children as young as eight years of age living in underground sewers beneath the city. When there was flooding, these sewers filled with water, and the children drowned like rats. He read about a Catholic man going down into the tunnels to help those wretched children who lived in the darkness without light.

What are the evangelicals doing? Dan wondered. He tried to awaken the churches to their duty to the poor but found that there was generally no interest in the *desachables,* or "disposables."

"Disposables" in Colombia smoked *bazuco*, a derivative of cocaine. Children sniffed glue to get high because it was cheaper than narcotics. He found it tragic that these outcasts needed to take mind-altering substances to numb their hunger and pain. From Proverbs 31:6–7, Dan gained a new understanding of their needs and of the way society usually brushed them aside: "*Give strong drink to him who is perishing, and wine to those who are bitter of heart. Let him drink and forget his poverty, and remember his misery no more."*

Instead of "strong drink," Dan reflected that these words could be replaced by *bazuco*, cocaine, or heroin. "Give *bazuco* to those who are perishing and drugs to those who are in anguish. Let them *sniff glue* and forget their poverty and remember their misery no more." Dan of course didn't agree with that heartless means of conveniently dealing with broken souls.

Dan and some pastors from Spain raised $20,000 in donations to support those who were ministering to these underground kids. In Bogotá, he visited a world-renowned charitable organization that raises funds to help needy children. The director's secretary gave him a tour of their facilities. The headquarters occupied a four–story building, filled with office staff and computers.

"But where are the children?" Dan inquired.

The secretary disclosed that they didn't run shelters or orphanages. Later Dan discovered that this charity really operated more like a financial agency, loaning money to small businesses at lower rates than commercial banks. Disappointed, Dan visited another well-known charity to find out how they were meeting the needs of vulnerable street children. After the director told him that they distributed millions of dollars' worth of seeds to farmers, Dan pressed him: "But what are you doing for *these kids*?"

"We give them a cup of hot chocolate once a week," he replied, informing him that this outreach took place on the most dangerous street in Bogotá. Undeterred, Dan and his daughter, Deborah, volunteered to hand out cups of hot chocolate.

"We must do something to help these kids," Dan resolved, deeply touched by their plight.

During the day, people living on the streets pushed a cart to collect cans, bottles, and scrap metals, or whatever they could sell.

At night, they covered themselves with tarps and slept in their carts in abandoned lots. Dan purposefully went out on the streets to talk with the homeless.

"I was shot by the police," one man confided as he showed the pastor the wounds in his hand.

"The police come by at night with machine guns," another told him. "They kill us while we're sleeping."

Tragically, they told Dan how off-duty police intentionally target street children because they're paid a certain amount per head. Abandoned children, who beg or steal for a living, are considered to be "vermin."

Dan located a wonderful home in the city of Bogotá that would be perfect to shelter destitute children. The Christian owner demanded that the pastor provide four guarantors to ensure that the rent would be paid.

"I'll pay the rent for a whole year in advance," he offered, not knowing where he, as a foreigner, would find such guarantors. But that wasn't enough for her. Fortunately, Dan was invited to speak at several of the large churches in Bogotá and found four guarantors. He rented a couple of rooms in the beautiful home.

While Dan and some visiting pastors from Spain were preaching in a nearby park, they encountered a twelve-year-old girl who'd been stabbed in the leg. She was living on the street and had no family. As she couldn't walk, they carried her to this refuge. The girl, who was wary of the foreigners, had insisted that her friend, a young boy, go along with them for her protection. When Dan and Deborah brought them to the house, the owner raised a ruckus.

"We don't want street children here!" she argued vehemently.

Dan was shocked. This woman was supposed to be one of the most prominent intercessors in Bogotá. He was astounded that she refused to allow these two urchins in. Dan considered street children to be closest to God's heart.

When Dan preached in another large church in Bogotá, he and Deborah brought this girl and boy, who were now living with them, along. Before he got up to address the congregation of one thousand, Dan noticed a commotion at the entrance of the church and wondered what had caused it.

"They threw my flesh out," the boy told him solemnly after the service.

What does that mean? Dan wondered, unfamiliar with the Spanish expression.

Deborah, who had witnessed what had happened, explained that a poor ragged man had come into the church and sat down. He wasn't drunk or begging or doing anything to disturb the service. His only fault was that he was a *desachable,* a "disposable," a castaway. Two deacons had grabbed this poor man by the arms and legs and had thrown him out onto the sidewalk.

Ironically, Dan had preached that morning on the scripture passage from the book of James that exhorts Christians not to differ their treatment between the rich and poor among them. Dan, who had been well received by the wealthy of that church, speculated: *What would happen if I let my beard grow and slept on the street for two weeks? If I then came back to this church, where I am honored and respected, would they throw me out?*

In Colombia, the warfare between the FARC guerillas[69] and the military had been raging on for over thirty years. The drug lords forced farmers in the countryside to grow cocaine. If they refused, they could be killed—but if they cooperated, they could be arrested

[69] FARC, or the Revolutionary Armed Forces of Columbia—People's Army, was a guerilla group involved in the Columbia conflict starting in 1964. They employed military tactics and terrorism and were funded by kidnapping ransom, extortion, and the production and distribution of drugs. For more information see: Wikipedia.org/ Revolutionary Armed Forces of Columbia.

by government soldiers. Trapped between two opposing forces, many farmers fled to the city. They lived in cardboard shacks on the outskirts of Bogotá, an area known as the *cinturón* (belt). Without skills, the girls often ended up prostituting themselves to survive.

Dan became friends with a former guerilla commander who had been converted. Together they ventured into these dangerous areas of prostitution, risking their lives. The love and compassion for souls compelled them.

"Don't go down that street!" a policeman warned them. "You might not come out alive."

Dan wasn't afraid, especially because he was accompanied by this former fighter. The ex-guerrilla didn't carry any weapons; he was bold and fearless. After entering a house of prostitution, they saw a couple of girls hanging around. One was a seventeen-year-old girl with a baby in her arms. The young mother confessed she had once been a follower of Christ.

"You must repent!" the ex-guerilla commander urged her.

"Brother," Dan interrupted him, "you can't ask her to repent when she has to make a living. She's got a baby now to look after. Let's find her a job."

Pastor Dan found jobs for two of the young women. He knew that they couldn't just tell these prostitutes to repent. They needed to give them an alternative. Thankfully, they were later able to establish a little church in the region. A dedicated couple began teaching unwed mothers sewing and other useful skills.

Eventually Dan and his ministry partners opened a wonderful home for street children in Columbia. Visiting known areas of prostitution, they implored the women to bring their children into this home. In the middle of Bogotá, apartment buildings were filled with women behind bars, selling themselves to the first man who came along. Dan entered these apartment blocks, seeking to help the children of these women as if they were his own children.

On one occasion, the ministry took in three children from the same family—a boy of thirteen and his younger brother and sister, all the product of incest. (Their father was also their grandfather.) Their mother came to the Lord, was filled with the Holy Spirit, and was able to break free from that abusive man. Dan heard not long ago that the boy, who is now twenty-five, has started a feeding program for street people.

Dan spoke about Jesus to a prostitute, a girl of thirteen who was living on the streets because of unbearable circumstances at home. She was pregnant. Dan invited her and the two boys who were protecting her to a church where he was preaching.

Before they arrived, Dan preached on Mary Magdalene and how she had been a woman of the street, but Christ freed her from seven demons. He exhorted the church to have Christ's attitude and to follow His example: to forgive, free, and restore every broken life. Dan spoke about the young girl he was expecting to join them as an honored guest and said that those who receive a child in need receive Christ Himself.

At that moment, the girl and the two boys showed up. "My guests of honor have arrived," Pastor Dan announced with a smile, recognizing them publicly.

All of the people in the church turned around to see these children. Some broke down in tears; others reacted with indignation. Dan viewed prostitutes such as this young unwed teen as victims of a corrupt government and degenerate society, trapped in overwhelming poverty, misery, and sexual slavery. Millions of children of prostitutes don't receive any kind of care.

"*When you receive one of these children, you receive me.*" Jesus's words had been burned into Dan's heart with the birth of David, forging one of the strongest areas in his life and ministry. Dan thanks God for giving him the strength to fight for other children for years, children whose needs were no less special than David's unique needs. Because of Dan, ministries in Argentina, Colombia, and Paraguay have served countless neglected children, giving them love and attention. Other churches have caught the vision and expanded the work.

Today there are an estimated 100,000,000 street children in the world who are rejected and abandoned—a whole harvest field untouched.[70] When people pass these poor homeless throw-aways on the streets, they're often blind to them. The children become invisible, but they are precious in God's sight! He loves them.

[70] "Unicef Report, 2002, accessed March 29, 2022, en.m.wikipedia.org/wiki/Street_children. The exact number is hard to quantify.

CHAPTER TWENTY-TWO
IT ONLY TAKES A SPARK

"For we do not wrestle against flesh and blood, but against principalities, against powers, against the rulers of the darkness of this age, against spiritual hosts of wickedness in the heavenly places." (Ephesians 6:12)

In the spiritual battles Pastor Dan has been engaged in throughout his life, he has won most and lost a few. One very significant battle he calls the "Battle of Trabuco." Perhaps the most effective ministry his wife, Rhoda, and daughter, Deborah, have been involved in during the last two decades is the summer camps for children held on the farm in Antequera. During the first week of August, children from eight to twelve years old attend, an age when they're most open to the gospel. During the second week, teenagers from thirteen to eighteen years old arrive. Two hundred youths usually participate in the camps, and forty adults supervise their activities. The summer camps are a spiritually decisive time.

Several years ago, Dan wanted to move the children's camps to the town of Trabuco, Spanish for an "old-fashioned musket." It wasn't an ideal situation to have all these children running around the dairy farm in Antequera, as they carried tubercular germs, which infected the cattle. For six years the farm had a real problem: every cow that became infected had to be slaughtered.

The crisis on the farm peaked when three thousand bales of dry barley straw caught fire—a dangerous emergency. Although the cause of this fire was never discovered, it was suspected that children playing with matches or a magnifying glass were responsible. The winds began blowing the sparks towards the discipleship house, and Dan was afraid it would totally go up in flames. Sparks then blew towards the corrals where the cows were fenced in. When fire engines arrived at the chaotic scene, they had no water! The community workers hurriedly filled the irrigation ditch with water from the well. Dan was about to give up in despair when the fire was finally brought under control. Although the bales of straw were totally burned up, the damage had thankfully been contained.

"We're not going to have any more summer camps here," Dan resolved firmly. "All of these children running around the farm like it's a zoo is too dangerous!"

Near the town of Trabuco, Dan discovered an idyllic location for the summer camps, an oasis in the desert. The land was beneath a mountain. On top of this mountain was a natural basin where water was stored as a reserve. Fifty pipes, drilled into the mountain, carried water down from the basin, forming a lovely flowing stream further below. The property Dan wanted was right on the edge of this stream. He could imagine children strolling through the woods and sitting by the stream under the fig trees.

"What do you think of my idea of holding children's camps there?" Dan asked the local mayor.

"It's a beautiful location," the mayor agreed, and he encouraged Dan to go ahead with his plans, neglecting to mention problems that the pastor could encounter.

Dan purchased the property, unaware that this land had been used as a public picnic ground for years. With his American mindset, he figured that if he owned a property, he was free to do what he wanted with it—misjudging the local culture. He instructed an architect to draw plans for the site, including children's dormitories, a restaurant, and a theater for showing Christian films.

The property, which was five acres in size, included fifty olive trees. Dan had purchased the land on one side of the stream, not knowing that his neighbor on the other side coveted this property. It had been owned by his brother-in-law, who had wanted to sell the land for nearly six million pesetas, but he had only offered to pay a third of that amount. The disgruntled neighbor gathered together a group of men of the "baser sort,"[71] as Acts 17 describes the mob who opposed the Apostle Paul.

"This man is going to bring drug addicts with AIDS here," the neighbor riled up the townsfolk. "He's going to baptize them, and the water will become contaminated!"

The neighbor created a riot, and an angry crowd mobbed the city hall in protest. The previous mayor, who had given Dan permission to purchase the property, had been replaced. Influenced and intimidated by the locals, the new mayor refused to give the pastor a building permit. When Dan tried to do anything, even prune the trees, the mayor sent the police to stop him.

For six years, Dan fought his case in the Andalusian court of southern Spain, which was a significant financial drain. Even though he won every legal battle, the mayor still blocked him. Mobs protested at city hall, shouting that the property belonged to them, even though Dan had purchased it. After six years, Dan finally conceded and let the property go.

Dan turned his attention back to the farm in Antequera. The community built two-story dormitories with twenty-four rooms accommodating six bunk beds in each room. They installed a special sewage purification system. Later Dan realized that God had

[71] Acts 17:5a: "… *lewd fellows of the baser sort*" (KJV).

been in it all. He would have had constant problems on the Trabuco property.

Over and over in his ministry, Dan has encountered this same battle, with the devil stirring up an angry mob. Whenever he enters "hostile" territory, the devil foments trouble. Dan believes this is the "*thorn of flesh*"[72] that the Apostle Paul speaks about: Satan working through people of the "*baser sort.*" He lost the battle for Trabuco but not the war of advancing his many other ministries in Spain, especially children's outreaches.

For over twenty years, the youth conferences and summer camps held in Antequera have been a great blessing for thousands of children. Many of the current leaders in Dan's affiliated churches today were saved at these summer camps. They are now the parents or family members of the children attending the camps and also serve as monitors. The camps have proven to be a strategic training ground for teaching and influencing children at an age when their hearts are most receptive to the gospel. God has also prospered and blessed the women's and men's meetings held at the farm. It also serves as an international Christian center for surrounding communities.

"Wherever we go as servants of Christ, we have to realize that we are battling supernatural forces that are strategically aimed at destroying God's work," Dan says. "We need to have the mentality of warriors. If we have the mentality of spectators, then we're at the mercy of these demonic forces that do have an agenda. We have to keep our purpose clear in mind that we're here to establish the Kingdom of God: '*Your kingdom come. Your will be done on earth as it is in heaven*'" (Matthew 6:10).

Another major battle Dan encountered concerned the Antequera farm and the national railway. When Spain joined the Eu-

---

[72] 2 Corinthians 12:7a: "*And lest I should be exalted above measure by the abundance of revelations, a thorn in the flesh was given to me, a messenger of Satan ...*"

ropean Union, the country upgraded its transportation system, including roads and railways. The government planned to have a train track running through the Antequera farm, which would have cut off access to their well. They could get by with losing some acreage on their property, but not having access to water from the well would have completely shut down the farm's operations. Community members protested these plans but to no avail. When Dan returned to Spain and saw the grim situation, he called the mayor and brought him to the farm.

"This is where the railway is supposed to go through." Dan pointed out the field. He explained all the rehabilitation treatment of addicts taking place on the farm: "Hundreds of young Spaniards have been helped through our care." In addition, he also told him about all the community events and retreats they hosted on the property. The track would be a hazard to carrying on with their good work.

"Well, it has to go through somewhere!" the mayor retorted.

"But it's not going through our farm!" Dan declared.

The decision was beyond the local jurisdiction, but because of God's mercy and the prayers and fasting of the people on the farm, the government eventually moved the train tracks about a quarter of a mile. The Antequera farm was saved—truly a miracle!

The farm in Antequera has now been in operation for almost four decades, with its continuing emphasis on social work, drug rehabilitation, and training followers of Christ. Youth, rehabilitated and prepared for ministry, serve in Spanish hospitals, nursing homes, street evangelism programs, and food distribution programs for the needy. The farm plans to open a Revival Training Center soon.

Caring for the sixty-five to seventy-five young people who live and work together on the farm at any one time has always been challenging. The farm continues to raise cattle for beef and exports sweet corn, but profit from the livestock and produce grown on forty acres of land is simply not sufficient to cover the rehabilitation center's enormous operational expenses. The farm has been experimenting with okra, but growing it is very time-consuming and labor-intensive. Those who live and work on the farm in Christian community really have to be dedicated. Staff, some of whom have been there for twenty or thirty years, are spiritual warriors committed to the Lordship of Jesus Christ. Many who have been converted, trained, and discipled on the Antequera farm have gone on to start their own ministries and outreaches.

Spain has profoundly changed over the years. When the Del Vecchios first arrived in 1964, the nation was under the dictatorship of General Franco, and religious liberty was restricted. In 1978, Spain changed to democratic rule and later was integrated into the European Union. Over time, Dan influenced many government officials, including mayors and governors. On one truly historic occasion, he was invited to speak in a cathedral to a number of bishops. He discovered that his book on the Holy Spirit had circulated for twenty-five years among priests.

In all the villages around Antequera, there is almost no gospel light. In Spain, there are seven thousand villages of eight to ten thousand residents with little or no active Christian witness. Much of the country is still besieged by idolatry. The spiritual resistance is extremely difficult to break through, even more difficult than traditional religion that has become nothing but empty ritual. For this reason, Pastor Dan is still fighting and still carrying on with his radio program, *Palabra de Vida* (*Word of Life*), which broadcasts the gospel to forty-seven cities in the nation five days a week.

Dan has written seventeen powerful books in Spanish, all available on Amazon. *The Holy Spirit and His Work*, now in its fifth edition, sparked revival in Spain. He has preached on radio and on television, at one point broadcasting on eleven channels, including Spain's TBN channel, *Enlace*. Later, he connected with Miguel Díez and broadcast on REMAR's stations based in Madrid. Dan continues to preach on forty-five radio stations, broadcasting 150 programs a month.

"Spain is just one country without the gospel, with less than 1 percent[73] who are evangelical believers," Dan points out. "We have so much more to do before the end comes. Don't look to heaven as a goal," he urges Christians. "Look to the unreached nations of the world. Go where Christ is not named!"

For sixty-five years, Dan has preached the gospel in twenty-eight countries, including fifty-seven years that he and his family have been involved in Spain. He has shared and invested what God has given him into the lives of others: his time, his resources, his very life. In all these nations, he can testify that the "Word of God is powerful and that God always gives a strategy to overcome the power of darkness and establish His Kingdom."[74] Preaching on the streets, in churches, and in home meetings, through records, cassettes, radio, television, and the internet, Dan has faithfully sown the Word of God.

"No one can extinguish its fire, fanned by the flames of the Holy Spirit in receptive hearts. The magnitude of the fire that a single spark can ignite is unimaginable! The fire of the Holy Spirit can burn in millions of hearts, if we don't allow the love of the world to extinguish it."[75]

"I'm now eighty-nine, but I'm going to continue to fight for the advancement of the Kingdom of God," Pastor Dan passionately declares. "Even though we lose a battle here and there, thank

[73] "Pray For: Spain," Operation World, accessed April 18, 2022, operationworld.org/locations/spain.

[74] Del Vecchio, *El Manto de José* , 113.

[75] Ibid., 127.

God we know that we are more than victorious. We have God on our side, and we are going to win!"

EPILOGUE

GLORIA A DIOS

According to the grace of God which was given to me, as a wise master builder I have laid the foundation, and another builds on it. But let each one take heed how he builds on it. For no other foundation can anyone lay than that which is laid, which is Jesus Christ. Now if anyone builds on this foundation with gold, silver, precious stones, wood, hay, straw, each one's work will become clear; for the Day will declare it, because it will be revealed by fire; and the fire will test each one's work, of what sort it is. If anyone's work which he has built on it endures, he will receive a reward. (1 Corinthians 3:10–14)

As a wise master builder, Pastor Dan preached the gospel in Cuba, Mexico, Spain, and South America, laying the solid foundation of salvation through Jesus Christ. The principles of God's "true fast" from Isaiah 58 inspired the formation of an international Christian community in Torremolinos, reaching out to drifting youth, delinquent drug addicts, and alcoholics. Besides birthing multiple ministries, churches, and rehabilitation centers in Spain, Dan's ministry spread to regions of South America and beyond. He became burdened by the needs of street children around the world. He and his ministry partners desired to practically show the love of God to those mired in poverty and misery, deeply traumatized by abuse, rape, and suffering.

In the late 1980s, Pastor Dan gave the Spaniards free rein to run their churches and outreaches. "And they ran!" Dan has exclaimed. Most of the drug rehabilitation centers continue to radically change lives through the work of the Holy Spirit. Through the mighty name and power of Jesus Christ, Pastor Dan trained pastors to free those who have been enslaved by Satan through exposure to the occult, false religions, sexual immorality, and other bondages. Besides visiting those bound by prison or hospital walls, the associated churches fight for those bound by economic, social, and religious injustices.

An outreach to the Spanish-speaking people of South America flourished. Today, missionaries David and Diana, working with Qechua Indians in Ecuador, are building a leadership training center; Rafa and Raquel are helping unwed mothers in Colombia; and Marion and Jamie have a nation-wide ministry in Paraguay serving school-children. In Spain, *Asociación Real Rehabilitación de Marginados* currently gives away literally tons of food to people who are designated by the government as impoverished or low-income. Nearly all of their associated churches have food distributions to the needy.

A Spanish businessman in Vitoria, inspired by Dan's teaching on the church's role in social work and self-supporting businesses, grabbed hold of this vision and multiplied it. Miguel Díez, president of REMAR International, has established 1,500 rehabilitation centers in Spain alone. He's involved with all kinds of businesses and Christian communities, ministering to the marginalized and bringing the gospel to those most in need. His foundation is now active in fifty-seven countries around the world. Sixty thousand people are being helped, housed, and cared for daily. With a budget of over one million dollars, its operating funds are raised primarily through its businesses. Dan recently preached at REMAR's international conference to 2,500 participants. Using this model of social outreach, another Spaniard, Elias Tepper, also opened ministries under the name "Betel" in more than twenty countries.

In 1988, the Hotel Panorama in Torremolinos was torn down. More than sixty community members had been living there at the time. This loss proved to be the catalyst for most of the internationals to disperse to their home countries, sparking a progressive exodus over the next several years. Adjustment to "normal life" wasn't easy, especially for those who had spent more than a decade or longer in the community. The transition to their native lands proved challenging, and many felt like "strangers in their own country." In Spain, the community had provided a "greenhouse" environment where they could be spiritually nurtured and grow in the Lord. Adjusting to the "real world" and finding similar fellowship back home wasn't easy.

While living on the farm in Antequera, Gordon and Mairi had been praying about their family's future. In December of 1988, they were riveted by the horrific bombing disaster of the Pan Am plane, which had exploded over their hometown in Lockerbie, Scotland.[76] Soon after, they returned with their children to Lockerbie. After almost a decade of living in Spain, they felt like "aliens" in their native country. They started a church, which they pastored for eight years. Eventually Gordon moved into working with drug

[76] Pan Am flight 103, en route from Frankfurt to Detroit, with a stopover in London, was blown up over Lockerbie, Scotland, on December 21, 1988. All passengers and crew were killed (259 fatalities) as were eleven people on the ground. It remains the deadliest terrorist act in the history of the UK (en.m.wikipedia.org/wiki/Pan_Am_103).

addicts, managing a rehabilitation center in nearby Dumfries, and Mairi returned to teaching.

During this period when so many international community members returned to their home countries, André and Irene felt that they should stay in Spain, where their four children had been born. The Swiss-German couple continued to serve in children's ministry, worship, prayer, and evangelism. As a handyman, Big André found plenty of work repairing broken items. In 1996, after living in the community for sixteen years, they moved to Switzerland, where André was eventually placed in charge of a workshop for unemployed people. Their transition was made easier because, for the first year, they lived in a community-like setting with other people hungry for God.

The year 1988 was a time of crisis for David and Ullie and their two boys, as they wondered where they should go. At this critical juncture, David contacted some of his previous piano-servicing customers. The nearby British territory of Gibraltar (famous for its "Rock") provided rich business opportunities, as it was full of untuned and damaged pianos! By faith, David and Ullie bought a house near Mijas and paid off their mortgage within five years—a house they have now lived in for over three decades. They serve on the pastoral team of an English church in Los Boliches.

Gus, the community electrician, was the last one to live in the Hotel Panorama. After spending a combined total of nine years in the community, Gus returned to Australia in 1989 and married Daniele, a leader of the Torreblanca girls' rehabilitation home for addicts. They became foster parents to fifty children, adopted a son from South Korea, and have recently become grandparents.

"I had an incredible time in the community!" Gus remarks. "It was exciting to see the Lord bring in people to His Kingdom from all over the world. I think I stayed in and worked on every house and church in the community. I'm just one of the many who grew out of Dan and Rhoda's ministry. What a great privilege to have been part of that move of the Lord and His Spirit."

Through Dan's various ministry endeavors, and the impact of the evangelical churches in Spain, a great revival has occurred that has changed the nation. It has spread to more than seventy countries through those who have caught the vision. These fervent emissaries have gone on to serve Christ in Great Britain, Norway, Sweden, Finland, Belgium, Germany, Switzerland, France, the United States, Canada, Australia, Mexico, Israel, Africa, Korea, Indonesia, China, South America, and other nations. Thousands of lives have been touched and transformed by the gospel.

Wonderful leaders have come out of the community in Spain. Dr. Dennis Lindsay, who slept on the floor in Dan's office decades ago, is now the President and Chairman of the Board of Christ for the Nations, Inc., a world-wide missions organization and Bible Institute. From its Dallas Texas campus, Christ for the Nations has trained over fifty thousand students from fifty countries to carry the Good News about Christ all over the globe, and it has ninety other campus locations around the world.

Wayne Hilsden, one of the first young men to move into Barbara's garage back in the early1970s, received a clarion call to ministry in the Torremolinos Church. Dr. Wayne Hilsden and his wife, Ann, partnered with another couple to pioneer the largest Christian fellowship in Jerusalem, King of Kings Community.

"We often get young travelers coming through Jerusalem who end up in one of our services at King of Kings," Dr. Hilsden remarks. "And I'm thrilled that in the same way that I was so powerfully impacted in Torremolinos, similar encounters were happening to young people when they came to King of Kings. I'm so deeply grateful to Pastor Dan for the significant role he played in influencing the trajectory of my life and ministry."

Dr. Daniel Lucero (PhD in Agricultural Science) and his wife, Martine, who met in the community in the 1980s and helped start the farm in Antequera, now co-pastor a church in Nice, France. As Global Director for Africa and Francophone Nations for the International Church of the Foursquare Gospel, and President of the Foursquare Church in France, Dan Lucero oversees ten thousand Foursquare Churches in Africa and throughout the French-speaking world.

"Pastor Dan Del Vecchio and his apostolic ministry has had the most profound influence on my spiritual walk. His nine words to live by—'Take God's side. Expect a miracle. Never give up'—have been bedrocks I have built my faith upon."

Dan is thankful for this spreading witness. Although through his ministry he has seen thousands come to Christ, miracles of divine healing, and demons cast out, the most important thing in his estimation is "the disciples who have been the result of these things and are now in ministry in many countries today. This is the most gratifying part of my ministry. I certainly am not special; God has no favorites. His promises are to all who believe."

"Each of us is a living stone placed by God in strategic places," says Dan. "Every member of the body, however insignificant it may seem, exercises an indispensable function for the health of the body and for the work of the ministry."[77] Each of us is a link in the chain of events that can touch millions ..."[78]

In 2014, almost one hundred former community members from around the globe gathered for a Jubilee Reunion held at the farm in Antequera, in honor of the Del Vecchios' Fiftieth Anniversary of ministering in Spain. It was a time of thanksgiving, joy, and laughter as memories were shared.

---

[77] Del Vecchio, *El Manto de José*, 37.

[78] Ibid., 129.

In 2019, ICEA,[79] the association of the Spanish Evangelical Apostolic Churches, celebrated the Fiftieth Anniversary of the first evangelical church planted by the Del Vecchios in Torremolinos. The ICEA's churches are located in Amposta, Antequera, Cartagena, Fuengirola, Granada, Guadalajara, Málaga, Torremolinos, and Vinaròs.

Today the Evangelical Community Church in Torremolinos continues to welcome hundreds of tourists. Bernard Grandjean and his wife, Danielle, who have resided in Torremolinos for the past forty years, faithfully minister to the Spanish and international congregation meeting in the church. An Indian fellowship has recently started meeting.

Pastor Dan is on regular Zoom calls with the fourteen associated Apostolic churches in Spain, keeping in touch with his ministry partners and community "graduates" spread all over the world. "I've just sent a message to our churches in Spain encouraging them to believe for a new move of the Holy Spirit. The work that we began with God's help in Málaga in 1964 spread throughout the country and became the first great revival of the charismatic Pentecostal movement in that nation."

Dan is grateful for the internet and its potential to reach hundreds of thousands of people—far more than he'd ever be able to speak to in person. He's active on social media sites, engaging with the nations and a new generation. Taking advantage of this great opportunity to get the gospel out, unhindered by physical limitations, he's pursuing and emphasizing ministry through these platforms.

Now in their late eighties, Pastor Dan and Rhoda spend most of their time on their blueberry farm in Albany, Georgia and a few months of the year in Spain. In 2020, they celebrated their sixtieth wedding anniversary. Australian Pastor Barry (who had been in

[79] Iglesia Cristiana Evangélica Apostólica.

the community in the 1970s) married their daughter, Deborah, a few years ago, and they minister in a nearby church affiliated with the Evangelical Apostolic Churches of Spain.

In 2021, Pastor Dan, Rhoda, and Deborah returned to Spain for a few months of fruitful labor. Dan sometimes preached three sermons in a row. Along with a team of leaders from various churches, Deborah helped organize two youth meetings, called "The Call," and young Spaniards came from all over to attend. Dan is encouraged that his sermons, broadcast over the internet through REMAR's stations, have received over a million views within the last six months in nineteen countries. He finds it rewarding that he can now instantly connect with hundreds of thousands, preaching from his own home.

During the COVID-19 lockdown, I joined Zoom sessions with former community members, organized by Irene. It was inspiring to find out what's been happening in people's lives. Many have served or are serving in various ministries and churches around the globe, like Warwick and Eeva (Belgium, Germany, UK), Dory and Anna (Indonesia, Germany, Canada), Margaretha (Bolivia), and Carter and Mirella (Korea, Spain). Others have gone "into all the world," working in professions such as teaching, law, social work, and medicine. Some have earned PhDs. Former community members have worked in diverse fields, such as aeronautics, skilled trades, deep sea operations for the offshore oil industry, investment banking, the arts, media, and telecommunications.

Several are parents and grandparents. (We've been interceding for these second and third generations.) Some are now widowed. Others are struggling with serious illnesses. A few, like Anne-Marie and Barbara, have already passed on to glory. As we pray and share together over the internet connection across various time zones, meaningful "community" is once again forming. At the time of this writing, the Zoom community has met weekly for over a year. More than five dozen people from four continents have participated.

I'm struck by how our lives are still linked by shared experiences in the community and our faith in Christ, even after more than four decades! My own life would have been so different if Mark hadn't been faithfully witnessing on the street in Torremolinos. If Barbara hadn't opened her villa to backpackers, an international community may not have started. And if Dan and Rhoda and their family hadn't been obedient to the call of God on their lives, and willing to make sacrifices, countless souls in many nations wouldn't have been impacted for eternity! We all have a part to play in God's extraordinary plan of reaching others, of Jesus's Great Commission to disciple the nations. In these uncertain times, we most certainly need a fresh outpouring of the Holy Spirit to go forward.

Time is short. We must re-establish friendships that have grown cold and re-connect to form networks for ministry. I pray that the Holy Spirit will breathe on the burning embers of our love for Jesus, like a blacksmith's bellows, igniting the flame again. I pray that the fire of the Holy Spirit will burn intensely in our hearts, consuming passivity and radiating His love for the lost.

Daniel Del Vecchio has been privileged to participate in the moves of God in many nations, including twenty revivals! God gave him a vision of what He wanted to do in the nation of Spain, and it "spread like wildfire." Through the overflowing power of the Holy Spirit, thousands of lives have been radically altered, healed, and restored. There aren't enough pages to chronicle all of these incredible testimonies. Only heaven will reveal the extent of the far-flung witness of the Del Vecchios' powerful Spirit-led ministry.

The fire of the Holy Spirit, *the flame of God,* is still sweeping across Spain and to nations beyond, igniting hearts with a burning zeal to know and serve the living Jesus Christ, Lord of Lords and

King of Kings. For the work that He is doing in the nations, all the glory, honor, and praise must be given to God. As the Spanish Christians heartily proclaim: "Gloria a Dios!" Glory to God!

A MESSAGE FROM PASTOR DAN

The experiences and testimonies recounted in this book are presented with the hope that each miracle illustrates a message, that in each test a measure of understanding is acquired, and that in each pain there is hope. I don't intend to presume that my experiences are unique or superior to those of others, as each of us has experiences we have lived and a story to tell. God guides His children through different paths—some through the waters, and others through fire, but all towards the final victory of inheriting the promises.

Now after more than sixty-five years of ministry in over twenty countries, I stand amazed at the goodness, faithfulness, and mercy of God that has sustained me and my family. He has given me favor with officials and opened doors beyond my wildest dreams. I can say as the apostle Paul,

> *Now to Him who is able to do exceedingly abundantly above all that we ask or think, according to the power that works in us, to Him be glory in the church by Christ Jesus to all generations, forever and ever. Amen.* (Ephesians 3:20–21)

At present, through the internet and radio, we're able to reach more than thirty countries with over one million people viewing our programs. Our ministry has exploded! Some messages have over 250,000 views in a very short time, especially the messages that refer to the end times and prophecy. Since the COVID-19 pandemic, people have been concerned and even fearful of the future.

It's evident that we're living in the last of the last days. When asked by His disciples what would be the *sign* of His coming and the end of the world, Jesus said, "*Take heed that no one deceives you*" (Matthew 24:4b).

The apostle Paul wrote: "*But evil men and seducers shall wax worse and worse, deceiving, and being deceived*" (2 Timothy 3:13, KJV).

Fear and insecurity have gripped the hearts of multitudes. Racial strife, ethnic wars, famine, and epidemic are now worldwide. Many are departing from the faith, and the love of many Christians has grown cold. Nevertheless, a remnant has held fast to the faith, in spite of wide-spread persecution. The Church triumphant is alive and well! The promise of Christ will never fail: "*I will build My church; and the gates of hell shall not prevail against it*" (Matthew 16:18b, KJV).

The last sign Christ foretold that would herald His coming was the outpouring of His Spirit upon all flesh:

> *And it shall come to pass in the last days, saith God, I will pour out of my Spirit upon all flesh: and your sons and your daughters shall prophesy, and your young men shall see visions, and your old men shall dream dreams.* (Acts 2:17, KJV)

He said, "*And this Gospel of the kingdom shall be preached in all the world for a witness unto all nations; and then shall the end come*" (Matthew 24:14, KJV).

Never before in the history of Christianity has this prophecy had the possibility of being fulfilled. It's now possible through modern media platforms to literally reach the world with the gospel. However, the lukewarm, complacent, self-indulgent Church will never do it. Jesus said "*This* gospel of the kingdom" shall be preached. Not a powerless humanistic gospel that requires little and promises much. It will be the gospel of the Lordship of Christ, confirmed with mighty signs and wonders that will convince the people.

The apostle Paul wrote:

> *And my speech and my preaching was not with enticing words of man's wisdom, but in demonstration of the Spirit and of power: That your faith should not stand in the wisdom of men, but in the power of God.* (1 Corinthians 2:4–5)

When the love of God is poured forth in your heart, it will find outlets to reach the needy, the oppressed, the sick, and the suffering. It is said that "We cannot heal the wounds we do not feel." There's a great cost to being used of God. There's no gain without pain and no crown without suffering. But it will be worth it all when we see Jesus. Life's trials will seem so small when we see Christ. One glimpse of His wonderful face, and all sorrows will be erased. Remember: "*Be faithful until death, and I will give you the crown of life*" (Revelation 2:10b).

The great commission is still in effect. The deeds of the apostles and disciples of Christ are still being written wherever there are Christians willing to pay the price. The latter glory of the house will be greater than the former. If God could and can use me, He can also use anyone who dares to get out of the boat and start walking on the water. Unexpected storms will come, but the Lord is still in control of the winds and the sea. The harvest is great, but the workers are few. Dare to live by faith, looking only at the Author and Finisher of our faith. He will supply your needs according to His riches in glory.

> *Trust in the Lord with all your heart, and lean not on your own understanding; In all your ways acknowledge Him, and He shall direct your paths. Do not be wise in your own eyes; fear the Lord and depart from evil.* (Proverbs 3:5–7)

My great desire for this book, describing the miracles and acts of God, and the testimonies of those whose lives were radically transformed, is that it inspires others to take steps of faith and obedience. May your faith increase to believe in the impossible, and may you have confidence that God cares for you—even the smallest details of your life. Meditate on His Word, listening carefully to the voice of the Spirit, and surely He will speak to you and call you.

My prayer is that this book will kindle a fire in your heart that will cause you to believe beyond all possible boundaries and limitations to fulfill all that God has called you to accomplish. My sincere hope is that these experiences serve as lessons to help you in your walk with God. Your future starts now. *Obey God's call,* for the world is waiting for the manifestation of God's children. If you persist, if you persevere, if you are filled with the Holy Spirit, if you know God has called you, there is nothing impossible with God.

I'm grateful to God for everything He has done! Whatever mantle I have, I want it to fall upon this next generation so that they can carry this further. The passion still burns in my heart to go into all the world and preach the gospel:

> *And Jesus came and spoke to them, saying, "All authority has been given to me in heaven and on earth. Go therefore and*

make disciples of all nations, baptizing them in the name of the Father and of the Son and of the Holy Spirit, teaching them to observe all things that I have commanded you; and lo, I am with you always, even to the end of the age. (Matthew 28:18–20)

Daniel Del Vecchio,
Albany, Georgia, USA

For more information and access to resources, visit this website: www.delvecchio.org.

APPENDIX A
APOSTLE TO SPAIN

"Are you not my work in the Lord? If I am not an apostle to others, yet doubtless I am to you. For you are the seal of my apostleship in the Lord" (1 Corinthians 9:1b–2).

APOSTOLIC PIONEERING MINISTRY

Dan Del Vecchio was sent by God to be an apostle to Spain. *Apostolos* means "a messenger, a sent one." A true apostle is a messenger of the Lord, sent as God's ambassador to establish churches in regions where Christ *is not named.* As the Apostle Paul states in Romans 15:20, *"And so I have made it my aim to preach the gospel, not where Christ was named, lest I should build on another man's foundation."* An apostle's authority is limited to the areas where he is part of establishing the church, setting the doctrinal position, and building it up—training and preparing followers of Christ.

THE BAPTISM OF THE HOLY SPIRIT

"But you shall receive power when the Holy Spirit has come upon you; and you shall be witnesses to Me in Jerusalem, and in all Judea and Samaria, and to the ends of the earth" (Acts 1:8).

Dan explains that "Jesus told his followers to wait in Jerusalem until they received power from on high. They had already been born again when He had breathed upon them to receive the Spirit. They had received the Spirit of Christ, and their souls were regenerated. Nobody can be saved without the influence and conviction of the Holy Spirit, and the revealing of Christ. The baptism of the Holy Spirit is the infilling, the impartation, the preparation."

When the Del Vecchios first arrived in Spain, the baptism of the Holy Spirit was virtually unknown. Throughout the country, there were no more than two dozen people filled with the Holy Spirit. In major cities like Madrid, Seville, and Málaga, there were no charismatic churches. Preaching the gospel with the power of the Holy Spirit, Pastor Dan pioneered the Charismatic movement in Spain. The church he planted in Málaga several decades ago now has a congregation of over one thousand. He spearheaded churches in Marbella, Córdoba, Torremolinos, Fuengirola, Torreblanca, Barcelona, Madrid, Seville, Asturias, and other cities. Today he encourages pastors affiliated with ICEA, the Evangelical Apostolic Christian Churches in Spain.

THE FIVE-FOLD MINISTRIES

> *So Christ himself gave the apostles, the prophets, the evangelists, the pastors and teachers, to equip his people for works of service, so that the body of Christ may be built up until we all reach unity in the faith and in the knowledge of the Son of God and become mature, attaining to the whole measure of the fullness of Christ.* (Ephesians 4:11–13, NIV)

Dan began as an evangelist—preaching the gospel, healing the sick, and bringing the Good News to the poor. Over time, his ministry changed, and he desired to be a father, to "generate spiritual children and disciples." Even today it's still his deep desire to "win souls, make disciples, and pastor pastors."[80]

In Madrid, Pastor Dan taught one hundred pastors, who were part of the "Renewal," on the gifts of the Spirit and the five-fold ministries. At the time, neither the role nor the importance of apostles and prophets in the body of Christ were understood in Spain. He clarified the need for the governing structure for the growth of the church. Like a wise builder, Dan laid the doctrinal foundation for apostolic ministry, which incorporates these five-fold ministry gifts. This historic teaching impacted many of the pastors, shaping their ministries and the spiritual destiny of the nation.

THE FIRST EVANGELICAL COMMUNITY

The first community of internationals started in Torremolinos. At the time, neither the Del Vecchios nor the young believers had experience in living together in Christian communities for discipleship and true transformation. The early months and years of the lives of new Christians are of vital importance for establishing the habits and priorities they will exercise later in life.

Today through this model of "community," thousands of Spirit-filled Christians have been trained and prepared to be disciples, leaders, pastors, and missionaries. The second generation of these young people rescued from the world is now serving God in various countries.

THERAPEUTIC REHABILITATION CENTERS

Due to the increase in drug and alcohol dependency in Spain, the evangelical community opened nine therapeutic rehabilitation centers to meet this need. Community-living laid a strong foundation to help those struggling with drug and alcohol addictions. With the internationals and Spanish working together, the

[80] Del Vecchio, *El Manto de José*, 205.

communities began to take in and care for the needier members of society—those living on the fringes. Instead of an institutional environment, the centers provided a more intimate family-like setting for rehabilitation and skills training.

INNER HEALING

Dan was one of the first pastors in Spain to teach on healing of the emotions and memories—a subject that is still relatively unknown in that nation. The community gained practical experience and spiritual insight while working with those grappling with alcohol and drug dependency, and with those who suffered traumas and verbal or sexual abuse.

DELIVERANCE AND CASTING OUT OF EVIL SPIRITS

> *"Behold, I give you the authority to trample on serpents and scorpions, and over all the power of the enemy, and nothing shall by any means hurt you"* (Luke 10:19).

Without the baptism of the Holy Spirit, a Christian will not have the anointing or discerning of spirits necessary to cast out demons. Soon after Dan was baptized with the Holy Spirit, God gave him the gift of discerning of spirits. Although he has cast out evil spirits en masse, most of the time he has ministered quietly to individuals, with one or two intercessors present: "Christ came to destroy the works of the devil and now has given His church this mandate. It is the power of the Spirit, the finger of God that casts out both demons and diseases."[81]

RESTORATION OF DANCE IN WORSHIP

Through the Holy Spirit's instruction, Dan restored dance as an expression of reverent worship to God. The community became

[81] Ibid., 211.

pioneers in introducing Hebrew-style choreographed dance into worship services in Spain. Dance is now incorporated into worship in churches all over the country. At Deborah's wedding to Barry a few years ago, it was very moving for Dan and Rhoda to see young women worship the Lord through dance during the ceremony.

THE FOUR SEASONS OF THE CHURCH

This is Dan's revolutionary teaching on the four cycles or seasons churches pass through. The first season is spring: evangelism. With the powerful seed of the Word of God and the anointing of the Holy Spirit, a church can be started anywhere. Dan thanks God that he is a sower of the gospel with a book full of "seeds"—and these seeds keep multiplying.

The second season is summer: discipleship. Jesus taught by His example and lived in close contact with His disciples. Dan believes that there's no better way to disciple believers than by living together in community. Discipleship takes time; it can take years. Men and women need to be trained, prepared, and sent out with the power of the Holy Spirit. "Our entire life is being made into His image, into His likeness, as we let the Word form us, reform us, and transform us," Dan teaches. Three basic precepts are: a) how we respond to God, b) how we react to circumstances, and c) how we relate to others.

The third season is fall: social work. Jesus will reward His followers who get involved with human needs:

> *... Come, you blessed of My Father, inherit the kingdom prepared for you from the foundation of the world: for I was hungry and you gave Me food; I was thirsty and you gave Me drink; I was a stranger and you took Me in; I was naked and you clothed Me; I was sick and you visited Me; I was in prison and you came to Me.* (Matthew 25:34–36)

The early church was involved with ministry to widows, orphans, slaves, the elderly, and the poor. Social work can be exhausting and stressful. Unless Christians are empowered by the Holy Spirit with the gifts operating, they won't be able to perform social ministry properly and will become burned out.

The fourth season is winter: becoming self-supporting. By providing vocational training and starting community businesses, churches can become self-supporting and assist the needy—a practical demonstration of faith and compassion.

APPENDIX B
REVIVAL FIRE

Cover Photo: As this book was being updated in 2021, the La Palma volcano erupted in the Canary Islands, a territory of Spain. The cover captures the fiery explosion of this volcano, showing the mighty force of nature but also symbolizing the explosive power of God's Holy Spirit.

Volcano Vision: In 2014, during the Reunion, Barry Butters had the following experience, which he related to Dan Del Vecchio, his future father-in-law:

While I was with you in Spain for our Jubilee Reunion, a great burden of prayer came on me, and I found myself in travail for God's plan to be birthed. It's been a long time since I've sensed such intensity in prayer.

One morning while I was praying in the Dome, I was caught up in the Spirit and could see what looked like a volcano of God's revival fire about to be released. I saw in the Spirit that Spain is central to Europe and Asia and Africa. I could see the fire of God being carried and transferred to different areas, all flowing out of the work in Spain.

I could see apostolic teams being set on fire and sent out in small clusters to minister revival fire and then return to Spain for rest and further re-firing. I could see a prayer center where we would worship God and teach and train regarding intercession.

I could see that this would be like a huge dynamo of spiritual power, building and growing and gaining force in the Spirit.

Is God's revival fire being ignited again? Is this the time for a revival school?

Printed in the USA
CPSIA information can be obtained
at www.ICGtesting.com
LVHW012321011124
795432LV00001B/225

9 781486 622719